D1099300

Promoting Pre-school Curriculum and Teaching

Henry E. Hankerson

LB
1140.23
H32
1987

 Wyndham Hall Press

PROMOTING PRE-SCHOOL CURRICULUM AND TEACHING

by

Henry E. Hankerson
School of Education
Howard University

Library of Congress Catalog Card Number 87-050867

ISBN 1-55605-016-X (paperback)
ISBN 1-55605-017-8 (hardcover)

ALL RIGHTS RESERVED

Copyright © 1987 by Henry E. Hankerson

Printed in the United States of America

This book may not be reproduced, in whole or in part, in any form
(except by reviewers for the public press), without written permission
from the publisher, Wyndham Hall Press, Inc., Post Office Box
877, Bristol, Indiana, 46507, U.S.A.

TABLE OF CONTENTS

i

DEDICATION AND ACKNOWLEDGMENTS

Realizing that "what we are is God's gift to us, and what we become is our gift to God," I praise God Almighty for making this accomplishment possible, and herewith dedicate this textbook to my Mother (Mrs. Willie Pearl Hankerson) and my late Father (James Hankerson) who instilled in me "THE LOVE" of God, my fifteen sisters and brothers, my precious relatives, dear friends, education, and mankind.

The completion of this textbook is the result of the interest, effort, cooperation, and involvement of many persons. I am indebted to my professional colleagues in early childhood and teacher education who have supplied foundational information and materials as the theoretical and practical framework for the textbook. One of my graduate students and an early childhood professional, Helen Battle Jones, has been especially supportive in providing technical assistance for which I am very grateful. Graduate and undergraduate students in my "Instructional Strategies" classes at Howard University have provided invaluable input and strength to this project and deserve a token of gratitude.

The photographs for this textbook have been provided through Mercedes Palmer, Director of Howard University Hospital Child Development Center, whose support has been unselfish, untiring, and endearing. I am also appreciative of the teachers, staff, parents, and children at the center for the many positive roles and help they gave to the successful completion of the project.

Crystal Medley Johnson handled the technical mechanics of typing, reviewing, and re-typing of the manuscript. I take this opportunity to thank her and to express my appreciation for a product of high quality.

To all caregivers of young children, interested persons, and advocates, this textbook was designed and developed with you in mind. Therefore, I hope that it is helpful and that it is used very often.

PREFACE

Promoting Pre-School Curriculum and Teaching is a text that combines curriculum and instruction and bridges the gap from curriculum theory to practical application. It serves as a practical resource and action guide for caregivers to obtain subject-matter content, methodologies, expected outcomes, and practical knowledge (know how) about curriculum and teaching to change a learning center or classroom into a stimulating world which "motivates pre-schoolers to learn." The text deals with pre-school curriculum from a dimensional pattern of correlated subject knowledge bases, growth and developmental needs of young children, and instructional strategies, as a single entity, to the teaching/learning process. It is a comprehensive instructional tool that comprises a systematic approach to teaching and learning for caregivers and pre-schoolers in a single edition.

This text is designed to fulfill the long overdue need for preparing caregivers who are capable of understanding, recognizing, and expanding/extending connections of "theory" into "practice." It is organized to depict information and materials in a manner befitting of promoting the enmeshing of curriculum and teaching into an integrated process. Caregivers responsible for providing challenging, sound, relevant, imaginative, resourceful planning and implementation of teaching/ learning of young children, ages three to seven, will find **Promoting Pre-School Curriculum and Teaching** an invaluable resource and action guide. Curriculum is presented in all subject-matter areas in a developmentally-sequenced manner to deal effectively with the age-appropriate needs of pre-schoolers. Teaching methods/resources and activities are given to show ways in which pre-schoolers' learnings can be supported in each subject-matter area, language arts, motor functioning, expressive arts, social studies, science, and mathematics. The text presents information and materials in a step-by-step, explicit and understandable manner to help caregivers to make the connections of "theory" to "application."

The text serves as a process of impartment (knowledges, skills, attitudes, and competencies) between the professor and the undergraduate student, as well as graduate students in methods of teaching early childhood education courses. It also serves as a practical applications reference tool (concepts, methods, techniques, etc.) for practitioners, parents, and early childhood professionals. In order to accomplish the aforestated features, the text is presented in easy-to-read formats while at the same time a scholarly approach has been maintained. The content in each chapter is organized in a "question-answer" format, whereby the questions were formulated in accord with important information and materials that are necessary in teaching and learning early childhood curriculum. This "question-answer" format will alleviate entanglement in unnecessary words, concepts, and rhetoric and, instead, present curriculum and teaching strategies in a simple, practical, productive manner whereby theoretical knowledge bases and instructional activities are illustrated for ease of accessibility and utilization.

Other distinctive features of the text include: 1) self-contained chapters that are designed to serve as curriculum models for subject-matter content, present a body of knowledge that can be independent, yet each chapter bears a direct relationship to each other in formulating the concept of holistic "curriculum and teaching" in the pre-school---while at the same time, the curriculum models can serve as written curriculum for many new and underdeveloped pre-school programs; 2) charts are used as a simple approach to providing visual representation of the conceptualization of "curriculum and teaching/learning" in a systematic manner to show the relationship of concepts to outcomes to activities to teaching methods to resources; 3) a correlation of each subject area is provided to show the relationship of one to the other in the total pre-school curriculum for continuity, relevance, and integration (of curriculum to teaching/learning) on a day to day basis without having to be implemented as separate subjects; 4) major contributors to pre-school curriculum and teaching from the past whose contributions have strengthened early childhood education, and live on today, are discussed in the text; 5) and the goals of early childhood education have been presented in an integrative fashion in accord with curriculum and teaching/learning. Emphasis has been placed on the culturally diverse pre-schoolers (Blacks and other minorities), and attention is focused on "management" and "intervention strategies." Each chapter also contains "activities for study and discussion" which may or may not pertain to the information presented. In some cases attention is given to assigning additional extended issues for research and demonstration. There is an Index to cross-reference words, names, and terms for all chapters of the text.

The text is organized by content-orientation to depict a three-fold conceptualization of pre-school curriculum and the teaching/learning process. First, Chapter One, "The Pre-School Curriculum: Key To Teaching and Learning," deals with an introductory review of curriculum, teaching, and learning as a holistic process. Theories of instruction and learning are discussed which serve as the foundation from which curriculum is learned, taught, and applied by caregivers in accord with the needs, abilities, and creativities of the learners. The dimension of discussing the contributions of renown scholars (Martin Luther, Comenius, Locke, Rousseau, Pestalozzi, Froebel, Montessori, etc.) to the pre-school curriculum and early childhood education is a key attribute in linking theory to practice, as well as providing a professional frame of reference and knowledge in the field. Chapter Two, "Material Resources and Computers For The Pre-School Curriculum," provides input for all of the chapters in that it expresses the concept that "pre-school curriculum has, as its foundation, experiences with materials as the key factor to the teaching/learning process in all subject areas." The use of computers in pre-schools is a feature that makes the curriculum current with needs, trends, and operations in our highly technological society.

Second, Chapters Three, "Understanding the Educative Value of Play and Motor Functioning;" Four, "Language Arts Experiences;" Five, "Social Living Experiences;" Six, "Experiences in the Expressive Arts;" Seven, "Mathematical Experiences;" and Eight, "Experiences in Science," cover information and materials relating to subject matter content in the pre-school curriculum. Each chapter presents a discussion of curriculum theory, instructional strategies, techniques for practical applications, specific activities and experiences as examples for the teaching/learning process, as well as related information and resources. Each chapter is self-contained and provides a "skeletal" curriculum model to be used, modified, and/or adapted in each of the subject areas.

Third, Chapter Nine, "Effective Teaching/Learning For All Pre-Schoolers: Integration, Intervention, and Management," deals with the teaching/learning process in reference to Blacks and other minorities in large urban areas. The subject matter content that has been included in other chapters as well as other materials in the text are covered in chapter nine through the framework of "addressing the goals of early childhood education." Information and strategies for classroom management and discipline of pre-schoolers are provided as an added dimension to effective pre-school curriculum and teaching/learning.

The text serves as an action guide that is relevant and applicable to "promoting pre-school curriculum and teaching" for all children. It, therefore, lays the pathway for preparing competent caregivers in early childhood education to be used throughout the pre-service and in-service years, as well as facilitate parents and others in the profession. The inference of this task is undergirded in this passage:

> Beautiful indeed and of great importance is the vocation of all those who aid parents in fulfilling their duties and who, as representatives of the human community, undertake the task of education in the schools. This vocation demands special qualities of the mind and heart, very careful preparation and continuing readiness to renew and to adapt. (Gravissimum Educationis, #5)

Henry E. Hankerson
Howard University
Washington, D.C.

CHAPTER ONE

THE PRE-SCHOOL CURRICULUM: KEY TO TEACHING AND LEARNING

CHAPTER 1

THE PRE-SCHOOL CURRICULUM:
KEY TO TEACHING AND LEARNING

- HOW DO CHILDREN'S LEARNING STYLES INFLUENCE CURRICULUM?

- HOW DO CHILDREN LEARN?

  - WHAT IS PERCEIVING?
  - WHAT IS THINKING?
  - WHAT IS DOING?
  - WHAT IS FEELING?

- WHAT IS THE RELATIONSHIP BETWEEN TEACHING AND LEARNING?

- WHAT ARE SOME PHILOSOPHICAL AND THEORETICAL BASES FOR UNDERSTANDING HOW CHILDREN LEARN?

- WHAT BEARINGS DOES CURRICULUM HAVE ON THE TEACH-ING/LEARNING PROCESS?

- HOW CAN WE TELL WHEN TEACHING, LEARNING, AND CURRICULUM ARE OPERATING TOGETHER?

- HOW CAN PLANNING, SCHEDULING, PROGRAMMING, AND ASSESSMENT SERVE AS INSTRUMENTS FOR TEACHING/ LEARNING?

- WHO ARE THE MAJOR CONTRIBUTORS TO THE PRE-SCHOOL CURRICULUM AND THE TEACHING/LEARNING PROCESS?: THE PAST AND THE PRESENT PROVIDED PATTERNS OF EXPERIENCE

- WHAT ARE SOME BASIC PRINCIPLES FOR TEACHING AND LEARNING?

- ACTIVITIES FOR STUDY AND DISCUSSION

- REFERENCES

2

HOW DO CHILDREN'S LEARNING STYLES INFLUENCE CURRICULUM?

Promoting pre-school curriculum and teaching/learning adheres to the concept that "curriculum" is a vehicle for influencing behavior of pre-schoolers by their interacting with the environment--people, places, things. Key to planning a comprehensive developmental curriculum (growth and developmental needs, chronological and mental ages, environmental and societal influences, needs, and ills, etc.) is the programmatic approach of organization, goals, objectives, concepts, activities, processes, materials, resources, assessments, and strategies that are interrelated into a system that operates on a daily basis. The nature of the curriculum must reflect the learning needs of the young children. Therefore, the caregivers must give careful attention to the pre-schoolers' learning styles.

The varying learning styles of children require specific preparation by caregivers in order to develop instruction and to determine what curriculum is to be taught. Caregivers respond to the ways children learn through comprehensive knowledge of basic assumptions about growth and development in relationship to environment. Each waking hour of the child's life is filled with a matrix of events that cause the human behavior to be in constant change. Much of the behavioral development is learned, modified, shaped and changed at very early ages. The caregiver's responses to the child's learning styles are entangled in the notion that the environmental process has its greatest effect in early childhood, due to this stage being the most rapid in the total development process. Therefore, learning styles affect curriculum as actions are taken to:

1. plan, organize and foster learning activities based on the idea that most human behavior is sequential in development.

2. give full recognition to the importance of basing learning experiences in an orderly fashion going from a concrete to an abstract form as suggested by Piaget's theory in order to link learning to age and maturation;

3. make careful observations of children's behaviors and have regular communication with parents for the purpose of providing new knowledge, attitudes, and skills in an effort to make learning more meaningful; and

4. provide individually prescribed learning events for children in order to effect specific desired behavior change.

3

"Learning styles" connote an array of high level as well as low level procedures for dealing with the issues in teaching and learning in early childhood education. For the sake of relevance and the expediency of practicality in the teaching process, let's treat the subject of "how" in a very practical manner. Learning styles begin at birth as the child's physiological and psychological environmental influences are initiated. However, the child is handled by parents, caregivers, and others around him/her who will influence the way he/she will express him/herself. Differences in how these expressions are revealed include:

1. Visual Learning Style -- the child selects and classifies information according to "seeing" and "looking" as his/her pattern of mental ability (i.e. facial expressions, reading newspaper, seeing pictures, objects, signs, notes, and displays, watching television, films, etc.).

2. Auditory Learning Style -- the child selects and classifies information according to "hearing" as his/her pattern of mental ability (i.e. listening to records, radio, and bands, using discussion and telling as key communications methods, using the telephone, etc.).

3. Kinesthetic Learning Style -- the child selects and classifies information according to "feelings" as his/her pattern of mental ability (i.e. body language, gestures, patting, hugging, movement, physical actions, etc.).

It is easily determined that the learning styles can be a combined process of utilizing logical skills (Barbe and Milone, 1980).

Two cognitive styles of learning have been identified by Cohen (1969). They are called the analytical and relational styles which refer to differences in the methods children use to select and classify information and utilize logical skills. Some characteristics of these styles have been compiled (Hilliard, 1976, pp. 36-40). The following examples are included in the compilation: Analytical Style -stimulus centered, parts-specific, finds nonobvious attributes, extracts from embedded context, relationships seldom involve process or motivation as a basis, long attention span, greater perceptual vigilance, and view of self tends to be in terms of status role; and Relational Style -- self-centered, global, fine descriptive characteristics, relationships tend to be functional and inferential, responses tend to be affective, emotional, short attention span and concentration, gestalt learners, tend

4

to ignore structure and self-descriptions, creative in the arts--visual, audio, and video, and tend to point to essence. Identification of and understanding ways in which children differ can be very instrumental in helping caregivers to determine learning styles and better understand how children learn.

Ultimate to the understanding of learning modalities of young children is observation of their behavior. It is the basic source of information. The child's reaction and performance to learning tasks set a pattern for his learning style. The effectiveness of teaching is measured by the desired behavior changes that occur in children being taught. If the desired behavior does not occur, attention can be given to the child's learning style. Oftentimes, learning, as determined by performance, is done by children in spite of the environmental stimuli, as previously discussed in reference to the teaching/learning process. The caregiver should make note of as many activities and modes of performances done by each child as possible in order to assess the strengths and weaknesses of the child's modalities for learning specific tasks. Instruction, then, can become more specific and related to the child's learning style. Such provision of strategies by the caregiver is truly a step toward diagnostic-prescriptive teaching.

In summary, the whole "art" of teaching relies, to a great extent, on the act of learning. It is without a doubt then, that either knowingly or unknowingly, caregivers respond to the ways children learn. Nevertheless, with the multiplicity of learning and achievement problems today, much of the response to learning styles has been more incidental and accidental than not. In some cases, and particularly for this textbook, the piecemeal teaching patterns might be due to a lack of knowledge and understanding about "how" children learn.

HOW DO CHILDREN LEARN?

In examining How a Child Learns, let's take the following considerations into account as described by Barbara Vance (1973).

1. The behavior of young children is less complicated than that of older children or adults.

    a. Young children have lived fewer years than older children and adults and therefore have had fewer experiences to complicate their behavior patterns.

b. Young children tend to "wear their personalities on their sleeves" (they seldom hide their feelings and attitudes and ideas).

2. What they learn tend to stand out in bold relief. Therefore, it is probably easier to study the process by which all people learn as the result of observing how young children learn. A depiction of the modes of perception, reception, retention and expression are herewith described in the following model.

3. This model begins with perception, moves on to forming a mental picture, then to actual performance, and finally to feeling.

STEPS:	ONE	PERCEIVE
	TWO	THINK
	THREE	DO
	FOUR	FEEL

An outlined account of ingredients of this model is as follows:

What is Perceiving?

o   all learning begins with a sensory experience (perception);

o   the learner has contact by one or more of his senses with objects, people, places, or events;

o   the average infant is bombarded with a wide variety of sights, sounds, smells, textures, and body pressures. (The variety of taste stimuli is probably small to begin with);

o   the infant has little ability to screen out stimulation except through the medium of sleep. This ability is increased as the child grows older. He is able to screen out certain stimuli while attending to others;

o   a bombardment of too many sensory stimuli at one time will cause the child to suffer from "perceptual indigestion;"

o   "perceptual indigestion" typifies a confusing situation in which behavior becomes erratic and uncontrolled;

o   learning is more effective and appropriate when sensory stimuli are available a few at a time;

o   Kagan (1968) refers to this as distinctive stimuli;

o   young children are natural explorers of their physical environment;

o   they receive information constantly in a variety of sights, smells, sounds, tastes, pressures, and textures;

o   they are building their sensory "data banks" (assimilation);

o   the quantity and quality of these sensory experiences determine the quantity of the child's THINKING (the next step in the learning process);

o   to assure less chance for error in the "THINKING" stage of the learning process, sensory experiences that are the result of DIRECT CONTACT with actual objects, people, places or events are best;

o   when one or more of the child's sensory organs are damaged or becomes nonfunctional, the learning messages received through the senses are limited in scope and complexity;

o   early identification of sensory handicaps and correction when possible will assure greater learning capacity for the child; and moreover,

o   LEARNING, then, begins when the child perceives something.

What is Thinking?

o   objects, people, places or events, ONCE PERCEIVED, become a part of the total realm of perceptual experience by which one thinks and performs;

o   the child formulates some sort of mental picture of his sensory experience;

7

o this mental picture is made up of past sensory experiences, feelings, and actions related to the present sensory experience;

o no two children form the same mental picture of the same sensory experience--for example: one child might have a frightening experience with a kitten, while another might have a pleasant one. Therefore,

> o the mental pictures formed by these two children are inferred from their actions;
>
> o forming a mental picture is an internal process that cannot be directly observed. This is why the next step in the learning process is so important. The ACTION step tells us what the child is thinking. This is the <u>DO</u> step.

What is Doing?

o what a person thinks and is reinforced for performing determines to a great extent how he will act;

o not all action is the result of conscious thought, nor does all thought produce action;

o sensory experiences lead inevitably to mental pictures that, in turn, lead to observable behavior or action under given circumstances. For example, one child in the previous illustration enthusiastically approached the teacher and real kitten while the other drew away. From this behavior inference can be drawn to say that each had a very different mental picture of kittens and what kittens do. We can be sure that the two experiences related to cats and kittens were very different. By knowing something about the past sensory experiences of each child, the inferences could be more accurate;

o basically, the consequences of a child's past experiences determine his actions in the future;

o the "<u>do</u>" step gives basic data on each child

> o it is the child's observable behavior, or "doing," that tells what and how he is learning;

o   some behavior patterns are psychomotor, cognitive and affective that implement "doing."

What is Feeling?

o   refers to the emotions as well as to interests, attitudes, and values;

o   certain consequences in the environment tend to accompany or follow each of our acts;

o   responses to these consequences are basically physiological and involuntary;

o   involuntary responses are called feelings and labeled: fear, anger, joy, happiness, frustration, shyness, and so on;

o   key element in the humanistic approach to teaching/learning.

WHAT IS THE RELATIONSHIP BETWEEN TEACHING AND LEARNING?

Let's look further at the four stages of learning as previously discussed and add the "levels" for teaching. The relationship between teaching and learning is illustrated in Figure 1 as discussed by Vance (1973).

This hopefully shows how teaching and learning relate. The curricular provisions would serve to enhance this process as objectives, lessons-- activities, and strategies are planned, programmed, and evaluated for the children.

WHAT ARE SOME PHILOSOPHICAL AND THEORETICAL BASES
FOR UNDERSTANDING HOW CHILDREN LEARN?

Barbara Vance's (1973) theoretical formulations are organized into three levels of learned behaviors: 1) Psychomotor, 2) cognitive, and 3) affective.

Psychomotor behavior is based on the utilization of the body's skeleton, its muscles and joints in skills of locomotion, manipulation, and body

Figure __1__

	Perceive	Think	Do	Feel
Child Activities	See Hear Touch Taste Smell	Recall (Memory) Imagination Concept formation Reasoning	Do the behavior	Feelings, attitudes, interest, values resulting from behavior. Desire or lack of desire to do again.
	Show*	Discuss*	Apply*	Reinforce
Teacher Activities	Show children what you want them to learn through: Firsthand experiences, vicarious sensory experiences	Ask questions, Pose problems, consider each child's idea. Ask for interpretations and feelings. Allow practice of desired behavior (verbal and motor)	Plan activities that allow children to exhibit desired behavior objectives, make assignments allow reports of related out-of-class behavior	Provide pleasant consequences for desirable behavior

Adapted from Teacher Development Program: Basic Course, Salt Lake City, Utah: Corporation of the President of the Church of Jesus Christ of Latter-day Saints, 1971, 63.

*These terms adopted from Woodruff, A.D. Basic concepts of teaching. San Francisco: Chandler Publishing Co., 1961.

Figure __1__ . Relationship Between Learning and Teaching.

balance. Cognitive behavior is dependent upon symbolic processes and language as one memorizes, imagines, forms concepts and solves problems. The basic emotions, interests, attitudes, and values of an individual comprise the affective behavior. Information presented in an area on "How Children Learn" reflects Vance's conceptualization of the levels of learned behaviors in detail based on: perceive, think, do, and feel.

The theoretical frame of reference presented by Jean Piaget, a noted psychologist, in regards to intellectual development parallels a close similarity to Vance's conceptualizations about how a child learns. Piaget (1971) believed that a child passes through stages as he/she grows and develops. The child's way of learning is molded into four stages of intellectual growth: 1) the sensorimotor stage (birth to twenty-four months), 2) preoperational stage (twenty-four months to seven years), 3) the stage of concrete operations (seven to age twelve), and 4) the stage of formal operations (twelve years and up).

The stages are infested with the concept of "readiness" as experiences are induced. The sensorimotor stage represents the period in the child's life when his/her actions portray how and what he/she learns. The usage of the basic senses are key factors as the child exercises his/her reflexes and impulses in experiencing environmental stimuli. The various schema utilized by the child during this stage operationalize Piaget's concepts of assimilation and accommodation. Readiness is implicated as this sensory thinking is tested in the real world for the child. Even though the child's ability to do expressive language is void, the essence of receptive language is apparent. Rowland Lorimer (1977), a communications specialist, conceived environmental experiences which are flavored by language into the focal awareness of the child. It is in the preoperational stage that Piaget sets forth the notion that the knowledge of symbols and concepts are acquired in the form of language.

The outstanding symbolic behavior of the child during the preoperational stage does not preclude the fact that capabilities of operational thinking are weak. His/her symbols, concepts and language abilities are immature. This creates the state of "readiness" for the cognitive process.

Four important cognitive processes are involved in the stage of concrete operations (Kagan, 1971). Mental representation sets forth the child's ability to represent sequences of events. Conservation entails the realization that objects do not change their essential volume or weight at the changing of shapes. The logical relationship of parts and wholes is explained through the process of class inclusion. Serialization is the fourth process which shows that objects can be arranged according to some quantifiable dimension. Piaget postulated that these cognitive processes are vital to successful school learning. However, Lorimer (1977) reinforced the premise of the cognitive processes, as theorized by Piaget, but alleviated the age factor as he expresses two propositions: 1) formal instruction must be grounded in the experiencing of full-sensory-perceptual capacities of the person, and 2) the experiencing of the person must be grounded in a "real" world. Such propositions, inclusive of Vance's and Piaget's views on how a child learns, are impregnated with implications for better understanding this position.

Regardless of age -- 3, 4, 5, or 6 -- when credence is given to "how" children learn, with careful observation and knowledge of their learning modalities---visually, auditorially, verbally and physically---as to which one or combination is more pronounced---a sound base for teaching and learning is established.

WHAT BEARING DOES CURRICULUM HAVE ON THE TEACHING/LEARNING PROCESS?

Children do not learn as the result of what caregivers do, but as a result of what caregivers get them to do. This basic principle is as important for children to understand as it is for caregivers. The caregiver who relies on the "I'll talk, you listen" type of teaching is not likely to see much learning take place. With threes, fours and fives it is not a natural behavioral response for them to just sit back and listen, therefore, if the caregiver expects this, he or she will be disappointed.

This is so because learning is change. The ingredients of the curriculum reflects this change as activities are geared toward evoking behavioral change of the individuals. This type of change does not truly become a part of a child until he/she has reinforced it through use. For example, a child can memorize a new word for his/her vocabulary or how to rote count to ten. But he/she doesn't actually "learn" those things until he/she practices using the word and numerals in meaningful situations. The child, in short, must in INVOLVED in the process of learning.

The most basic element of learning is probably MOTIVATION. It is the key factor which forces a person to move toward a goal. Motivation can be instrumental in making a child want to know, to understand, to believe, to act, in order to gain skill. It is up to the caregiver to recognize the importance of motivation and to find out ways to bring motivating factors into the teaching/learning process. Some motivating factors are:

1. The need for security
2. The need for new experience
3. The need for recognition
4. The need for self-esteem
5. The need for conformity and
6. The need to help others

Learning is an ACTIVE process and the actions must focus primarily on the child rather than on the caregiver. The caregiver therefore, plans a variety of participating activities for the children--OBSERVING, LISTENING, THINKING, REMEMBERING, IMAGINING, WRITING, ANSWERING, QUESTIONING, FEELING, TOUCHING, MOVING, AGREEING, DISAGREEING, AND DISCUSSING. The more the participation on the part of the child, the more learning will take place. To put it another way, the more we use our various senses, the greater will be the learning.

Caregivers must be in tune with "how" people learn; they must adjust, develop and/or practice changing their techniques, methods, materials, and behaviors to be more eclectic in their teaching strategies. For example, to teach the concept "red"--the child can identify many "red" objects--mix red paint--a display of "red" objects is organized--stories, poems and riddles are told about the subject "red" as objects are described--i.e., red balloon, red apple, robin red-breast, etc.--the word "red" is printed and displayed in the environment where the child might write it, draw it, trace it, paint it, feel it in different textures, etc.--and then given an opportunity to select the color "red" from a few other colors, as a discriminating task. Much of the teaching failures have been attributed to the ways in which information is presented to the learner. It stands without reason that anyone engaged in the work of teaching young children should have as his/her major goal that he/she understand "how" children learn. This brings the teaching/learning process into focus with curriculum as it suggests appropriate activities and materials for various subject-matter content.

John Blackie, a British Head Master, used this premise in 1969:

> Put a 3 year old down on a seashore, with sand and stones and rock-pools, you will not have to tell it what to do.

Using this premise, one can see the high emphasis placed on careful observation of the child's intellectual capabilities. Such techniques enable caregivers to plan instructional tasks that are broad enough to accommodate a wide variety of learning styles and make teaching and learning more compatible.

HOW CAN WE TELL WHEN TEACHING, LEARNING AND CURRICULUM ARE OPERATING TOGETHER?

Pre-School Curriculum is the total spectrum of experiences for children that happen as they play in their environments. These experiences are characteristic of content areas (i.e., language, sensory perceptions, motor activities, creative arts, science, social studies, and mathematics) which enhance growth and development of the total child--physically, mentally, socially, and emotionally. The play environments include home, school, neighborhood, and community.

Teaching for pre-school is the guidance, care and leadership provided by a caregiver to meet the growth and developmental needs of children. It requires reaching the expected objectives and goals of teaching as achieved through the planning, programming, and evaluation of the curriculum by that caregiver. The caregiver may be a teacher, parent, or interested adult.

"Learning," as defined by Munn (1965), is a process of more or less permanent sequential behavior change resulting from an individual's own performance, special training, and/or observation.

Vance (1973) interpreted this meaning to connote that learning is inferred from the observable behavior of an individual and that the sequential nature of the behavior change indicates that one behavior is built on the foundation of another that precedes it. For example,

o   the young child learns to sit on his tricycle and propel himself by pushing both feet against the ground at the same time;

o   later, he learns to put his feet on the pedals and slowly push alternately with one foot and then the other; and

14

o after practicing this skill for a while, the child eventually rides the tricycle rapidly, negotiating turns around corners and play equipment with greater and greater ease.

As described here, the skill was developed sequentially. Step-by-step the child was able to develop such skill through the accommodating efforts of bodily structure and muscular strength (maturation). Appropriate environmental conditions must be utilized, i.e.,

o availability of an adequately-sized tricycle;

o other children riding tricycles to serve as models of trike-riding skill (observation); and

o perhaps a lot of verbal instruction by teachers and/or children-- such as what comes first, and what comes next (special training).

Still, the child would not have developed his trike-riding skill without applying what he had been taught (performance). Vance further contended that changing behavior reveals whether or not he is learning.

The teaching strategies that influenced the learning of this skill could have taken one or a combination of learning behaviors or styles. For example,

o the child could have learned the skill solely from trial and errors...just by experimenting with the mechanics of the instrument (trike) and its parts (pedals, wheels, handle-bars); or

o the child could have learned the skill from carefully watching the actions used by his peers in the environment;

o nor can we rule out the possibility that the child could have learned the skill from verbal instruction and special training (telling him and showing him what to do); and

o then, there is the chance that it could have taken all of these teaching episodes to enable the child's learning of this trike-riding skill.

Therefore, it is safe to assume that learning changes behaviors, and behaviors are results of observations, special training, and/or the child's own performance (verbal, motor or both). Almost all human behavior is a result of the process called learning. It is, therefore, an integral part of teaching which requires curriculum.

The teaching/learning process and curriculum begin as early as birth. Much of the newborn infant's first few weeks of life is based upon spontaneous and random response to physical stimuli (loud sounds, variety of light intensity or color, various textures, the contractions of an empty stomach, etc.). These responses are limited by the infant's immature bodily structure and poorly developed motor skills (he cries, waves his arms and kicks his feet but cannot move toward the source of satisfaction of his need.) As a matter of fact, in the beginning weeks the baby is not even aware of the source of that satisfaction. His/her need just <u>IS,</u> and his response is <u>SPONTANEOUS</u> as the result of maturation (physical structure and physiological functions). Vance contended that learning is not apparent in such early random and spontaneous behavior. But as the child grows and becomes a more viable part of the surroundings, he begins to learn only what his physical and social environment teaches him within the limitations of his mental and physical capacities.

HOW CAN PLANNING, SCHEDULING, PROGRAMMING, AND ASSESSMENT SERVE AS INSTRUMENTS FOR CURRICULUM AND TEACHING/LEARNING?

The pre-school program should be designed to help young children engage in worthwhile, interesting, and fun-provoking activities. Pre-school curriculum and teaching/learning focus on social, emotional, physical, and mental growth and development. Therefore, the curriculum must be developed to implement the program having diverse learning experiences to provide opportunities for:

o   Participation in sensory experiences.

o   Observation of adult work activities which provide experiences for thinking.

o   Self-selection activities that require manipulative and experimental experiences.

o   Vicarious and simulated experiences.

o   Activities which provide opportunities for conversation and sharing as involvement is carried on in all subject areas.

<u>Planning</u> for teaching/learning is essential in order to help caregivers to predict the future course of study. Classroom experiences must be planned to reveal the scope, sequence, and content of subject

16

area. Planning also includes designing the activities to be used, the pre- and post- assessments, and the extent of defining the curriculum. It is herewith advocated that planning be done in reference to Unit Planning to include: 1) A Resource Unit; 2) A Teaching Unit; and 3) Lesson Plans. Unit planning and teaching make provisions for a holistic (comprehensive) approach to quality curriculum and teaching/ learning. The Resource Unit provides for a "planned curriculum" on each subject area from which the caregiver will be able to select topical teaching episodes--strategies, methods, techniques, concepts and resources (Teaching Unit) that are already selected and organized. The Teaching Unit is the organized plan of related instructional and evaluational experiences that are already contained in the (Resource Unit). This organized plan (Teaching Unit) can be divided into selected instructional strategies to be taught on a daily basis (Lesson Plan). The Lesson Plan constitutes those specific learning activities which evolve from the Teaching Unit. Each lesson plan contains information and materials germane to dealing with specific topics for which guided processes of curriculum and teaching/learning are structured to produce reflective thinking and performance. More specific information about each of the planning processes is as follows:

o   RESOURCE UNIT. A planning episode whereby the caregiver determines what major ideas or dimensions will be emphasized in the pre-school curriculum during a broad period of time (a year, six months, three months). An exploration is undertaken to obtain any and all information and materials in all subject areas for the pre-school curriculum. A complete survey of textbooks in the area of pre-school curriculum, curriculum guides, various courses of study, and books and materials is done to formulate this plan. The nature of planning the Resource Unit calls for individual planning by caregivers collective planning by groups of caregivers. This planning consists of a collection of materials to provide information for all subject areas in the pre-school curriculum. Moreover, a textbook alone cannot provide the caregiver with a Resource Unit plan. Therefore, the information and materials should represent a plan including:

    o   Purposes for teaching each subject area: expressive arts, language arts, mathematics, science, social studies, play and motor development.

    o   List the goals and objectives for teaching each subject area.

17

○ List concepts (ideas, facts, common sense understandings, basic givens, etc.) to support each subject area.

○ Compile strategies (methods, activities) to be used to implement each concept in each subject area. These can be identified by listing sources obtaining examples and samples of teaching/learning strategies.

○ List appropriate teaching resources (material and human) for the children and for the teacher to be used in implementing the teaching/learning.

○ Specify assessment plan for each subject area (pre- and post- evaluation ideas), recognizing that much assessment information will be included in instructional strategies.

○ Write a brief and concise statement to show each subject area will be correlated with each other in order to support incidental and planned teaching/learning from the vantage point of being able to recognize learning and provide teaching in both structured and non-structured environments and situations.

○ TEACHING UNIT. A planning process whereby information and materials are drawn from the Resource Unit around meaningful topics comprising a subject area. The curriculum focuses on a central theme in order to attain some degree of unified teaching/learning. These related concepts are unified for instructional purposes and provide opportunities for critical thinking, generalization and application of information and materials to many topical situations. The pre-school curriculum is more creatively implemented when teaching units focus upon practical, central ideas (themes) to be explored in blocks of time much shorter than those planned for the Resource Unit. A period of six weeks is probably a good maximum time for implementing the Teaching Unit, with a period of three weeks being the minimum time. There are some phases of unit planning involved in the Teaching Unit like initiating activities, developing activities, and culminating activities that are necessary to effective implementation of the curriculum and teaching/learning process. The Teaching Unit must be consistent with, and fit into, the overall framework established in the Resource Unit.

° LESSON PLAN. A more detailed analysis of a particular activity that is described in the Teaching Unit is a Lesson Plan. The essentials of a Lesson Plan are similar to the important elements of the unit plans. The forms and styles of Lesson Plans are different, but the plan should in all cases include essential elements like:

  ° Topic/Theme.

  ° Goal or objective (stated behaviorally).

  ° Approach or introduction (explanation of content).

  ° Activities (including methods, procedures, techniques).

  ° Evaluation Plan (including special needs provisions).

  ° Materials to be used.

Lesson Plans must be modified in accordance with teaching methods, instructional purposes, various requirements of jobs, and so forth. A sample Lesson Plan is provided to set a visual image of the elements. See Figure 2. The Lesson Plan is designed around the concept of utilizing the children in the planning. This helps to enhance the teaching/learning process due to the inclusions of motivation, interest, and individual differences of pre-schoolers.

Scheduling is the process of organizing curriculum and teaching/learning endeavors into structured time frames. These time frames can differ from program to program in accord with planning and organizing for individual and group instruction. The curriculum is broken into subject area groups and living circumstances, like experiences in play, mathematics, science, arrival, breakfast, art, music, and so forth. The best use of the time of caregivers and pre-schoolers is structured into a "schedule." There is common understandings about approximate time periods to be used for different parts of the schedule. For example, subject area content might use time periods scheduled as follows: Outdoor Play (30 minutes per day); Expressive Arts -- Music, Visual Arts, Drama, Dance and Movement (15-30 minutes); Language Development (20 minutes); Mathematics and Science Concepts (20 minutes each); Snacks (10 minutes); Lunch (30-45 minutes); Arrival and Free Play (10-30 minutes); and so forth. The following sample of a schedule could be helpful in organizing a typical day in the pre-school program. See Figure 3.

Figure __2__.

<u>SAMPLE LESSON PLAN</u> (SKELETAL)

Subject Area _____ Date _____

Age Level _____Time for Lesson _____ ( ) Minutes

OBJECTIVES OF LESSON: (Stated Behaviorally)

MATERIALS NEEDED:

MOTIVATION:

ACTIVITIES (PROCEDURES):

EVALUATION: (Teacher and Children)

Figure __2__. Sample Lesson Plan

20

Figure __3__

Activity	Individual/Group	Time
Greet Children at Arrival Health Check Breakfast Snack (preparation and clean up time) FREE PLAY and PLANNING	(Individual Children)	8:30 to 9:15 (45 minutes)
EXPRESSIVE ARTS (Exploration with materials, blocks, etc. (The Work Period, Preparation Time and Clean-Up Time)	(Small groups in several interest groups)	9:15 to 10:25 (70 minutes)
GROSS MOTOR PLAY (Outdoors or in Play Room inside)	(Whole group)	10:25 to 10:50 (30 minutes)
CONCEPT DEVELOPMENT (Mathematics, Science, Language, Social Studies, etc.	(Small groups, Individual Children)	10:50 to 11:10 (20 minutes)
EXPRESSIVE ARTS (Music, Drama, Dance, etc.)	(Small groups, Individual children, some instances of whole group)	11:10 to 11:30 (20 minutes)
LUNCH (Preparation and Clean-Up)	(Whole group)	11:30 to 12:30 (60 minutes)
REST AND RELAX-ATION TIME	(Whole group)	12:30 to 2:00 (90 minutes)
CONCEPT DEVELOPMENT AND FREE PLAY (Clean-Up and Dis-missal)	(Individual, Small group, Whole group)	2:00 to closing (30 mins. – 180 mins.)

Figure __3__ .   Sample Schedule of Activities

The sample of the full-day schedule of activities for three, four, and early five year olds can be further explained as shown in the following information.

EXPLANATION FOR A SUGGESTED DAILY PROGRAM
AS DESCRIBED

Greeting Children:

Children arrive and as they enter, warmly greet each child and address by name.

Health Check:

Give special attention to the appearance of each child. Look for running noses, red and/or watery eyes, rashes on skin, signs of fatigue, abuse, hunger, and neglect.

Breakfast/Snack:

After checking for health reasons, prepare children for breakfast or snack by washing their hands and then seating them at tables set with juice, cereal, toast, and milk. Hold conversation with them concerning weather, family, or news items.

Free Play and Planning:

Children can select any activity to engage in play. Planning is done with children in accord with their interest and ideas.

Expressive Arts
Experience with Materials:
(The Work Period)

This period includes opportunities for freedom of activity and children are not necessarily limited to the use of creative arts materials. Give children the freedom of choosing activities relating to dramatic play, block construction, library corner, musical instruments, housekeeping corner, and listening corner, if available. Allow adequate time for cleaning up area.

Gross Motor Play:	Use large equipment, balls, tricycles, hoops, ropes, and rhythm instruments on the outside (weather permitting). Can be done in large spacious indoor area.
Concept Building Experiences:	Provide opportunities for <u>planned</u> science, mathematics, social studies and/or language experiences.
	Use enrichment activities like, puppets, magnetic and flannel board, experiences with the tape recorder, viewing TV and listening to radio programs geared to pre-school, records, listening center, if available, and social learning episodes.
Expressive Arts:	Have children engage in singing, rhythmical experiences, music appreciation, dancing and movement activities.
	Read or tell a story or poem to children or have them create original stories or poems, retelling stories by children and acting out (dramatizing) can be done.
Preparation and Clean-Up for Lunch :	Toileting and hand washing before and after lunch, and removing trash after eating.
Lunch:	Caregivers, teacher aides, and volunteers should dine together in small groups (one adult to every five children), allowing opportunity for conversation, the forming of friendships, and intellectual interaction.

	Clean-up is an accepted part of lunchtime routine. Each child should be responsible for cleaning up the place where he eats (table and floor).
Rest and Relaxation Time:	Give children opportunities to rest (many will go to sleep) for a period during the day.
Dismissal:	Prepare for sending children home (dress, wash-up, have snacks, prepare environment, and so forth).

A good order to follow when programming/curriculum and teaching/ learning for pre-schoolers is outlined in the following six steps. This model (Barbara Vance, 1973) summarizes the presentation on planning, scheduling, programming, and assessing.

STEP ONE: | Determine Focus of Instruction |

STEP TWO: | Determine Instructional Objectives |

STEP THREE: | Assess Pre-Instructional Behavior |

STEP FOUR: | Determine Learning Activities |

STEP FIVE: | Determine Reinforcement Procedures |

STEP SIX: | Evaluate Instructional Outcomes |

Step One, "Determine Focus of Instruction;" Step Two, "Determine Instructional Objectives;" Step Four, "Determine Learning Activities;" and Step Five, "Determine Reinforcement Procedures" have been addressed already in this chapter. The two steps, "Three" and "Six" are described in the following presentation on assessing pre-schoolers in reference to curriculum and teaching/learning.

The primary purpose of assessment is to provide a basis for individual guidance. Each child is assessed in order to determine strengths and weaknesses so that pre-school experience can enhance learning. A survey is made before pre-schoolers begin the teaching/learning process to determine what the child already knows. Then instruction is carried on. Afterwards, the pre-schoolers are again evaluated with the same instruments, strategies, and sources to see how much learning took place over a set period of time. This process constitutes "assessing pre-instructional behavior" (Step Three) and "evaluating instructional outcomes" (Step Six).

In order to assess a child's learning in any area, the caregiver must have a clear idea of the goals and objectives for the child's learning. Progress or growth assumes a direction. They assume movement from one level to another. When a child's learning is evaluated, three steps are involved:

Step One: Information is gathered to determine the child's strengths (skills and understandings)

Step Two: A comparison is made between the present assessment and previous assessments

Step Three: A comparison is made between the present assessment and goals for the child's learning

Although these steps are based on an underlying structure which requires an organized idea of a progression in understandings and skills, this does not mean that children's learning must be RIGIDLY SEQUENCED.

FOR EXAMPLE: IF THE CHILD CAN RECOGNIZE AND NAME SETS WITH NUMBER PROPERTIES UP TO FIVE, THE CHILD IS PROBABLY READY TO:

     o   Learn to recognize and name sets

     o   Learn about relationships among numbers from one through five

     o   Learn to recognize written numerals for numbers through five and match them with the proper sets

Children need not be restricted to specific steps along a narrow path. This example shows <u>pre-instructional behavior.</u>

Pre-instructional assessment involves securing information about what the child knows or can do. There are basically two ways to collect such data:

One: Directly through observation

Two: Indirectly through written work or other products and assessments

It is sometimes helpful to combine the two methods. This is done as described below:

Directly Through Observation

○ The teacher must observe the child to see if he/she can name sets correctly, when he/she cannot yet write his/her name and read.

Indirectly Through Written Work or Other Products

○ It is extremely difficult to think of a way to collect data about computational skills without the use of pencil and paper. (The teacher looks at the finished product, since it is not necessary to watch the child as the work is being done).

Combining the Direct and Indirect Ways

○ In collecting data on the child's ability in art, the teacher might find it helpful to observe while the child works on an art project as well as to examine the finished product.

The teaching/learning process is implemented (after the pre-instructional assessment) in an orderly manner. Every caregiver should have an individual theory of instruction. Each should understand and use learning theory in his/her teaching. Included should be a rationale of the ideas considered important in teaching and learning. Based on this rationale, curriculum is built and teaching strategies are developed and implemented. The caregiver must continue to learn and to revise and expand a storehouse of ideas, methods, activities, and resources.

Post-assessment is done through various means. There are principally two methods of testing that are used in addition to "observation" of performance to obtain post-assessment. These two methods of testing are "norm-referenced tests" and "criterion-referenced tests."

Criterion-reference testing, as opposed to norm-referenced testing, evaluates the individual on the basis of a set of criteria established by the teacher/examiner. The criteria are explicitly stated in the behavioral objectives and the individual's success depends on meeting the stated criteria. As the child's performance is not compared to that of other children in the same age/grade level (as in norm-referenced testing), this type of test is recommended by those who want to minimize the effects of bias, competition, and anxiety in testing. Also, norm-referenced testing is not a good measure to use for assessment with pre-schoolers due to their (pre-schoolers) changing behavior patterns, the need for frequent testing, and the need for cultural free tests (especially in the cases of culturally diverse pre-schoolers (i.e. Blacks, Asians, Hispanics, etc.). This assessing of learning must be done continuously in order to serve as the greatest assurances of progress or non-progress we can provide for pre-schoolers and their parents.

WHO ARE THE MAJOR CONTRIBUTORS TO THE PRE-SCHOOL CURRICULUM AND THE TEACHING/LEARNING PROCESS?: THE PAST AND THE PRESENT PROVIDED PATTERNS OF EXPERIENCES

As early as the Fifteenth Century, great men and women have made contributions to curriculum and teaching. They provided a conceptual base that tied curriculum to the teaching/learning process in order to improve life in their times. The lives of young children, then, and at the present time, have been affected by the imagination and drive of great men and women who formulated early childhood programs (theories and practice).

Ever since the initiation of various ideas and programs to facilitate pre-school curriculum and teaching, educational practices have been adapted to meet the goals, objectives, purposes, and implementation of "education" to change behaviors. This historical perspective of contributors to pre-school curriculum and teaching will enhance the background and knowledge base for caregivers. An appraisal of the programs and ideas that were contributed is an excellent learning experience for caregivers to study to provide a framework for using curriculum purposefully. Contributors of the past have made indelible footprints in curriculum and teaching as their ideas and theories are very much apart of educational practices today (Davis, 1963).

o   MARTIN LUTHER (1483-1546) spoke as an educator through the Ninety-Five Theses of October 31, 1517.

   o   The teaching of MUSIC is a contribution that Luther made to pre-school curriculum and education. To him, music was the salve for tired souls. Placing great importance on music, Luther believed that primary teachers should be skilled it it. His interest and background made it possible for him to stress music as a major curriculum area that took root and branched out over the world throughout the centuries. Soothing music and singers that were esteemed by kings and princes, as well as their place and use in the Bible helped to provide strong support for Luther's belief. Of his many contributions to children's education, making music a major curriculum area is the one that is seldom recognized. The song "Away In A Manger" is a singing experience that provides heritage from the work of Martin Luther.

   o   An obligation on all society to teach all children of all people was pronounced through the thesis Docendi Sunt Christiani (Christians Are To Be Taught). Luther supported the concept that primary schools of the church extend their services to all the children of all the people by broadening the educational goal to include not only piety but an understanding of the social obligation to make the community Christian.

   o   Luther presented and crystallized two ideas relevant to pre-school education: 1) All towns and villages were challenged to be responsible for good primary school; and 2) This responsibility was to be split between the two institutions of the church and the local government.

o   JOHN AMOS COMENIUS (1592-1670) saw education beginning in early infancy at the age when learning is absorbed, not forced.

   o   Comenius believed that attractive appearance of the classroom teaches the child, when he grows up, to beautify his home and make it more pleasant. He was responsible for encouraging ART as a part of the curriculum. Pleasant classroom atmospheres for learning, the use of visual aids, and the use of pictures for teaching vocabulary are a few of Comenius' brilliant innovations in pre-school curriculum. One of his books, **Orbis Sensualium Pictus,** (the great picture book), has played an important part in the direction and encouragement of art as a curriculum area.

o   Comenius, the father of the primary school, provided rich concepts to pre-school education. The efforts of teachers utilizing art forms -- visual aids, books, pictures -- and remembering reflective thoughts pertaining to mass education, interest, motivation, preparation, and methodology will result in quality teaching/learning.

o   JOHN LOCKE (1632-1704) presented to the educational world the "tabula rasa" belief which assumed that the mind of a child at birth is a blank tablet upon which all experience will make impressions. This gave adults and professional educators the signal to present, select, and organize the best and most correct impressions to young children. Today, this assumption is contradicted, but the stimulus that it provided benefited the field of education.

o   Locke concerned himself with "constructive instruction" which implied that the adult teaching the young children should approach learning from a positive standpoint. For example, if the child displayed a wrong habit, the teacher would not emphasize the wrong habit, but she/he would present the right method for the child (or a better way to handle the situation).

o   Locke's contribution to a specific area of the pre-school curriculum is LITERATURE. He saw literature as having great value to the education of young children. It was through the influence of Locke that publishers printed these books: **Reynard the Fox** and **Aesop's Fables.**

o   JEAN JACQUES ROUSSEAU (1712-1778) is best known for using a fictional approach -- Emile -- which showed how Emile was educated under a plan designed according to nature. He believed that education for young children should be away from organized society.

○ Rousseau's contribution to pre-school education is broad and those that have been attributed most profoundly to him are enmeshed in the curriculum area of PLAY. He felt that play was the keystone to learning. Also, derived from Emile are concepts like, education is a process of growth; lessons should be learned from free activity whereby the child can interpret life from personal experiences with nature; education is comprised of adaptation and adjustment; and to maintain the good of nature in balance with the good of society should be the goal of education, since the child is born good.

○ The early stages of education, according to Rousseau, should be done through taking the infant through the unconscious state of existence and then the period whereby the child learned from environmental contacts through the pleasure-pain principle. The child would not receive any punishment during these two periods; all pain would be learned from natural reactions to contacts in experiences.

○ Rousseau saw early education taking place through natural contacts in the environment and, therefore, no books or abstract ideas should be given during the formative years. He believed that it should be the eleventh year when the child would see written literature. Because of the nature of the content of the book **Robinson Crusoe,** he would suggest using it for the adventure, natural exposure and dealing with the environment, rather than using **Aesop's Fables.**

○ JOHANN HEINRICH PESTALOZZI (1746-1827) impacted upon pre-school education through the power of love and gratitude (in his writings and his philosophy).

○ Pestalozzi's own school emphasized curriculum in accord with the importance of sound, form, and number as found in each subject area and experience. INDIVIDUAL READING and individualized assignment approaches are contributions made to pre-school education by Pestalozzi.

○ Pestalozzi taught and believed that human equality was tempered and directed by individuality. Therefore, the child who understood his/her individual nature would be assured of equal rights to attain productivity, and would most assuredly find happiness.

o FREIDRICH FROEBEL (1782-1852) was the innovator of many concepts relevant to the kindergarten -- self activity, gifts, occupations, and unity -- and the quotation, "Come, let us live for our children," brings to the mind of pre-school educators the Froebelian concept that the kindergarten was the essential element for so doing that.

    o Froebel, known as the Father of the Kindergarten, systematized young child education and made it possible for the "training" of teachers rather than relying on the natural intuition for instruction.

    o Froebel's concept for teaching, "Gifts and Occupations," was a famous early childhood method. His contribution through this methodology cut across the pre-school curriculum and enhanced BLOCK PLAY, MANIPULATING MATERIALS, and FINGER PLAYS as major considerations in pre-school. The gifts, concrete-tangible objects (primary color yarn balls) had been given to children to play with and observed by Froebel for fifteen years, were chosen for the inherent and indirect endowments he believed they had. The occupations were the play activities that Froebel directed the mother or teacher to use with the gift. The gifts and occupations were selected on the premise that each would enable the child to interpret his/her surroundings and give expression with movement, gestures, and words.

    o He did not believe in having males trained to teach young children. Females were seen as the ones most capable of guiding the young children as they used their senses and emotions as the key elements in learning in the kindergarten (and in infancy - **Mutterund Koselieder**, his book, Handbook for Young Mothers with Babies in Arms).

    o Froebel's concept of kindergarten, "the garden where the young child may grow like a flower if nourished with the essential training," is still a popular one in pre-school education.

o   SUSAN BLOW (1843-1916) was a pioneer in establishing kindergartens in the public school systems. Naturally, she utilized Froebel's curriculum in implementing an experimental kindergarten in St. Louis, Missouri.

   o   Blow paved the way for others to use the Froebelian concepts (Mrs. Carl Schurz, Miss Elizabeth Peabody, Mrs. Quincy Shaw, and Mrs. John Kraus) in private schools and philanthropic efforts.

   o   Blow made many speeches and published materials to state the values of Froebelian philosophy in the educational arena. She published, "Educational Issues in the Kindergarten," in 1908 to further pronounce her cause in pre-school education.

o   MARIA MONTESSORI (1870-1952) was a pioneer in the education of exceptional children.

   o   The pre-school curriculum and teaching/learning process have Montessori to thank for the concept of FREE PLAY and its spontaneous manifestations. The equipment and activities were planned and stationed in the environment to facilitate the child's selection and involvement for any length of time. Much of the routine organization in pre-school education today follows the pattern of the Montessori -- health and personal check-up time, putting on smocks for art work, toileting, and performing chores in the room -- as a part of planning.

   o   Montessori's teaching materials were didactic -- self-corrective. These didactic materials included lacing boards, insert boards, measurement sticks, and hooking boards. This concept was operated in a manner similar to today's teaching machines. Awards were reached when all materials were placed back in order by the children.

   o   Some Montessori methods to remember today include: ideas and lessons for teaching attention, for teaching silence, for teaching habits of quick thinking, and for teaching tactile sense.

o   A practical concept of Montessori's teachings include the idea of the physical plant necessary for the education of young children being constructed as a "real house" (a set of rooms with a garden of which the children are the masters). Furniture in the house should be light enough for the children to move it around, and painted in a light color so that it can be washed with soap and water. A little flower plot is necessary for each child to sow the seeds of an indoor plant. These attributes were basic construction designs that are followed in Montessori schools today, however, many modifications have been made based on financial affordability and restraints.

o   PATTY SMITH HILL (1886-1946) applied the theories of John Dewey in the primary grades. She expressed the significance of purposeful activity and meaningful material that would stimulate the creative thinking of young children.

   o   Hill advocated "a conduct curriculum" (published book) which comprised nature study, literature, music games, gifts and occupations, dolls and doll families, conversation, industry, blocks, health and values.

   o   She is perhaps noted for her contribution to the pre-school curriculum (also) through designing the LARGE HOLLOW BLOCKS that are commonly found in pre-school environments today.

People like Blow, Comenius, Froebel, Hill, Locke, Luther, Montessori, Pestalozzi, and Rousseau have made provisions for theoretical-curriculum frames to be used at present and to be projected well into the future of pre-school education. Caregivers and others interested in early childhood education must give recognition and understanding to the significance of borrowing from our past and other cultures. These attributes should be fused into pre-school programs today for greater quality of "curriculum and teaching/learning."

WHAT ARE SOME BASIC PRINCIPLES FOR TEACHING AND LEARNING?

The Principle of Effect. -- In learning theory and practice, pleasant and satisfying experiences, stimuli and responses are accepted and repeated. Those that are unpleasant and annoying evoke "avoidance behavior: in the individual. Knowing this, caregivers must provide curriculum that will assure successful, motivating and useful experiences in the children's play environment--at home and at school.

The Principle of Primacy. -- In teaching and learning, the caregiver must make sure that initial experiences are successful. The first impression is the most lasting one. The curriculum must provide for interesting and creative subject matter and performance experiences. The strategies used in the teaching/learning process must insure success in the beginning in order to become a lasting learning experience.

The Principle of Exercise. -- Take heed to repeating skills in the teaching/learning process. If the practice is appropriate, the children will benefit a great deal. A desirable habit will be formed in accord with the repetition of the act. Use meaningful drill and recall processes during experiences. The caregivers must make sure that the children are performing the operations correctly. This ensures learning, and at the same time alleviates misconceptions and inadequate performance.

The Principle of Disuse. -- Constant care must be given to foster practice of a skill and rational use of knowledge in the environment. The more a child uses the tools for learning -- listening, talking, seeing, acting, asking, moving, etc. -- the more the child will retain. If the child does not use the skills and knowledge, they become meaningless and are forgotten.

The Principle of Intensity. -- Children will remember the vivid, dramatic and exciting learning experiences. A routine or boring experience will be meaningless in the pre-school, therefore, learning will be void. A caregiver must be an actor. This does not mean that the classroom should be a circus or a theatre-in-the-round, but, the caregiver can make teaching/learning dramatic and realistic by using vivid examples and supporting materials.

The pre-school curriculum, therefore, becomes the key to teaching and learning. It takes into consideration the caregivers roles and responsibilities to provide for meeting the needs of the children as they grow and develop. The needs include providing the children with actions that will foster learning from physical, mental, social and emotional perspectives. Contained in the premise of pre-school curriculum and its relationship to the teaching/learning process are characteristics which have been discussed in another section of this chapter -- "planning, scheduling, programming, and assessment."

ACTIVITIES FOR STUDY AND DISCUSSION

1. Review the Goals for Early Childhood Education and discuss them in reference to curriculum...
   º What experiences must be fostered?
   º What interpretation can be made from curricular activities to show goals being implemented?

2. Find and make a list of concrete examples of curricular activities for theoretical implications of learning patterns by Piaget, Vance, Bruner and others to depict psychomotor, cognitive and affective experiences. Use references to extend/expand beyond the ones in this text.

3. From your reading and discussion of Chapter One, write an essay (500 words) to substantiate the concept that -- "Pre-School Curriculum is the Key to Teaching and Learning."

4. What are your perceptions and attitudes about role delineations in teaching, learning and curriculum for teachers, parents, and young children?
   º How do you fit into this picture?
   º What changes, revisions, deletions do you visualize as necessary to build strong pre-school curriculum?
   º Do you feel comfortable with the teaching/learning process as presented in this text? If not, why not? Be specific and give constructive reasons, suggestions, and recommendations.

5. Do an in-depth review and study of people who have made contributions to the pre-school curriculum; to pre-school theory; and to pre-school practice and applications. Other topics can be included to fit many situations in early childhood education.

REFERENCES

Allen, K.E., B. Hart, J.S. Buell, F.R. Harris, and M. M. Wolf, "Effects of Social Reinforcement on Isolate Behavior of a Nursery School Child," **Child Development**, 1964, 35, 511-518.

Ausubel, D.P., "Can Children Learn Anything That Adults Can--And More Efficiently?", **Elementary School Journal**, 1962, 62, 270-272.

Barbe, Walter B. and Michael N. Milone, Jr., "Barbe Modality Checklist (Parents)," Zaner-Bloser Educational Publishers (163 Coronation Dr., Amhurst, N.Y. 14226), 1980.

Boutwell, R.C. and R.D. Tennyson, "Instructional Objectives--Different By Design," Working Paper No. 13, Instructional Research and Development, Division of Communication Services, Brigham Young University, 1971.

Brown, P. and R. Elliot, "Control of Aggression in a Nursery School Class," **Journal of Experimental Child Psychology**, 1965, 2, 103-107.

Bruner, J.S., **The Process of Education**. Cambridge: Harvard University Press, 1960.

Cohen, Rosalie, "Conceptual Styles, Culture Conflict and Non-Verbal Tests of Intelligence," **American Anthropologist**, 1969, 71:828-56.

Cratty, B.J., **Perceptual and Motor Development in Infants and Children**. New York: Macmillan, 1970.

Davis, David C., **Patterns of Primary Education**. New York: Harper and Row Publishers, 1963.

Eisner, E.W., "Instructional and Expressive Educational Objectives," In M.D. Merrill (Ed.), **Instructional Design: Readings**. Englewood Cliffs, N.J.: Prentice-Hall, 1971.

Eliason, Claudia F., and Loa T. Jenkins, **A Practical Guide To Early Childhood Curriculum**. St. Louis: The C.V. Mosby Company, 1977.

37

Gage, N.L., "Theories of Teaching," in E. Hilgard (Ed.), **Theories of Learning and Instruction. Sixty-Third Yearbook of NSSE, Part 1.** Chicago: University of Chicago Press, 1964.

Gagne, R.M., **The Conditions of Learning**. (Second Edition). New York: Holt, Rinehart and Winston, 1970.

Gagne, R.M., "The Learning of Principles," in M.D. Merrill (Ed.) **Instructional Design: Readings**. Englewood Cliffs, N.J.: Prentice-Hall, 1971.

Gagne, R.M., "The Learning of Concepts," in M.D. Merrill (Ed.), **Instructional Design: Readings**. Englewood Cliffs, N.J.: Prentice-Hall, 1971.

Hendrick, Joanne, **Total Learning: Curriculum for the Young Child**. Columbus, Ohio: Merrill Publishing Company (A Bell & Howell Company), 1986.

Hildebrand, Verna, **Guiding Young Children** (Third Edition). New York: Macmillan Publishing Company, 1985.

Hilliard, Asa, "Alternatives to IQ Testing: An Approach to the Identification of Gifted Minority Children," (Final Report to the California State Department of Education), 1976. In Hale-Benson, Janice E., **Black Children: Their Roots, Culture, and Learning Styles**. (Revised Edition) Baltimore: The Johns Hopkins University Press, 1986.

Mager, R.F., **Preparing Instructional Objectives**. Palo Alto, California: Fearon Publishers, 1962.

Maier, Henry W., **Three Theories of Child Development** (Third Edition). New York: Harper and Row Publishers, 1978.

Martin, Beatrice D., **Teaching Young Children**. Albany, New York: Delmar Publishers, A Division of Litton Educational Publishing, Inc., 1975.

Munn, N.L., **The Evolution and Growth of Human Behavior**. (Second Edition), Boston: Houghton Mifflin, 1965.

Vance, Barbara, **Teaching the Pre-Kindergarten Child: Instructional Design and Curriculum**. Monterey, California: Brooks/Cole Publishing

Co., (A Division of Wadsworth Publishing Company, Inc.), 1973.

Woodruff, A.D., **Basic Concepts of Teaching**. San Francisco: Chandler, 1961.

CHAPTER TWO

MATERIAL RESOURCES AND COMPUTERS FOR
PRE-SCHOOL CURRICULUM

CHAPTER 2

MATERIAL RESOURCES AND COMPUTERS FOR
PRE-SCHOOL CURRICULUM

- WHAT ARE THE PURPOSES OF "EXPERIENCES WITH MATERIALS FOR THE PRE-SCHOOL SUBJECT AREAS?

- WHAT TYPES OF MATERIALS ARE BASIC TO THE PRE-SCHOOL CURRICULUM FOR CHILDREN? FOR CAREGIVERS?

- HOW DO CAREGIVERS SET STANDARDS AND GUIDE ACTIVITIES FOR PROPER USE OF MATERIALS?

- HOW CAN FIELD EXPERIENCES SERVE AS MATERIAL RESOURCES FOR THE PRE-SCHOOL CURRICULUM?

- WHAT ARE THE THREE C'S FOR OBTAINING MATERIALS FOR PRE-SCHOOL CURRICULUM?

    - COLLECTING MATERIALS
    - COMMERCIAL MATERIALS
    - CONSTRUCTING MATERIALS

- HOW CAN COMPUTERS BE EFFECTIVELY USED IN THE PRE-SCHOOL CURRICULUM AND TEACHING/LEARNING PROCESS?

- ACTIVITIES FOR STUDY AND DISCUSSION

- REFERENCES

WHAT ARE THE PURPOSES OF "EXPERIENCES WITH MATERIALS" FOR THE PRE-SCHOOL SUBJECT AREAS?

An Introduction

Loving guidance and adequate materials can open the door for a child to a world where he/she can unfold and learn to understand him/herself and those with whom he/she lives. The Pre-School Curriculum has as its foundation "experiences with materials" as the key factor to the teaching/learning process in all subject areas. Therefore, providing the right types of materials, facilities and equipment is a serious responsibility. Shoemaker (1963) believed, and many others concurred, that in order to make an intelligent selection of toys the caregiver must know what values might accrue to the child from their use and be knowledgeable to certain well-established standards or criteria for their selection. The materials and equipment must be provided in absence of caregiver preference or by surface appeal. Young children need simple but challenging materials and equipment that will build strong bodies and a broad base of understandings.

Each subject area, i.e., pre-reading readiness, language arts, science, mathematics, social studies, and motor learnings, is considered a work period in the pre-school curriculum. In the teaching/learning process the children are free to use materials to express their personal ideas and ideals in a free and exciting manner. The significant activities in all of the subject areas provide an array of opportunities for the children to manipulate objects, explore and experiment with materials and use computers in the instructional process. The caregiver directs the performances of the children at their own levels of development and creativity. A vital point to remember is that when children work with materials, "the process is the most important objective and not the product."

A collection of criteria for identifying proper materials include the following:

1. Materials must be free of detail as possible.
2. Materials must be versatile in use.
3. Materials must involve the child in play.
4. Materials must be large and easily manipulated.
5. Materials must be warm and pleasant to touch.
6. Materials must be durable and work as intended.
7. Materials must encourage cooperative play.

8. Materials must be easy to comprehend in accord to the construction.
9. Materials must be safe and flexible in function.
10. Materials must be enjoyable.

During the pre-school years and the minutes, hours, and days in the pre-school classrooms, centers, and in the homes, the child receives his/her first and basic experiences. A wealth of material resources for each of the child's learning activities will ensure concrete understandings, positive attitudes about learning, and competent beginnings in social, cognitive, emotional, and physical growth and development. These skills and abilities will influence all future learning in later years. The purpose of "experiences with materials" in the pre-school curriculum is dire to the proper care and guidance of pre-schoolers in the teaching/learning process. Therefore, the pre-school curriculum in all subject areas must be enhanced by a rich array of materials and equipment in order that the child may grow and develop to his/her fullest capacity during these experiences.

WHAT TYPES OF MATERIALS ARE BASIC TO THE PRE-SCHOOL CURRICULUM FOR YOUNG CHILDREN? FOR CAREGIVERS?

The pre-schooler needs a wide variety of materials to use when he/she plays in the activity areas. The caregiver needs these materials in order to provide a rich environment for teaching and learning. The educational value of materials in the pre-school and in the home is depicted through innovative devices that enable the child to intelligently experience his/her world with excitement and understanding. The utilization of educational materials in the pre-school curriculum is based upon many philosophies and learning theories. Two of the most known theoretical concepts in material construction and utilization are based on the work of Piaget and Montessori. Therefore, materials and equipment must be multi-purposeful for the regular and the exceptional child--gifted, retarded, physically handicapped, and disadvantaged. The pre-school curriculum is designed to meet the needs of all children, and the materials and equipment must be congruent with the subject area activities.

The pre-school curriculum is dependent upon materials to enrich the teaching/learning process by: encouraging manipulative skills and abilities; by building confidence; by arousing interest and excitement; by facilitating creativity; by providing sensorial experiences; and by providing an abundance of skills, attitudes, and abilities in creative arts, fine and gross motor activities, language arts, pre-reading, science, mathematics, and social living concepts. The following material resources provide specificity for the pre-school curriculum and serve as a guide for caregivers to use in the careful and strategic planning and scheduling of activities. One of the caregiver's primary responsibilities in the teaching/learning process is the task of selecting appropriate materials (Schickendanz, et. al., 1983). These are minimal listings taken from a series of materials to give the basic or primary types for each curriculum area. However, this does not preclude their usage in other areas and for multi-purposes, especially in adapting and renewing use for special needs children, multi-cultural needs, and special projects. Many of the same materials will be listed under two or more subject areas.

The competent caregiver will make sure that the child has a wide variety of basic materials to use in the learning environment. The pre-school curriculum encompasses material resources as a vital, integral part of its experiences. Rather, it coincides the goals and objectives of the teaching/learning process to the direction and use of material resources. Without a doubt, the child, then, is provided with the best possible learning environment for positive growth and development--physically, socially, emotionally, and intellectually.

Chart 1

MATERIALS/RESOURCES: GROSS MOTOR AND SMALL MOTOR EXPERIENCES

GROSS MOTOR MATERIALS/RESOURCES

- tumbling mats • jump ropes • large nesting cubes
- hand puppets • see-saws • coaster sleds
- stair steps • jump boards • teeter totters
- balance bridges/beams • climbing apparatus
- large cars, trucks, scooters for peddling
- broad jump pads • large hollow blocks
- scooter boards • tricycles • wagons
- push-pull toys • hobby horses
- crawling tunnels • rocking boats
- rocking horses • balls for throwing and catching
- swings • slides • playground accessories

SMALL MOTOR MATERIALS/RESOURCES

- stacking cubes • wind up music toys • matching sorting pieces
- bottle caps for counting • paint brushes
- pinch items--dried beans, pebbles, shells, macaroni
- busy board/box for assembling small items
- parquetry (small squares for counting and sorting
- scissors and construction paper for cutting
- small building blocks • unit blocks
- beads • puppets • puzzles
- pegs and peg boards • wind up toys
- fat pencils/crayons • stacking toys
- pounding bench and pegs • thread and empth spools
- string and buttons • sorting tray • buttoning apparatus

45

Chart 2

MATERIALS/RESOURCES: EXPRESSIVE ARTS, LANGUAGE ARTS, MATHEMATICS, SCIENCE, AND SOCIAL STUDIES CURRICULUM

EXPRESSIVE ARTS	LANGUAGE ARTS	MATHEMATICS	SCIENCE	SOCIAL STUDIES
• Visual Arts Paper, crayons, play dough, paints, brushes, clay, paste/glue, scissors, chalk/chalk board, macaroni, rice, string, yarn, masking tape, easels, felt pens, finger paints, pipe cleaners, felt materials; • Dramatic Play dress-up clothes, full length mirror, dress-up accessories--shoes, hats, wigs, purses, jewelry; uniforms-- police, fireperson, nurses, doctors; play telephones, house corner "stuff"--dolls and accessories,	• Pre-Reading, Speaking, Listening, Writing puzzles, record player, records, games--for reading/language, earphones, sequence cards, picture dictionaries, tape recorder, writing paper--lined and unlined; fat pencils/crayons, chalk and chalkboard, paper bags for puppets, flannel boards, large picture books, letter charts, flash cards, writing charts, flip charts for writing stories, story books, puppets, old socks for puppets, large hollow blocks, large pasteboard boxes	• Numbers/Numeration objects, unit blocks, abacus, number line, number readiness posters, bead bars, counting boxes and spindles, number cards/flash cards, number puzzles, number puzzle boards, cash registers, play money, number games, calendars, pegboard and pegs, clocks • Measurement buckets, pails, shovels, spoons, cans, pans; weighing scales, thermometers, rulers, yardsticks, meter sticks, popsicle sticks	• Exploration and Sensory Perception soluble/non-soluble substances-- sugar, salt, pepper, sawdust, sand, gelatin, clay, rice; nests, pictures, leaves, balloons, pots and pans, fan, magnifying glasses, telescopes, nets, pulleys, lock and key, small animals, seeds, plants, textures, magnets, scales, rock and mineral, odor jars--mint, peanut oil, garlic, banana, paint, cloves;	• Socialization name tags, labels, games, maps, globes, mirrors, records, record player, tape recorder, camera, photographs, pictures of people, places, and things; dress-up clothes and costumes, posters of costumes and sceneries for other countries, books, atlas, blocks, puzzles, puppets, flag of the USA, flags of other countries, seasonal pictures, charts, graphs, pictures of animals, weather charts, thermometers

Chart 2

MATERIALS/RESOURCES: EXPRESSIVE ARTS, LANGUAGE ARTS, MATHEMATICS, SCIENCE, AND SOCIAL STUDIES CURRICULUM

EXPRESSIVE ARTS	LANGUAGE ARTS	MATHEMATICS	SCIENCE	SOCIAL STUDIES
child sized stoves, refrigerators, sinks, irons and ironing boards, cupboards, tables, chairs, sinks, dishes, spoons, forks, knives, cups, glasses, pots, pans, tea set, mops, brooms, sponges, empty containers • Music record players, re-cords, drums, wrist bells, tone blocks, tambarines, symbols, rhythm sticks, tri-angles, xylopipes, maracas, wooden bell, cubes, bongos		• Geometry geometric form board, shape disks, geo-metric figures and solids, fraction blocks, unit blocks, geo-boards, geometric insert templates, geometric form cards, rulers and straight edges, dimensional objects--tubes, cans, boxes, balls, carpet squares	• Health and Safety first aid kit, danger signs (posters), traf-fic signs, street signs, adequate toilet facilities, wash basin, drinking water foun-tain, stove or hot plate, refrigerator, toilet paper, paper towels, soap, thermom-eters, snack foods, trash cans, cotton balls, eating utencils, (i.e. forks, spoons, knives, plates, etc.)	

HOW DO CAREGIVERS SET STANDARDS AND GUIDE
ACTIVITIES FOR PROPER USAGE OF MATERIALS?

The effective use of pre-school curriculum materials by both the caregiver and the child benefits the teaching/learning process. One of the best ways to use materials properly is to define them under specific subject areas and assign specific spaces for activity areas. The activities or experiences are planned and scheduled in reference to ages and stages of development. Each teaching objective is the ignition for the child's learning opportunities to manipulate, experiment, examine, and explore the use of a wide variety of materials.

Careful consideration must be given by the caregiver to avoid imposing standards and methods or techniques on the child's work. It is the caregiver's role to encourage and guide the child toward freely expressing his/her ideas and interests. Some methods the caregivers may employ in guiding the activities or experiences are to:

○ carefully <u>observe</u> the child as he/she works in the activity areas;

○ move among the children, often, and <u>spot evaluate</u> the performances;

○ give <u>help</u> and <u>guidance</u> to the child based on observed assessment;

○ ask <u>questions</u>, <u>show pictures</u>, and <u>provide supplementary material aids</u> to arouse and maintain interest levels of the children;

○ require <u>awareness of directions</u> for using computers and other equipment before operating them;

○ <u>demand relevance</u> of activity or experience based on objective or purpose;

○ keep materials on the <u>maturational level</u> of the child;

○ provide for <u>individual experiences;</u>

○ provide for <u>small group</u> experiences; and

○ <u>encourage free choice</u> of materials to aid in building discipline and self control and self direction.

The caregiver is charged with the role and responsibility of setting standards for proper usage of materials. Material resources must be kept in proper condition and utilized in a safe and orderly manner in the activity areas. This ensures derivation of maximum satisfaction of usage as well as the child's development of desirable work habits and work attitudes. Ultimate to setting standards and guiding activities for proper use of materials is the caregiver in the teaching/learning process. The following criteria is helpful to the pre-school caregivers as they select, care, and maintain material resources for pre-school curriculum. Figure 4 shows a Materials Standards Guide. This guide sets forth the beginning criteria, and as the caregiver gains more exposure to the teaching/learning process, the material resources, standards, and caregiver's role will be expanded and strengthened.

MATERIALS STANDARDS GUIDE

Figure 4

MATERIAL RESOURCES	STANDARDS	ROLE OF THE CAREGIVER
Activity Areas Work Space	Home shelves & counters for toys, cots, records, and block carts or shelves for building blocks and unit blocks; have shelves for storing accessory materials, music equipment, art materials and supplies, science materials, and play materials; 35 sq. ft. of open floor space per child.	Orient children to activity areas and teach rules for using and returning materials, toys, and equipment to storage spaces. See that floor space is adequate for group or individual child.
Storage Space	High cabinets to store poisonous items--kitchen and household cleansers, drugs and health aids. Food storage cabinets and shelves and sterilizing equipment for cooking and eating utensils.	Watch children and make sure they do not have access to these cabinets. Keep them high and locked. Know how to use first aid equipment, drugs, etc. and cooking-eating utensils.
Furniture and Equipment	Child-sized chairs, tables, bathroom facilities (basin, toilets, etc.), beds or cots, and housekeeping activity area furniture-- stove, refrigerator, sink, ironing board, table and chairs.	Order, purchase and make sure funiture and equipment are appropriate for the age, size, and abilities of the children.
Telephone	Have at least one in the center/classroom or near by for emergencies.	Post all emergency numbers (police, hospital, fire station) and have numbers for parents or significant others of children at work and at home readily available.

MATERIAL RESOURCES	STANDARDS	ROLE OF THE CAREGIVER
Carpeting	Select a Washable, durable carpet that is fireproof (nylon in-door/outdoor type).	Check local fire safety regulations. Use in work area more appropriate for conducive learning activities for carpet, i.e., reading, language, dramatic play area.
Good Temperature Control	Proper equipment for cooling and heating environment. Proper insulation and ventilation.	Check thermostats and building equipment to enact health and safety regulations.
Blocks (Building, Unit, and Hollow)	Hardwood, non-splintering, smooth rounded edges and clear lacquer finish; or other materials like fiberboard, plywood, and plastic that are durable, lead-free paint, wipe clean and light enough to tumble safely.	Guide children toward stacking in orderly fashion (size, shape, type) in storage space and/or block carts. Arrange for block play in area free of clutter to avoid accidents. Make limitations on number of blocks and on number of children in the blockbuilding area.
Reading Area (Books, Magazines, and Pictures)	Well lighted area in the room; out of the main flow of traffic; tables and chairs scaled to size of children; a carpeted area in case children want to sit on floor; relatively quiet spot in the area; reading materials that are varied to include: large picture books with realistic, large, clear pictures; colorful books and pictures;	Provide a reading center in the room; keep the materials displayed in an orderly and neatly arranged format; introduce new materials to the children; browse through the materials with and without the children periodically to keep abreast of the contents and encourage children to model after you; and help the children to keep the reading area

51

MATERIAL RESOURCES	STANDARDS	ROLE OF THE CAREGIVER
	magazines for cutouts and some for observations and conversations; books with cloth covers; pictures covered with plastic for protection of handling and long usage; and a variety of reading materials that fit the curriculum areas.	quiet, neat, and interesting.
Mathematics and Science Area (Tools for measuring--rulers, yardsticks, blocks; for weighing--scales; for telling time--clocks, hour glass; for counting --small objects, number lines, abacus; for geometric concepts--models of shapes and solids, materials for tracing, drawing, and constructing shapes and solids and pictures to see the different shapes and solids; tools for using the metric system--meter stick, containers for measuring liquids; thermometers. Items for scientific discovery--plants and small animals; planetary system; smell jars; hot plate for boiling water and cooking; materials of various fabrics for sensory perceptions).	Make sure that all tools are in good condition for using; tools should be easily understood-- clear numbers, large digits for counting and measuring; easy to handle or manipulate; fairly easy to dismantle or put back together; proper housing for small animals and room temperature and food supply adequate; have proper storage space for materials; and keep area functional with materials of interest and related to the topic of discussion, etc.	Set up learning areas; make sure items for use are relevant to the interest and topic of discussion; take relevant materials from other activity areas and replace them after usage in the mathematics and/or science experiences; make rules for caring for the plants and animals; see that children have responsible chores as well as learning experiences.

Materials Standards Guide
Figure 4 (continued)

MATERIAL RESOURCES	STANDARDS	ROLE OF THE CAREGIVER
Music, Games, and Large Motor Activities (Record Player, Records, Simple Instrument--Bells, Tamborines, Triangle Ring, Drums, etc. Jump Ropes, Wheel Toys--Tricycles, Wagons, Scooters, Push-Pull Toys, Large Hollow Blocks, Mats for Tumbling, Puppets, Climbing Apparatus, and Balls).	Large, open area with space to move and interact; storage space for equipment and toys; have at least 35 square feet of open floor space per child; set rules for playing games, and using toys; have time limits for activities.	Encourage free choices; spearhead active learning, plan movement activities; make sure the rules are clear and understood by each child; supervise removal and placement of materials and equipment; take an active part in the activities.
Activity Area for Small Motor Experiences (Table Games, Stringing Beads, Manipulating Small objects, pencils, crayons, puzzles, puppets, pegs and peg boards, wind-up toys, nesting and stacking toys, unit and small building blocks, busy box and form boards and box).	Tables scaled to the size and height of children; toys, in proper working condition; blocks of hard wood or plastic that can be easily handled or manipulated; objects should be colorful and interesting to the eye; storage space and shelves for small items; pencils and crayons should be fat; and space for working is adequate for number of children.	Set up activity area; provide a variety of activities on a daily basis; encourage play in various activities for children; demonstrate the use of toys and materials of children; set rules for using and storing materials; encourage eye-hand coordination and grasping skills during the actual experiences.
Creative Activities Area (Art Experiences--Clay, crayons, chalk, paint, finger paint, paste, scissors, collage; wood work experiences; and water and sand play).	Children wear aprons/ smocks when working with clay--keep covered in damp cloth or in container with top, make balls of clay, keep at proper consistency for modeling and manipulating, keep out of the sink drains, store scraps for future use; chalk	Make sure children are properly attired for art activities; arrange space for completing projects--painting and drying, etc.; label the child's work; limit the time and number of children to participate in the various activities; set rules and

53

MATERIAL RESOURCES	STANDARDS	ROLE OF THE CAREGIVER
	should be used on the chalk board or on paper with a rough surface, very effective to use wet chalk on dry paper; paint is better at a consistency of cream, or bright colors, in containers that are easily identifiable, and can be handled by the children, never fill the container completely, use a different brush for each color, wash brushes often and daily, compact hair of brushes together and store on wooden ends, children should wear smocks or aprons, use the easels and construction and/or art paper for painting; paste should be mixed to a consistency easy for spreading, keep in tightly sealed containers, keep in small amounts, use brushes and/or wooden sticks for spreading, hands are also used to spread paste, clean materials immediately after use on a daily basis, and keep a variety of pastes for different art activities; Fingerpaint should be made to possess the proper consistency for spreading, have a variety of bright	regulations for doing work and putting away materials and finished/unfinished projects; check materials to make sure they are stored properly and labeled correctly; demonstrate a variety of usages and make children feel comfortable in exercising the process and not too concerned with the product; extend the art project beyond the classroom to the home and the neighborhood; provide a variety of models--pictures, objects, other projects, etc.; have puppet and art shows with the children; plan activities and provide adequate amounts of materials for each child; spot check the work and projects of each child periodically; give suggestions by asking questions and showing pictures and models of other projects; stress safety in use and storage; demonstrate proper handling of tools; keep area free of loose sand and water spills; show trust and confidence in the children as they perform in the wood work area and during other art activities.

MATERIAL RESOURCES	STANDARDS	ROLE OF THE CAREGIVER
	colors, be clear and smooth, use on proper paper (glazed or wax type), children should wear aprons/smocks and stand to do the finger painting, can be done on clear, clean table tops, or on large pieces of paper on the table as a group project (mural); clean construction paper strips and scraps, newspaper and other materials may be used for constructing a collage, pictures of faces, objects, etc. can be cut and pasted to make a collage, store these materials in small containers-- boxes, jars, cans; scissors can be blunted or sharp on the ends, store in small cans with points down, carry to and from work area in these containers; keep crayons in con- tainers for each color, use the fat pieces and not too short so that chil- dren can handle and use effectively, keep points peeled and ready for use, and use with con- struction paper and art paper; sand play requires sand that is free from foreign items, dry or wet, and keep in containers large	

Materials Standards Guide
Figure 4 (continued)

MATERIALS RESOURCES	STANDARDS	ROLE OF THE CAREGIVER
	enough for children to play when standing or sitting inside the sand box; water play requires containers to hold water, objects to use in filling and dumping just as in sand play, children usually stand at containers, or use wading pools of plastic/rubber, sprinklers are also used in Summer-time, change water daily and keep clean and free from food items; and wood work requires proper demonstration of the use of the tools, use soft wood of a variety of sizes and shapes, use nails with large heads, small hammers, and small hand saws.	
Puzzles (for use in all subject area activities)	The name of the puzzle should be written on the back with magic marker or in ink on a piece of masking tape, only complete puzzles should be used by the children, children can share in the use of the puzzles in a helping fashion, display puzzles on tables, on shelves, and/or in puzzle racks; mark puzzles with handles for easy manipulation of	Write the names of puzzles on each one; check after use to see that all parts are there; remove uncompleted puzzles by nature of missing pieces from puzzle racks; check/evaluate completion of puzzles per child on a regular basis; and demonstrate use of puzzles that may be unfamiliar to the children.

56

MATERIAL RESOURCES	STANDARDS	ROLE OF THE CAREGIVER
	accord to age, size and maturity of the children.	
Housekeeping and Dramatic Play Areas (Blocks and Accessory Materials, dolls, furniture, dress-up clothes, mirrors, telephones, household objects-- mop, broom, dishes, pots, pans, silverware, etc.)	Ample storage spaces, materials in good condition neatly arranged, properly defined territory for play, keep furniture in good shape for use by children in both dramatic play and in imitating housekeeping duties, keep doll clothing and old clothes for dress-up activities clean and uncluttered for use, materials should be scaled to the size, age, and maturation of the children.	Stress safety in use and storage; provide adequate materials and equipment for activities; provide adequate space and theme atmosphere, spot evaluate but do not interfere with play; involve children in a variety of experiences denoting family life and life in general to enhance dramatic play scenes; and encourage creativity on the part of the children--free expression, exploration of ideals/ideas, and wide use of imagination.
Computers for instructional purposes (hardware and software--floppy disks)	Proper computer tables, placed in cool area of room for use and for storage (protection from theft), properly maintained by contractual services by company.	Provide complete and detailed instructions for operation and use by children. Supervise use of computers closely, for assessment of instruction and for appropriate use and care of equipment.

HOW CAN FIELD EXPERIENCES SERVE AS MATERIAL RESOURCES FOR THE PRE-SCHOOL CURRICULUM?

Field experiences through trips, nature walks, neighborhood visits, and extended classroom study through the outdoors are very important to the child and to the pre-school curriculum as material resources. This is the vehicle toward extending experiences and compounding information for making learning more relevant and real to the children. Ideas are made more clearer; language is facilitated; and more contact can be made by the child to his/her physical world. The environment is full of resources for the child to use in his/her learning experiences. When assessing these resources from subject areas in the pre-school curriculum, one might find these answers to the question: "How can field experiences serve as material resources for the pre-school curriculum?"

o   <u>Small and gross motor experiences</u> are enhanced through field experiences when children pick up rocks, pebbles, insects; through walking, climbing hills, climbing trees, swinging on limbs, running through the fields, and other active involvements in the neighborhood and community.

o   <u>Pre-reading skills and language arts</u> are nourished through the child's exposure to the environment as he/she listens to sounds of animals, automobiles, and nature; through exposure to the printed pages like the newspapers, signs, and posters; through talking with peers and others about things in the environment; through trips to the library, and television shows.

o   <u>Mathematics experiences</u> are received through familiarity of home addresses of children, street numbers, counting objects, cars, trucks, and people; through measuring shadows, observing heights of trees, and sizes of houses; through looking at shapes of houses, streets, road signs; through identifying numerals and temperatures; and through estimating distances, sizes, and amounts of places, people and things.

o   <u>Science experiences</u> are obtained through the child's contacts with the environment through weather conditions, times of years, month, day; through observing the plants and animals and their means of survival; through feeling the tree trunks, bark, leaves, buildings; through tasting the foods from the gardens, orchids, and farms; through smelling the air for various aromas of foods cooking, automobile fumes, fragrances of flowers, and other substances used for building and making things; through seeing nature in full bloom, and seeing people do many things.

o   Social living experiences are facilitated by the field experiences as children interact with themselves and the environment; through seeing the balance of nature in the sense of plants and animals needing one another to survive; through respecting the rights and property of others--fences around yards, signs posted to give directions and information, and models of walking on the walks and not on the lawns; through observing the various offices of community workers, the community workers in uniforms--policemen-women, bus drivers, sanitary workers, etc.; and through obeying rules of the neighborhood, community and schools; and through seeing peoples of all nationalities.

o   Creative arts experiences are expanded through the children's observations of various art forms in the community; through the various colors of plants, houses, clothes, automobiles, and objects; through musical sounds made by people, things, and nature; through seeing building constructions, and architectural designs; and through incorporating sights and scenes into art medium and movement.

Field experiences are ways to provide the children with direct contact with the environment which adds dimension to the teaching/learning process. They are excellent accessory materials for enhancing the pre-school curriculum. The children are reinforced in their understandings, knowledges, skills, attitudes, and abilities as they explore and examine the learning objectives and perform the tasks.

WHAT ARE THE THREE C'S FOR OBTAINING MATERIALS FOR PRE-SCHOOL CURRICULUM?

The three C's for obtaining materials for pre-school curriculum are: 1) Collecting; 2) Commercial; and 3) Constructing.

There are many common items around the house and in the neighborhood and community that can make effective materials for using with the pre-school child. When all of these "thing" are collected and made part of the curriculum the young child is given an opportunity to manipulate, explore and experiment with materials that are effective, yet do not cost anything to acquire for the program. This only takes imagination on the part of a skillful-competent caregiver.

There are several companies that are in the business of selling materials--toys, equipment, computers and accessories, etc.--that are safe, durable, colorful, and effective in supplementing the pre-school curriculum. This commercial material is available in many brands and varieties for both retail and wholesale costs. The astute caregiver is aware that there are many commercial materials that encourage free expression and creativity that are too complex and detailed to find in the scraps and junk around the house and the neighborhood-community or that can be easily constructed by children and facilitators. Therefore, when materials are being considered for the pre-school curriculum, some commercial materials are necessary to help enrich the total spectrum of material resources.

However, too much "store bought" materials--toys, equipment, etc.-- can be a turn-off to some children, parents, and teachers as well. McAfee (1976) attests to the idea that homemade materials that are constructed by parents, children, and teachers generate some tangible values in view of involvement and conservation of the makers. The art of constructing materials for the pre-school curriculum is a way of maximizing the talents and creativity of many in producing "things" that can be used to derive satisfaction in the teaching-learning process. This technique requires careful inspection of products to insure durability and safety for usage. Constructing materials will induce a small cost to the program or individual. However, this small cost will be compensated in the wide use and educational values accrued by the young children.

There are many companies that sell commercial materials for the pre-school curriculum. These companies advertise very widely and are many in number. The names and addresses of these commercial companies can be obtained from the public libraries; libraries at the public elementary schools; child care and nurseries may have catalogs and information about them; media centers at the colleges and universities usually have information and advertised literature on these companies; and many of the toy stores can give you information about companies that sell commercial materials for young children.

The concepts of collecting and constructing materials for the pre-school curriculum are publicized in many books, magazines, booklets and leaflets. A caregiver might start a collection of ideas for producing his/her own manual to have on hand. A loose leaf notebook can be used to store many ideas that are in the form of leaflets; information from books can be reproduced and placed in the notebook; and booklets can be punched with holes and placed in the notebook.

Examples of the materials that can be collected from the home, neighborhood and community are: plastic containers, fruit and vegetable containers, egg cartons, empty spools, bottle caps, baby food jars, small and large cardboard boxes, old clothes for dress-up play, cylinders from wax paper and aluminum foil, buttons, string, cord, scraps of cloth, popsicle sticks, carpet squares, milk cartons, milk cases, soda cases, lamp shades, jewelry, pots, pans, dishes, silverware, phonograph records, pieces of wood, calendars, plastic bags, safety pins, sea shells, seed, tiles, tin cans, keys, locks, and hundreds of other things.

Examples of toys and play materials that can be constructed from items collected at home, in the neighborhood, in the community, and through purchasing from the stores are: wheel toys from boxes and spools; busy boards from gadgets and a board; blocks from wood scraps, soda cases, and cardboard boxes; puppets from socks, and small plastic containers; storage cups for crayons, paint brushes, and small objects from large plastic jugs, tin cans, and boxes; trays for pegs, small objects; and puzzles from boxes, and egg cartons; and many more useful materials for manipulation, exploration and experimentation.

HOW CAN COMPUTERS BE EFFECTIVELY USED IN THE PRE-SCHOOL CURRICULUM AND TEACHING/LEARNING PROCESS?

Most recently there has been a move towards using more instructional technology in pre-schools for teaching and learning. The environment is full of computers and pre-schoolers are exposed to them in various informal ways. They are seen in schools, businesses, restaurants, department stores, and in doctors' offices. There are computers all around us that do not look like computers--washing machines, gas stations, refrigerators, microwaves, cash registers--almost any place in the environment. Computers have become a natural way for keeping records, recalling information and materials, allowing faster and better service to people, and providing more jobs. Almost any work place can use a computer. More and more computers are being placed in homes for use by parents and children. Everyone must understand what computers can and cannot do for him/her. Pre-schoolers, alike, must understand and know what computers can do for them. They should be taught not to be afraid of the computer because it is such a complex machine. Today, more high technology has become an integral part of children's toys and educational machinery which demands a different kind of teaching/learning experience for caregivers and children. This trend draws attention to the need to enhance the pre-school curriculum and teaching/learning process by including computers as an instructional tool for early childhood. There have been, of course, pros and cons regarding the inclusion of computers in the pre-school curriculum.

The curriculum is a part of the controversy in view of provisions being made to keep the subject matter content abreast with societal demands. Pre-schoolers must be provided with experiences to prepare them to live productively and successfully in this highly technological society. There are articles and research studies presented in educational journals, newspapers, and reports about the purposes, uses, and needs manifested by the computers in making life simpler. The pre-school curriculum, then, must be made relevant to the needs of socializing pre-schoolers into our high technological society. Therefore, one point of view is that "any good pre-school classroom will have one or more microcomputers" to be used in instruction on a daily basis. Another point of view is that "computers could make the pre-school curriculum too electric or novel while losing the developmental, more basic, competencies gained through play as young children manipulate concrete objects." Experiences designed for the computer to be used in the classroom will depend on electrically operated equipment, unlike the classroom where pre-schoolers have to manually operate objects. Both of these conceptual operations influence the teaching/learning process.

The teaching/learning process must deal with the use of computers in view of how children learn. This process will be determined "effective" when the experiences allow the child to assimilate and accommodate (Piagetian) in a satisfactory manner. The technological experiences, like the manual ones, must provide for pre-schoolers the conceptualization of learning which includes perceiving, thinking, doing, and feeling. These operations defining how children learn have been presented in detail in Chapter One of this text. The important concept to keep in mind in dealing with "using" or "not using" computers in the pre-school as a teaching/learning strategy is the fact that any effective curriculum will include technology as an important part. Therefore, the teaching/learning process will be enhanced through using real-life (firsthand) experiences and technology--multi-media, AV materials, and instructional kits--through the means of: chalk boards, pictures and posters, books and magazines, films, filmstrips, tape recorders and cassettes, overhead projectors, slide projectors, television, typewriters, field trips, cooking, self-care activities, and "computers" (Lee, 1984). Naturally, the learner (pre-schooler) is affected during the teaching/learning process.

The learner is taken into consideration as the issue is explored. Lee presented a discussion that summarized the feelings projected by early childhood educators in reference to "using" or "not using" computers. She connoted on the one hand that some educators and parents viewed the use of computers as an important beginning for pre-schoolers to be socialized into our highly technological society. They (pre-schoolers) need to be equipped with experiences that will prepare them to work and live competently on a daily basis. While on the other hand, she connoted that educators and parents questioned whether pre-schools are becoming too electric or novel, which means their losing the developmental, more basic knowledge provided through manipulation of real objects in play. This is to say that perception and differentiation are developed from direct interactions with many manipulative objects in time and space on a concrete level. More and more the pre-school is incorporating electrically powered equipment, which means that pre-schoolers must use symbols instead of real objects. The concern here is that the pre-schoolers stand the risk of having to function "symbolically" before they progress from innate concrete stages of doing. The learner, then, is left at the care and direction of the caregiver in reference to how he/she will be involved in the teaching/learning process. The learner's principal caregiver (parent) becomes an important factor in this effort.

Parents are making decisions about curriculum and teaching/learning in the lives of their children. Their thoughts and expressions are ranged from little or no comment to much commentation on "using" or "not using" computers in pre-schools. For parents who can afford the computer, the children can experience using it in their homes. The parent, however, that cannot afford to buy the computer could be concerned with the exposure, or non-exposure, of this technology in the lives of their children. Since our society is set on equality of educational experiences for all children regardless of race, color, or creed, ways and means for so doing are placed in the hands of the educational system (and in this case the pre-school is the system). Surely the benefits derived from experiences with computers are sought by all parents for their children. Seemingly, computers are an integral part of our society and a need for every individual to become "computer literate" is profound. A statement by Harleston (1983, p. 95), "we must teach for a global perspective and an international focus; and we must teach for technological literacy and intelligence, including critical thinking," made it clear that computers are here to stay as a major component of our society. Therefore, it is advantageous for young children to become familiar with them in their critical stages of learning which begin in pre-school years.

The concern, then, is <u>how computers can be effectively used in pre-school curriculum and teaching/learning</u>.

The following statements are germane to effective use of the computers in pre-schools:

○ Caregivers must be computer-literate in pre-schools (able to teach pre-schoolers what a computer can/cannot do; operation of computer; procedures for programming; and programming strategies, etc.)

○ Pre-schools must examine the advantages and disadvantages of using computers (expenditure of maintenance, purpose congruent to learners, computer-literacy rate of caregivers, purchasing of different brand names, using brands that are adaptable to a wide variety of software (programs of study, motor ability of children, symbolic reasoning ability-readiness of pre-schoolers, etc.)

○ Microcomputers should be used as "a learning center" exercise in the same manner, purpose, and situation as would teaching machines and other technology.

○ Computer activities and experiences must be monitored to insure proper use and results for pre-schoolers.

○ Involve parents in the operation of computers as a curriculum and teaching/learning component of the pre-school program (provide training to help parents become computer-literate and supportive of "learning center" concept for computers.)

These are some of the ways and means for pre-school programs to address the issue of using computers effectively in curriculum and teaching/learning. Too, the "pros" and "cons" previously addressed concerning the curriculum, the teaching/learning process, the learner, and the parent, must be treated seriously and used as support knowledge, attitudes, and information in planning, programming, and implementing "computer" experiences in the pre-school program.

ACTIVITIES FOR STUDY AND DISCUSSION

1. Find out the different kinds of computers (microcomputers, etc.) that can be used in the pre-school and discuss the advantages and disadvantages in terms of their use in the pre-school curriculum and teaching/learning process.

2. Discuss more broadly the elements of a computer program that make it effective in the curriculum and the teaching/learning process.

3. Formulate a debating team and use the topic: "Pros and Cons for Using Computers in Pre-School."

4. Make a list of the various "software" materials that can be used in the pre-school. Give complete bibliographical data in order to obtain the materials.

5. Design a "Computer-Literacy" Workshop for Caregivers--teachers, parents, and staff.

6. Design a "computer learning center" for the classroom--including equipment, materials, environmental conditions, etc.--that can serve as a model for pre-school programs.

REFERENCES

Harleston, B.W., "Higher Education for Minorities: The Challenge of the 1980s," **The Journal of Negro Education**, 52, 94-109, Spring, 1983.

Lee, Marjorie, "Strategies for Teaching Young Children: Guides for Improving Instruction," **Early Child Development and Care**, Volume 14, Numbers 3 and 4, 1984.

Lee, M. and Houston, E., "An Electric Preschool: Pros and Cons," (Paper presented at Annual Conference of the National Association for the Education of Young Children, Los Angeles, California, November, 1984).

Leeper, Sarah H., Dora S. Skipper, and Ralph L. Witherspoon, **Good Schools for Young Children.** (Fourth Edition) New York: Macmillan Publishing Company, 1979.

McAfee, Oralie, "To Make or Buy?" in **Selecting Educational Equipment and Materials for Home and School.** (Edited by M. Cohen), Washington, D.C.: ACEI, 1976.

Osborn, D. Keith and Dorothy Haupt, **Creative Activities for Young Children.** Merrill Palmer Institute, Detroit, Michigan, 1964.

Project Head Start, "Suggested Activities for Child Development Centers," The School District of Philadelphia: Division for the Education of Young Children, 1968.

Schickendanz, J., Mary E. York, Ida S. Stewart, and Doris A. White, **Strategies for Teaching Young Children.** (Second Edition) Englewood Cliffs, New Jersey: Prentice-Hall, Inc., 1983.

Shoemaker, Rowena M., **All in Play, Adventures in Learning**. Play School Association, 120 W. 57th Street, New York, New York, 10019, (First published in 1958), 1986.

Stant, Margaret A., **Let's Try This in Nursery School and Kindergarten.** College Park, Maryland: San Mar Publishing Co., Box 174, 1963.

Weikart, D.P., M. Hohmann, and B. Banet, "Arranging and Equipping the Classroom," **Young Children in Action.** (Chapter 1) Ypsilante, Michigan: High/Scope Educational Foundation, 1979, 35-57.

Wood, J.M. (Editor), Hankerson, H. (Project Director), and (Contributors) House, D., Meddaugh, G., Sallach, L., Storm, P., and Strausbaugh, L., **Making The Young Child's Class Go: An Action Guide.** D.D.I.E.O. Project, The Nisonger Center, The Ohio State University, 1580 Cannon Drive, Columbus, Ohio 43210, 1975.

CHAPTER THREE

UNDERSTANDING THE EDUCATIVE VALUE OF PLAY AND MOTOR FUNCTIONING

GROSS MOTOR PLAY, FINE MOTOR PLAY, DRAMATIC PLAY, BLOCK PLAY, ADVENTURE PLAY, WATER PLAY, SAND PLAY

CHAPTER 3

UNDERSTANDING THE EDUCATIVE VALUE OF PLAY
AND MOTOR FUNCTIONING

- WHAT IS THE ROLE AND IMPORTANCE OF PLAY IN PRE-SCHOOL?

- WHAT IS THE EDUCATIVE VALUE OF BLOCK PLAY AND DRAMATIC PLAY?

- HOW DO OUTDOOR LEARNING ACTIVITIES FIT THE PRE-SCHOOL CURRICULUM?

- WHAT ARE DEVELOPMENTAL MILESTONES IN MOTOR FUNCTIONING?: A MODEL

- WHY IS PLAY THE FOUNDATION FOR PRE-SCHOOL CURRICULUM?

- ACTIVITIES FOR STUDY AND DISCUSSION

- REFERENCES

WHAT IS THE ROLE AND IMPORTANCE OF PLAY IN PRE-SCHOOL?:
AN INTRODUCTION

Today in the United States we face considerable unfinished business in education. The pre-school is gradually becoming recognized as an essential part of our schools (public and private). There is an increasing recognition by professional educators and laymen alike that the pre-school must develop a planned curriculum, inasmuch as it is an important part of the child's education. Practice and research show that much of the knowledge that children receive from any learning experiences can, in many instances, be obtained through "play." Therefore, the question remains: "Is 'play' the young child's means of discovery, of communication, and of expression?" Children's play, whether spontaneous or structured, is an important opportunity for pre-schoolers to learn. "Through many repeated play experiences, children can clarify and master many fundamental physical, social, and intellectual skills and concepts" (Isenberg and Jacobs, 1977).

The role and importance of play in pre-school is set forth through the conceptualization that follows (N.V. Scarfe, 1962, p. 119).

> A child's play is his way of exploring and experimenting while he builds up relations with the world and with himself. Play is a learning activity. It serves the function of a non-verbal mode of communication of a figurative language which satisfies a felt need of young children. Play is educative because while thus employed the child is self-directed, wholly involved and completely absorbed. It secures concentration for a great length of time. It develops initiative, imagination and intense interest. There is tremendous intellectual ferment, as well as complete emotional involvement. No other activity improves personality so markedly. No other activity calls so fully on the resources of effort and energy which lie latent in the human being. Play is the most complete of all of the educational processes for it influences the intellect, the emotions and the body of the child. It is the only activity in which the whole educational process is fully consummated, when experience induces learning and learning produces wisdom and character.

The eminent Swiss psychologist, Jean Piaget (1962), defined the important play and learning stages as follows. They are: a) sensory motor stage (birth to two years), b) play and imagination in early education (two to seven years), c) accommodating to the adult world (eight

70

to thirteen years), and d) grown-ups and family living (fourteen and up). The sensory motor stage (birth to age two) is the time when the infant makes the fastest growth and developmental changes--physically, mentally, verbally. From the neonatal period to four months of age, the child discovers himself by seeing, hearing, feeling, touching, and tasting. The next four months, the child becomes aware of and interested in objects outside his/her own body. An understanding of cause, effect, and time is established by the child during the eighth to twelfth months. After the child reaches one year of age, and up to two years of age, certain changes in growth and development take place. Namely, the child stands, begins to walk and talk. This is a time for practice play--when the toddler needs many opportunities and experiences to exercise his/her powers of seeing, hearing, touching, and manipulating. This is a time for reacting to the environment, reflecting experiences, exploring with materials, and learning to understand the environment and the content within. The play experiences must be directed by skilled caregivers; enhanced by a variety of stimulating toys and activities; and implemented in a conducive environment (in the home or in a child care center).

Play is a sure way two-to-seven-year-olds learn. From "practice play" during the sensory-motor period, play takes on "symbolism" and "imagination." Children throw themselves whole-heartedly into role playing, which involves the mind as no formal education can. Language is employed. This is sometimes referred to as the period of "symbolic play." It is further believed that without this five-year period of imaginative play, the child has missed part of his normal development. Piaget continues to describe this as the time of confidence-building and great drive ("Look how tall a building I can build!"); of exploring the community around him/her (as in block cities); of thinking through family relationships (with doll and doll play) (**Creative Playthings**, 1967). This becomes a time to provide healthy, happy experiences in an enriched play world, and in doing so, the two-to-seven-year-olds build steps that will lead them to confidence and creativity in later years. The importance and role of play can be seen as an initial educative value in denoting the idea that children learn through play.

WHAT IS THE EDUCATIVE VALUE OF PLAY?

There are ways in which children can learn through play. Children can take and create an idea and adapt it to their experience when they play. Through play they gain mastery over ideas they have learned at leisure time, at home, at school and in the community. A child's experiences will determine the way in which he or she will play out an idea. It will also depend upon the teacher's ideas or persons in the community, not to mention experiences of other children in the group. The children can discover for themselves. They bring their ideas to play; the caregiver brings the play spirit to their learning ideas. Caregivers in the pre-school must treat children's ideas lightly yet seriously and often humorously, but always with wisdom, dignity, and an understanding of their developmental needs. The most vital things children learn are not necessarily the ones that grownups plan for them, but rather what children themselves find out. However, the caregiver needs to take an active part in encouraging creative play. In doing so, the caregiver will see more than just the final results of children's play--a painting, a piece of woodword, a structure from block-building or an assembly program. Inexperienced caregivers are apt to say, "This is too good to be true." However, experienced caregivers appreciate "how it began" (Shoemaker, 1963). Nevertheless, in pre-school the degree to which a child expands his knowledge and experiences will depend upon the caregiver's understanding and use of appropriate materials and equipment.

Providing suitable play materials and equipment is a serious responsibility. Young children need simple but challenging materials and equipment that will build strong bodies and a broad base of understanding. Good playthings should have a combinatioin of these characteristics: a) free of detail as possible, b) versatile in use, c) involve the child in play, d) large, easily manipulated, e) warm and pleasant to touch, f) durable and work as intended, g) encourage cooperative play, h) construction easily comprehended, and i) enjoyable (**Community Playthings,** 1966). See Chart 3 for suggestions. Proper guidance and adequate materials and equipment can open the door for a child to a world where he/she can unfold and learn to understand himself/herself and those with whom he/she lives.

Play provides occasions for children to exercise their varied capacities in spontaneous activities which are largely self-regarding and usually enjoyable. Play has both psychological and physiological benefits. To relieve the tension of today's industrialized and technological world, a child requires more than recess and a so-called 'physical fitness' program several times a week (Frank, 1964). A child, we should remember, is initially a young organism with all the "Wisdom of the body," as Cannon (in Frank, 1964) called these inherited capacities for self-organization, self-regulation and self-repair. If we deliberately ignore the psychological benefits of play, we can still say that play is essential to wholesome development of a young organism be-

CHART 3

SUITABLE MATERIALS AND EQUIPMENT FOR CREATIVE PLAY

BLOCK AND DRAMATIC PLAY	OUTDOOR PLAY EQUIPMENT	HOUSEKEEPING	TRANSPORTATION	CREATIVE ART AND BOOKS	CLASSROOM FURNISHING & MISC.
hollow blocks, unit blocks, wooden figures, doll house, small dolls, furniture, puppets, puppet theater, derrick, and boxes (cardboard and wooden) for construction	walking board, rocking boat, doll wagon, tricycle, simple climbing equipment, climbing steps, hollow blocks, large wooden nesting boxes, planks, wheelbarrow, scooter, swings, slides, shovel & pail, rake, coaster wagon, triangle set, sand boxes, water tubs, and ladder	unbreakable doll, simple doll, clothes, doll blanket and carriage, childsize furniture such as: sink, table refrigerator, stove, cupboard, pots and pans, ironing board, iron, broom, dust pan, aprons, wooden telephone, rocking chair, chest of drawers, wash basin, clothesline and pins, basket, apron ties, cradle, childsize bed, carriage, and wardrobe	models of big cars and trucks for hauling and riding; cars and trains for pushing, airplanes, tractor and trailer, riding train	easels, paints, brushes, large crayons, books, records, record player, blunt scissors, clay, and magazines	bookcase, clothing lockers, storage shelves, block cart, work and library tables, chalk, pegs, sand & water, tool cabinet, tools, workhorse, wood bench, storage cart, bulletin board, softball, wooden puzzles, portable screen (room dividers), cots, plants, aquarium, pets, giant dominoes, construction set, household junk-- empty cans, spools, bottle caps, etc.

cause in his/her play activities the child exercises these varied functioning processes essential to his/her health and well-being. The important fact is that the child does this spontaneously in his/her own individual way. She/he usually regulates the time, intensity and extent of the play activities by these inner regulatory processes that are different and difficult, if not possible, for an observer to replace by external regulations and rules.

An educative value that "play" provides for growth and development of pre-schoolers is that it promotes cognitive learnings. Scarfe (1971) connoted that "play is education and may be described as spontaneous, creative, desired research activity carried out for its own sake." She further described play "as a child's way of exploring and experimenting while he/she builds up relations with the world and with himself/herself--in learning to learn; in discovering how to come to terms with the world; in coping with life's tasks; in mastering skills; in learning how to gain confidence; in discovering himself/herself anew; and in escaping into fantasy for it is not easy for the child to accept the patterned conduct of the social cultural living."

The educative value of play has been discussed by Piaget in reference to using play as a vehicle through which the child develops new and better cognitive skills. He saw play as assimilation, the process of taking information from the environment and incorporating it into already learned knowledge. Moreover, Piaget (1962) and Yawkey (1980) saw play as a dynamic process in its own right in view of its being interrelated with thinking skills and intellectual development. The new concepts that children learn are shown in spontaneous and guided play, and language is a vital factor in the play experience as interactions are pursued with peers. Many other early childhood educators (Garvey, 1977; Yawkey, 1980; Lieberman, 1977; Sutton-Smith, 1971) have provided information and research to verify the fact that play is an important, natural, and fun-fulfilling activity for pre-schoolers since it is their way to learn about the world in which they live.

Play sets forth its educative value through displaying functionality in all of the areas of growth and development and learning: personal-social-emotional, physical, and intellectual. Pre-schoolers will be exposed to the educative value of play as a means of:

° Serving the function of a non-verbal mode of communication of a figurative language.

° Involving and absorbing the whole child in self-direction.

○ Securing concentration for a great length of time.

○ Developing initiative, imagination and intense interest.

○ Stimulating intellectual ferment, as well as complete emotional involvement.

○ Improving personality

○ Inducing learning which produces wisdom and character.

○ Employing language.

○ Building confidence and great drive.

○ Exploring the environment.

○ Thinking through family relationships.

○ Gaining mastery over ideas learned at leisure time, at home, at school, and in the community.

WHAT IS THE EDUCATIVE VALUE OF DRAMATIC PLAY AND BLOCK PLAY FOR PRE-SCHOOLERS?

Dramatic play activities help the child to symbolize activities and information, and put them into a meaningful framework. The child's conceptions of the world are tried out on a small scale as he/she plays through various roles and situations. New ideas are tested and are associated with others. They are practiced and solidified until meaningfulness arrive. Dramatic play alone will not guarantee conceptual learning. This form of play is simply one important path of the total learning process. Its success and usefulness rest upon the existence of other conditions in the classroom.

Dramatic play is the natural expression of the kindergarten child, so it is used more than story dramatization for the five year old. Dr. Arnold Gesell's comment, "There are endless opportunities for dramatic assimilation of experiences," (Ward, 1952) is illustrated by children seeing a film and then coming back and playing it, laying out streets and sidewalks with blocks, being safety patrol members, pedestrians and others. The movie without the play would not teach its lesson half as effectively.

It would be a great pity, however, if dramatic play were not very often used for pure fun. Our children live in a hurried, tense world. They need to know how to relax, to have fun. "Laughter dissolves tensions. If we can laugh together, we can live together" (Robison and Spodek, 1965). So let us not forget the importance of cultivating a sense of humor.

Play is the chief, almost the only, mode of education for the child in the years of later infancy (Dewey, 1933). Dewey pointed out that when children play with toys they are living not with the physical things but in the large world of meanings, a store of concepts (so fundamental in all intellectual achievement), is defined and built up.

By recognizing the fact that play, and particularly dramatic play, is not only a universal expression of childhood, but childhood's own way of learning, the modern school relates its curriculum to the nature of the child. A child becomes one with his/her world through exploring his/her environment and through participating in activities in which she/he uses things she/he has made or acquired or which exist in his/her imagination. Provision should be made for the use of dramatic play, not only in the pre-school, but throughout the primary grades.

In denoting the educative values of dramatic play, it must be recognized that this kind of play offers a variety of opportunities for children to understand the world about them, to acquire new and worthwhile information, and to become increasingly efficient in the use of basic skills. A few of the reasons for using dramatic play as a method of guiding children's learning activities are as follows: (Teachers Guide to Education In Early Childhoood, 1956, p. 206).

1. Dramatic play is a natural and therefore easy way of learning.

2. Dramatic play provides dynamic, integrated learning situations that move forward on the self-impelled drives of children.

3. Dramatic play creates the best possible provision for democratic social living.

4. Dramatic play provides opportunities for teachers to note behavior which reveals incorrect concepts.

5. Dramatic play provides opportunities for teachers to observe unsocial attitudes and behavior and to aid in removing social conflicts.

6. Dramatic play provides opportunities for the teacher to discover emotional conflicts and home and neighborhood conditions that are conducive to the best type of learning.

7. Dramatic play affords an opportunity for the children to become somewhat aware of the social problems with which adults of today are confronted.

8. Often dramatic play has genuine therapeutic value.

Appropriate materials should be available for children to carry out their ideas in dramatic play. Of all the materials used in dramatic play, perhaps the most important are blocks.

Blocks are a prime example of flexible equipment, because they can be used in countless ways. Children can build anything with blocks, and the structures so built can relate to a limitless variety of activities. Blocks can aid children to develop social science and mathematical concepts of many kinds.

Whether the blocks become a tool for developing social science concepts in a particular class depends mainly upon the teacher, the planning he does, the accessories he makes available, and the program he develops. The blocks themselves are a neutral element for learning. Block building can lead to significant intellectual goals if the caregiver continually contributes ideas and information to the program. She/he does this through trips, language experiences, books, films, filmstrips, and a host of other communicative experiences. This is also done through the caregiver's guidance of the play situation. The props the caregiver offers, the suggestions she/he makes and the questions she/he raises as the children go through their block building, can help the children advance in their learning with a framework of freedom of action, opportunity for creative expression, and minimal structuring by the caregivers.

In the "Conduct Curriculum Classes" of Patty Smith Hill, a set of large floor blocks was devised. Long blocks could be fastened to corner posts with pegs to create structures for the dramatic play of children. The structures so created were large enough to allow children to play within them and sturdy enough to take an occasional knock that might occur when a group of robust five-year-olds become involved in their play activities. The stability of structure built with these blocks allowed the children to use buildings over a period of time so that their dramatic play could be extended and elaborated.

Several variations of these large blocks are available today, including the hollow floor blocks, the vari-play set and similar structural units.

Unit blocks were developed by Caroline Pratt at about the same time. The unit block, looking much like a length of 2" x 4" lumber, is based upon a unit of measure. Each block is either the size of the unit, a multiple of the unit, or a fraction of that unit. Thus, there will be half units and quarter unit blocks as well as double units and quadruple unit blocks. Various shapes are added, such as columns, wedges, curves, and semicircles, to make a set. A good set of unit blocks is constructed of hardwood so as not to splinter or wear excessively, and is finished carefully so that each block is in exact proportion to the unit. This allows the children to become involved in precision construction. If they build a structure with four walls, each consisting of a large number of blocks, every wall will be equally high, and if the same number of blocks is used in each, their buildings will stay built.

Unit blocks are much smaller than the larger floor blocks such as the Patty Hill blocks. They cannot be used for dramatic play in the same way, since the children will not fit into the constructions. Instead of involving her/himself in the dramatic play with unit blocks, the child further miniaturizes the world and manipulates it. In the early stages of block play, which can be observed in nursery schools, the young child is content first to simply pile blocks and then to build abstract structural designs, often without plans. This type of block building gives way to the building of individual purposely designed structures, and then large elaborated interrelated structures. Ideas for structures may come from the child's fantasy world or from the reality world, depending upon the kind of caregiver guidance that has been offered (Spodek, 1968).

In every classroom there are children of varying backgrounds and intellectual capacities; therefore, the teacher provides for individual as well as group work and selects materials that possess a variety of possible uses. He selects materials that are: a) durable, b) safe, and c) flexible in function. These materials should be thought of, not in terms of end products but, in terms of media through which ideas are conveyed and expressed. Therefore, in an attempt to formulate a list of suitable materials, Chart 4 serves as a guide for caregivers and others to use.

Creative play demands equipment and materials, but this equipment and materials do not need to be elaborate or expensive. Different

CHART 4

PLAY MATERIALS FOR DRAMATIC PLAY AND BLOCK PLAY

BLOCK AND DRAMATIC PLAY	ACCESSORY MATERIALS (Block Play)	HOUSEKEEPING	CREATIVE ART AND BOOKS	CLASSROOM FURNISHING AND MISCELLANEOUS
Unit blocks, wooden figures, doll house, small dolls, furniture, puppets, puppet theater, derrick, hollow boxes, wooden boxes, large hollow blocks	trees, people, men women, boys, girls, workers in community, signal lights, signs, airplanes, trains, trucks, farm animals: pigs chickens ducks roosters	unbreakable dolls, simple doll clothes, doll blanket, dollsize bed and carriage, childsize furniture, such as: sink, table, refrigerator, stove, pots, cupboard, pans, iron- ing board, iron, wooden telphone, or plastic one, rocking chair, broom, dust pan, aprons, chest of drawers, wash basin, clothes line and pins, basket, ties, etc. childsize bed, cradle, carriage, and wardrobe	easels, paints, brushes, crayons, large – books, records, record player, large pieces of paper, sponges, large folders for work, blunt scissors, clay, clay boards, clay jars, pottery crock (or galvanized garbage can that won't rust)	bookcase, clothing lockers, storage shelves, block cart, work and library tables and chairs, play tables and chairs wooden puzzles, portable screens, (room dividers) cots, plants, storage carts, chalk, pegs and bulletin boards, sand and water play table and chairs, work horses, wood working bench, tools, tool cabinet, aquarium, pets, giant dominoes, and construction set

(From Los Angeles City School District)

environments will provide different opportunities for play. The Los Angeles City School District (1962) compiled a list of play materials for "understanding the educative values of block play" that has been adopted in Chart 4.

Children are guided to respond to dramatic and block play in a receptive, spontaneous, and happy manner. Block play aids in the physical development of the child. It provides opportunities for: a) free bodily movement, b) muscular coordination, c) manipulation and experimentation, d) eye-hand coordination and e) freedom of movement. Emotional stability and social development may be encouraged by means of intelligently guided block and dramatic play, as follows. As children learn to work and adjust their behaviors to good group living, they realize a feeling of personal accomplishment, satisfaction, and security. By working and living with others through means of block play, children assume responsibilities for good group living by: a) entering into group planning for dramatic and block play, b) taking part in group discussion, c) taking part in the good housekeeping activities, d) respecting the rights and feelings of others in the group, e)taking part as a leader in some situations, and f) taking part as a follower in many situations.

During the dramatic play experiences, children are given opportunities for desirable intellectual development. They are given opportunities for entering into the following worthwhile experiences:

1. Participating in activities which will broaden and enrich the vocabulary by means of questioning, listening, and using new words in varied meaningful situations.

2. Using correctly a functional and meaningful vocabulary.

3. Making choices of materials and meaningful vocabulary.

4. Formulating a simple plan of action.

5. Following through a plan of action.

6. Following through a plan suggested by another member of a group.

7. Using oral expression during the play-work period.

8. Meeting simple problems and solving them. Such a problem may be as simple as the following:

   a. When there are too many children in a given play-work space, where should we (children) work?

   OR

   b. Where should we (children) place the blocks that represent the silo in the farm experience?

   OR

   c. How shall we (children) make the airport of blocks?

9. Finding answers to questions by going to various sources for aid. These sources may include:

   a. A trip for the purpose of gaining first-hand experiences by means of observation.

   b. The use of audio-visual materials such as illustrations, study prints, motion pictures, transcriptions, and others.

10. Using suggestions represented by other members of the group.

11. Developing quantitative concepts through estimating, counting, and manipulating. Such learnings may include the concepts of:

    a. large - small
    b. big - little
    c. rough - smooth
    d. long - short
    e. high - higher
    f. few - many
    g. light - heavy
    h. not enough - less than
    i. too many - more than

12. Using dramatic play in worthwhile activities. Some of these activities may include living the part of a worker in a market, a store, a gas station, a home, a garage, a farm, or many other workers in a community (Nelson and McDonald, 1954; Forman and Fleet, 1980).

Social concepts are only part of the total development which the child receives through guided experience in block construction, yet within this and other aspects of childhood education lies the foundation for many significant social understandings and skills (Leonard, Deman and Miles, 1963).

The educative values of block building justify its inclusions as an integral part of the early childhood education curriculum and, as such, it demands the caregiver's careful thought, planning, guidance, interest, and enthusiasm.

As in everything else, children do their best work in block construction in a calm and happy environment, free from tension and strain. The time devoted to block building needs to be long enough to develop whatever individual or group project is in progress, allowing the children to build without a feeling of pressure; yet equally important is the caregiver's alertness to signs of fatigue, lack of ideas, and the misuse of blocks, which indicate that the children need a change of activity.

From time to time there needs to be "on the spot" evaluation of a construction which will offer a challenging point to a particular group, or possibly to all of the children, especially if the group is at approximately the same stage in their building. Even children working in other centers on a given day may evidence a clear concept of vocabulary and sound thinking as they participate in the valuation of block structures developed by other children.

In conclusion, taking young children where they are, the creative caregivers guide them through growth commensurate with their potentialities. She/he seeks to help each personality develop to its fullest. At the same time, he/she helps each youngster make his adjustment to child society through the teaching/learning process.

Experiencing the many wonders of the brave, new young children's world with each group of children, the caregiver finds a joy and satisfaction that can come through understanding the educative values of block and dramatic play.

HOW DO OUTDOOR LEARNING ACTIVITIES FIT THE PRE-SCHOOL CURRICULUM?

Outdoor learning activities take on a reality for young children that is not possible to achieve by indoor classroom experiences alone. It has been thought by many that outdoor play is the way to get rid of energy and as a time for filling an otherwise dull routine by a change of pace. This is truly a misconception, as outdoor play activities facilitate the young children's need to explore, imitate, test, and construct. The value of outdoor learning activities is very comprehendable. Learning outdoors gives children a chance to understand and appreciate their own world more fully. They have many opportunities for expressing the pleasures they find from experimenting with the outdoors through words. For example, they have the pleasure of knowing: how the grass feels and smells, and how the blowing winds make the leaves rustle in the trees. They will be able to predict where the shadow of the school building will fall in the afternoon; to discover various shapes based on objects that are found in the outdoors; and to gain a sense of orderliness and predictability of the outdoor environment. Teaching from the perspective of outdoor learning activities is a provision for linking the indoor activities with the outdoor ones, which provides an extension of growth and development in cognitive, social, and motor skills and abilities (Houts, 1976).

Curriculum planning and development must take into consideration "outdoor play activities." The young child is curious, is interested in exploring and experimenting, and is desirous of mixing and matching the parts of his world together. In this, the image of the young scientist, the brainy mathematician, the future sociologist, the geologist, the economist, the teacher, and the human services specialist is beginning to make its imprints in the slate of education. A rich, varied, and safe outdoor environment can be the key to launching all of these vocations, advocations, and adventures for young children. There are, then, some aspects that must be considered in preparing the curriculum for outdoor learning activities.

Consideration must be given to play space and safety. The size of space that is required by most state licensing agencies is seventy-five square feet per child. A more desirable figure as suggested by The Child Welfare League of America is two hundred square feet per child. Having the outdoor play area easily accessible to the indoor facilities is desirable. Oftentimes, the indoor play and other learning activities can be extended to the outdoors. Bathroom facilities should be adjacent to the immediate play areas. The space must be conducive to creating an environment which invites learning. Fencing in this area can give children the security of safe limits and is therefore an important consideration.

A place to use and operate wheel toys is desirable. Children enjoy wheel toys for building gross motor skills and abilities. Riding the big wheels, the tricycles, scooters, pulling wagons, and pushing large toys are activities that should be included in the curriculum.

A place for digging in the sand and playing in water is also desirable. Both sand play and water play provide therapy (relaxation, displaced energies, ridding self of frustrations, etc.) for young children. There are various accessories that should be included in this aspect of outdoor play, such as plastic bottles, buckets, wash tubs, funnels, paint brushes, sifters, spocns, pots and pans, garden scoops, plastic dishes, and so forth. These toys give greater dimension to learning. The children's involvement in mathematics, science, social studies, language arts, and creative arts is enhanced through water and sand play. The curriculum must include planned activities for the children. There should be directions given to the children in regards to what is expected of each as he/she becomes involved in the sand and water play activities. For example, they should take turns sharing accessories, not splashing water, storing containers, staying in designated areas and so forth.

Outdoor play environments must include a place for dramatic play, like outdoor tree houses, doll houses, large boxes, hollow blocks, unit blocks, props for puppet shows, stores, circus shows, sawhorses, and wood crates to create scenes and so forth is necessary. Young children should have the opportunity to experience dramatic play in their curriculum. The caregiver can suggest play themes, spearhead activities through telling a story or reading a poem, sharing music and rhythms with children for movement activities, and providing props.

The landscaping of the play area is very important. Considerations must be given to: 1) variety of surfacing--grassy areas, hard surfaces, rocky areas, inclines, or hills, and sandy areas; 2) sunlighted and shady areas--shrubs, trees, and building constructions; 3) areas for carrying out play activities--a place for climbing, swinging, sliding, digging and planting, hiding, building, being quiet, and other areas conducive to healthy, enjoyable, and safe playing; and 4) suitable materials and equipment for outdoor play follow the same standards as for indoor play. This topic has been addressed earlier in the chapter.

Outdoor learning activities play a critical part in the pre-school curriculum. Children develop and grow physically, socially-emotionally, and cognitively through interaction with their environment. When activities are conducted outdoors they take on a reality for young children that is not possible to achieve by classroom experiences alone. The out-of-doors, then, might reasonably be viewed as an extension of the room, having similar characteristics such as quiet and noisy areas, wet and dry areas, and a variety of colors, textures, and shapes for utilization. Adequate planning and considerations of the principles of child care and development are just as important in constructing an "outdoor" play environment as they are in designing the classroom or center for "indoor" play/curricular activities. One advocate of outdocr play activities summed it up thusly: "If we are convinced of the importance of the early years of childhood, we must see outdoor play as a part of the educational process, not simply as a means for letting off steam, amusing oneself or passing time" (Stone, 1970, pp. 18-19).

WHAT ARE DEVELOPMENTAL MILESTONES IN MOTOR FUNCTIONING?: A MODEL

The young child from infancy to kindergarten is excited with the tasks of performing physical skills. These skills are repetitive patterns that cause change--exploring, examining, cause and effect happenings, and challenging events. Healthy bodies and minds are developed through play experiences. It is important to be familiar with developmental milestones of young children (infancy through pre-school) in order to determine what the child is ready to learn in accord with neuro-muscular development. This aids in determining the maturation of the body parts which will allow the child to perform certain skills. Many times the young child is eager to imitate skills and actions of other children and adults, but his/her body might not be ready and able to perform the motor tasks. The caregivers must be ready and willing to assist the child in being successful in motor functioning in both indoor and outdoor play activities. The curriculum must make provisions through its subject content to include play (free play, adventure play, dramatic play, socio-dramatic play and doll play) as a basic concept for the young child to be successful in motor functioning.

The model (Chart 5) herewith provided will be beneficial to caregivers as they plan, design, develop, and evaluate many areas for indoor and outdoor play activities for young children. The major aim of this implementation should be making these play activities in motor functioning contribute to healthy social, emotional, mental, as well as physical development. Prescott (1957) made an educational assumption that fits the need for adults being knowledgeable and skilled in the area of "developmental milestones in motor function." He pointed out that:

Chart 5

EXPERIENCES FOR TEACHING/LEARNING MOTOR FUNCTIONING

Developmental Sequence by Age:		Methodologies/ Activities	Materials/Resources
GROSS MOTOR	FINE MOTOR		
4 year old			
Balances on one foot 5 seconds; strong overhand throw of ball; hops on one foot; heel to toe walk; can skip to some degree; is sturdy and able to walk fairly long distances; runs; skips (considerable agility); plays along side and in cooperation with others; plays hard; tires easily; climbs	Can button coat; can fold paper three times; cuts paper in two with scissors; picks the longer line; dresses and undresses self with ease;	-Have the child stand on one foot first and then on the other; Ask him to hop (if he has trouble, hold one hand); -Provide avenues for self-expression in physical activity as well as intellectual curiosity -Prepare for a superactive, talkative, question-asking, loud noisy, boastful, self-centered, "show-off." Its all 'normal', be patient and accommodating!	Developmental Diagnosis Developmental Screening 0-5 years.
5 year old			
Can skip smoothly; catches a bounced ball	Copies a square; Draws a three part man;	-Provide lots of avenues for socialization.	Developmental Screening 0-5 years.

Chart 5

EXPERIENCES FOR TEACHING/LEARNING MOTOR FUNCTIONING

| | Developmental Sequence by Age: | | Methodologies/ | Materials/Resources |
	GROSS MOTOR	FINE MOTOR	Activities	
5 year old (cont'd.)	balances on one foot 10 seconds; climbs; catches (12 inch ball or beach ball) hops (on one foot alone - four steps or more); skips (hops on one foot, then the other, in continuous move- ment from place to place); hammer nails	reproduces with blocks from picture; strings or threads beads and spools; uses scissors; ef- fective self- help skills (dresses, uses utensils, brushes teeth, fastens and ties)	independency, and seriousness -Have dress-up apparel (adult- like). -Provide many school like games, materials, books, arts and crafts (writing, drawing and manipulating puzzles, etc.) -for copying (model from picture) -for constructing (bridge, gate) -for observing usage of tools	Developmental Scales as previously describ- ed in this manuscript Evaluating Children's Progress: A Rating Scale for Children In Day Care

the ability to manage the body well in a wide variety of activities and the possession of specific game skills are major assets for each child in winning peer-group roles and greatly affect relationships with other children. They also greatly affect the individual's feelings about the concept of himself and therefore, play an important part in his emotional adjustment" (p. 355).

Motor functioning activities and teaching methods to be included in the model include the following:

1. Body Movements -- squirming, wriggling, crawling, creeping, creeping with knees straight, walking, walking on tip-toes, running, trotting, bouncing, hopping, galloping, twirling, spinning, scooting, jumping, bending, stooping, skating, sliding, skipping, shuffling, shaking, rocking, turning, swaying, dancing, balancing, hiking, climbing, playing ball, and rolling over.

2. Hand and Arm Movements -- swinging, touching all parts of the body, pounding, patting, shaking, clapping, slapping knees, reaching, stretching, drooping, swimming, boxing, punching, jumping rope, pulling, tugging, lifting, waving, sweeping, brushing, scrubbing, shaking, grabbing, grasping, throwing, and catching.

3. Finger Movements -- patting, intertwining, snapping, holding, rolling, touching, tickling, pinching, pointing, tracing, lacing, winding, rubbing, pulling, scratching, squeezing, tapping, folding, typing, and cutting.

4. Leg(s) and Foot (feet) Movements -- bending knees only, clicking heels together, standing on tip-toes, standing on one foot, wriggling toes, stamping, kicking, tapping toes, tapping heels.

5. Teaching Methods -- (Activities for demonstrations and to get children to do):
   - Use games and activities requiring no hands, standing, lying down, sitting
   - Place abdomen on floor and act like worms, caterpillars, etc.
   - Imitate a baby, cat, dog, bugs, mouse, turtle, tugboat
   - Imitate spiders, lobsters, crabs

- Move like dolls, people; fast, little, loud, soft, slow, big
- Movement when baby is asleep; when hiding; like Indians
- Take big steps, little; act like leaves, wind, balloons
- Movement like a ball, jumping beans, Ten Little Indians
- Move on alternate feet
- Move like horses, ponies
- Move like a dancer
- Move like a spinning top
- Move on seat, abdomen, and like a tugboat
- Move over, off of, onto, like a frog, kangaroo, grasshopper
- Touch toes, walk like an old person
- Mimic leaning forward, moving on ice or roller surface
- Move in sloping fashion sideways (back and forth)
- Play game like Skip To My Lou
- Walk like a shuffling old man
- Do the hula dance, move standing, sitting
- Move on abdomen or back while sitting or lying down
- Stand and move in one place, small circle, large circle, around space or objects
- Hold someone's hand and move or move alone
- Move total body to music or rhythmic beats
- Walk on beams, pretend to be on tight rope; move sideways and backward
- Move up and down ladder
- Moving to music
-Throwing, rolling, and catching balls
- Playing games and activities to enhance all of the movements(body, hand, arm, finger, leg, and foot).

Assessment of motor functioning, providing experiences, providing resources and providing materials as suggested in the model should be done on a regular, continuous basis. Make notes of the activities to be used, the references like books, records, video-tapes, and others so that a record is made and kept of the performances in motor functioning. Use materials that have been suggested as listed in the reference guide of this chapter.

WHY IS PLAY THE FOUNDATION FOR PRE-SCHOOL CURRICULUM?: A SUMMARY

Play activities must be an integral part of the pre-school curriculum. Play on the "outside" should and could be an extension of "indoor" play. It is true that play is a child's way of experiencing life. Almost everything that children do in their everyday living is "play" in one form or another. Play enhances every curriculum area for pre-school: mathematics, science, pre-reading, language arts, creative arts, and social studies. Through play the young children are exploring, creating, asserting, experimenting, thinking and doing actions that show skill and competency in one or more areas of the curriculum. Since the curriculum is developed and implemented to provide knowledge, skills, attitudes, and abilities for young children, the values and purposes of play fit into the context of ensuring involvements in order to ascertain those attainments. Play is also examined within the context of growth and development. Play, then, becomes the foundation for teaching/learning in the pre-school curriculum.

Young children are involved in learning many socio-emotional skills through play. Play helps them to put their ideas and feelings into action; play provides strength for them to deal with the powerlessness of being a child in an adult society; play is an excellent way for young children to work out interpersonal conflicts, personality difficulties and emotional disturbances; play helps them to learn to control aggression and hostility and how to express these feelings in socially acceptable ways; and play helps young children to interact with others and learn to cooperate with and be considerate of others. Much of this can be done through outdoor and free play activities as well as those subject content activities.

Motoric skills and abilities are necessary for physical growth and development and children do learn a multitude of them as they play. Gross motor development is being fostered as young children run, jump, skip, pedal, push, pull, slide, hop, throw, creep, crawl, kick, tumble, roll, swing, climb, and move vigorously. Young children also gain and improve small motor skills and abilities through gross motor play. They are involved in body coordination and balance; they gain strength and endurance; they develop agility and grace; they develop confidence in handling their bodies; they develop perception and precision in performance; and they gain self-confidence in their strengths and acceptance in their weaknesses, hopefully with a desire to continue to grow and develop into a sound, physically fit individual. The young child's physical growth and development is enhanced through involving the body's system to help bring motor patterns, nerves, muscles and bones under harmonious control. It is through play activities (small and gross motor) that a momentum is set whereby young children can make a balanced thrust toward maturation. Their understanding of the body and its functions is easiest learned through "play" as they interact within the environment. The curriculum area of health and science, utilizing the essence of play activities, can be the vehicle for young children to make an impact on their environment--to examine, feel it, test it, make it change before their eyes, and master it, eventually (Stone, 1970). It is further recognized by early childhood educators that there is a relevant connection between physical activity and well-adjusted children. This concept is substantiated by Baker (1968) in stating her belief that, "outdoor play helps lessen the burden of pressures on children...healthy children are likely to be those who spend a great deal of time outdoors where they can play actively and imaginatively" (p. 59).

Play promotes cognitive growth and development. Both theoretical and empirical data are available to show that young children's mental capabilities are enhanced through play activities. Play provides a foundation for the pre-school curriculum as it represents the vehicle through which young children develop new and better cognitive skills (Piaget, 1962). Piaget felt that play is assimilation, which is the process of taking information from the environment and incorporating it into what the child already knows. Yawkey (1978) suggested that play is interrelated with thinking skills and intellectual development which constitutes a dynamic process. "Its link to mental development is through transformation and language" (PDK Newsletter, 1982). Transformation--to think and act as if oneself is another person, thing, or situation--and language--share and communicate thoughts in words that are understandable--are linked to intellectual development in play activities.

Studies show that play can lead to divergent thinking. Five personality traits were used in one study: 1) physical, 2) cognitive, 3) social spontaneity, 4) manifest joy, and 5) sense of humor (Lieberman, 1977). The results indicated a significant relationship between children's playfulness scores and aspects of divergent thinking. Problem-solving behaviors have been tested through play. The results of one study show that young children who were allowed to use free play with specific materials exhibited more problem-solving ability than young children who were not allowed free play activities. Young children who were engaged in free play activities exhibited more goal-directed behavior and greater persistence than those who did not participate in free play activities (Sylva, Bruner, Genoa, 1976).

While engaged in play, indoors and/or outdoors, young children have opportunities to make decisions and choices. Teachers and other adults must give recognition to the sophisticated thinking processes of the pre-schooler who successfully climbs on a piece of equipment, surveys the ground from its summit, and lands unscathed from the jump down. "Choice is the beginning of the process of discrimination and discrimination is learning" (Friedberg, 1969, p. 8). Mental learning happens as young children use play to exert visual, auditory and tactile memory skills in mathematics, science, social studies, and expressive arts. These skills are developed and practiced through the impact of the environment on the child's senses. There are many objects, people, and situations which evoke the young children to see, hear, touch, feel, and/or smell while engaged in play within the classroom or on the playground. Speech and language development which is a cognitive process is enhanced through free play (less structured environments) activities. Dramatic/socio-dramatic play facilitates speech and language development, especially for nonverbal, education-ally disadvantaged pre-schoolers (Belt, 1980). These types of play are encumbered symbolic play and are fostered in curriculum content areas as music, movement, visual arts, housekeeping, doll play, language arts, and social studies. Symbolic play is a way for young children to do abstract thinking. "Children who engage in symbolic play advan-ces in general emotional growth, speech fluency, persistence at tasks, an ability to distinguish reality from fantasy, cooperation with others, the ability to tolerate delays, empathy and leadership" (PDK News-letter, 1982, p. 2).

The pre-school curriculum is the master plan for learning, and play is education. In summary, Rousseau stated in Emile (reprinted 1962) a probability in view of children's learning:

> Children will only learn what they feel to be of actual and present advantage either because they like it, or because it is of use to them. Otherwise what motive would they have for learning (p. 51).

If "play" is nature's way of expressing individual education (learning), and curriculum is the master plan for education (learning), then play is definitely the foundation for pre-school curriculum. The definitions, theories, and stages of play are appropriate to outdoor play activities as curriculum is planned, developed, evaluated, and implemented. Outdoor play manifests active discovery and develops strategies for problem-solving which are essential to the growth and development of complex cognitive structures. The mere fact that outdoor play activities are germane to the context of the growth and development processes of the young child connotes its foundational emphasis for curriculum and the teaching/learning process.

ACTIVITIES FOR STUDY AND DISCUSSION

1. Based on the information found in this chapter, a review of the literature on play, academic and experiential background, write a generic definition of "play" in view of its relationship to curriculum.

2. Delineate the major types of play and explain each. Use examples of the types of play and differentiate the types in reference to the theorists and specialists, i.e., Piaget.

3. Do a series of observations of children in school settings for the purpose of finding information to answer the following: a) identify the types of play that the children are engaged in within the pre-school; b) substantiate the growth and developmental areas being influenced by the various types of play--give examples; c) record instances of extensions of indoor/outdoor play situations; d) make an annotated list of books that can be used in explaining the "educative values of play;" and e) comment on the types, amounts, appropriateness and conditions of the play materials and equipment in the center/school.

4. Write an essay on a theorist that you feel has made a great contribution to the area of "play" and advocates play as an educational resource.

5. Practice designing "play space" for both indoor and outdoor activities; include dimensions pertaining to size, locations of various areas, types of materials, equipment, and furniture, and the number of children to utilize the play space.

REFERENCES

Baker, Katherine R., "Extending the Indoors Outside," in **Housing for Early Childhood Education.** Washington, D.C.: ACEI, 1968.

Baker, Katherine R., **Let's Play Outdoors.** Washington, D.C.: NAEYC Press, 1976.

Belt, Marilyn A., "The Positive Effects of Dramatic Play and Socio-Dramatic Play on Language Development in Young Children: A Case Study," (Unpublished Masters Thesis) Howard University, School of Education, Washington, D.C., April 1980.

_____, "Criteria for Selecting Play Equipment for Early Childhood Education," **Community Playthings.** Rifton, N.Y.: Sept. 2, 1966.

_____, "The Power of Play," **Creative Playthings, Inc.** Princeton, New Jersey, 1967.

Dewey, John, **How We Think.** New York: D.C. Heath and Company, 1933 (Revised Edition).

Forman, G. and Hill Fleet, **Constructive Play.** Monterey, California: Brook/Cole, 1980.

Frank, Lawrence K., "The Role of Play in Child Development," **Childhood Education.** October, 1964.

Friedberg, M. Paul, **Playgrounds for City Children.** Washington, D.C.: ACEI, 1969.

Garvey, Catherine, **Play.** Cambridge, Mass.: Harvard University Press, 1977.

Houts, Mary, **Lesson Plans for Using the Outdoors in Teaching.** Danville, Illinois: The Interstate Printers and Publishers, 1976.

Isenberg, J. and J. Jacobs, **Playthings as Learning Tools: A Parent's Guide.** New York: Academic Press, 1977.

Leonard, E.M., Van Deman, and L. E. Miles, "Block Construction in Developing Social Concepts," **Foundations of Learning in Childhood Education.** Columbus, Ohio: Charles E. Merrill Books, Inc., 1963.

Lieberman, J.N., **Playfulness: Its Relationship to Imagination and Creativity.** New York: Academic Press, 1977.

Nelson, Leslie and Blanche McDonald, "Selected Procedures in Teaching Social Studies," **Guide to Student Teaching.** Dubuque, Iowa: Wm. C. Brown Co., 1954.

Piaget, J., **Play, Dreams, and Imitation in Childhood.** New York: Norton, 1962.

Prescott, Daniel A., **The Child in the Educative Process.** New York: McGraw-Hill Book Company, Inc., 1957.

_____, "Practical Applications of Research," **Newsletter** of Phi Delta Kappa's Center on Evaluation, Development, and Research. Vol. 5, No. 2, Bloomington, Indiana, December, 1982.

Robison, H.F. and B. Spodek, **New Directions in the Kindergarten.** New York: Teachers College Press, 1965.

Rousseau, Jean, **Emile.** New York: Teachers College Press, 1962.

Scarfe, N.V., "Play is Education," **Childhood Education,** November 1962 (Based on Address at 1962 ACEI Study Conference).

Scarfe, N.V., "Play is Education," (Speech at ACEI's Study Conference in Indianapolis, Indiana, April 1971).

Shoemaker, Rowena M., "Children Learn Through Play," **Play—Children Business,** ACEI, 1963.

Spodek, Bernard, "The Role of Materials in Teaching Social Studies to Young Children," (Written Speech for Teachers on the Child and the Real World) University of British Columbia, Vancouver, B.C., October 4-5, 1968.

Stone, Jeannette Galambos, **Play and Playgrounds.** Washington, D.C. NAEYC, 1970.

Sutton-Smith, B. and R.E. Herron, **Child's Play**, New York: John Wiley and Sons, Inc., 1971.

Sylva, K., J. Bruner, and P. Genova, "The Role of Play in the Problem-Solving of Children 3-5 Years Old," in **Play**: Its Role in Development and Evolution, J.S. Bruner, A. Jolly, and K. Sylva, eds. New York: Basic Books, 1976.

_____, **Teachers Guide to Education in Early Childhood.** Sacramento, California, State Department of Education, 1956.

_____, "Understanding the Educative Values of Block Play," School Publication No. 477, Guiding the Learning Experiences of Young Children. Los Angeles City School District, California, 1962.

Ward, Winifred, **Stories to Dramatize.** Anchorage, Kentucky: The Children's Theatre Press, 1952.

Yawkey, T.D., "More on Play as Intelligence in Children," **Journal of Creative Behavior.** Vol. 13, No. 4, 1980.

CHAPTER FOUR

LANGUAGE ARTS CURRICULUM (PRE-READING EXPERIENCES)

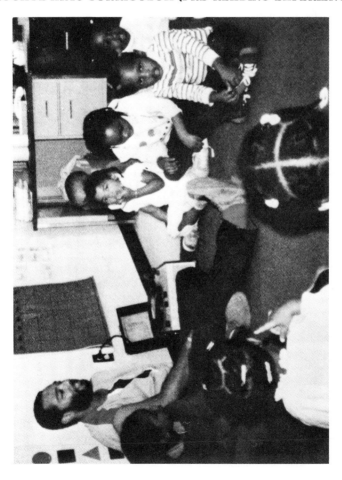

SPEAKING, READING READINESS, LISTENING, AND WRITING

CHAPTER 4

LANGUAGE ARTS CURRICULUM (PRE-READING EXPERIENCES)

- WHAT IS THE ROLE OF LANGUAGE ARTS IN THE PRE-SCHOOL CURRICULUM?: AN INTRODUCTION

- WHAT ARE THE SUBJECT AREAS THAT COMPRISE THE LANGUAGE ARTS CURRICULUM IN PRE-SCHOOL?

- WHAT ARE THE GOALS AND OBJECTIVES FOR TEACHING? THE LANGUAGE ARTS?

- WHAT APPROACHES TO USE TO EXPAND/EXTEND CURRICULUM THEORY INTO TEACHING/LEARNING APPLICATIONS FOR THE LANGUAGE ARTS (PRE-READING EXPERIENCES)?

- HOW IS EVALUATION CONDUCTED IN THE LANGUAGE ARTS CURRICULUM?

- HOW DO THE LANGUAGE ARTS CORRELATE WITH THE TOTAL PRE-SCHOOL CURRICULUM?

- ACTIVITIES FOR STUDY AND DISCUSSION

- REFERENCES

WHAT IS THE ROLE OF LANGUAGE ARTS IN THE PRE-SCHOOL CURRICULUM?: AN INTRODUCTION

Language Arts is the curriculum area which provides the foundation upon which pre-schoolers grow and develop in the manipulation and appropriate application of communication skills and language competence. Pre-reading experiences, listening skills, speaking skills, and writing skills comprise the core of the pre-school curriculum which provide a link to all of the activities within the school environment. Therefore, the role of language arts in the pre-school curriculum becomes one of grave importance in providing a stimulating climate for fostering desirable and appropriate communication and language skills, usage, and understanding. It is through the language arts that the pre-schoolers will gain knowledge, skills, attitudes, and abilities to communicate their needs, feelings, beliefs, ideas, and concerns within their environments and society.

The teaching/learning process in early childhood education must be designed to use the curriculum to express, clarify, and implement information and materials germane to thinking and understanding. The language arts (speaking, listening, reading, and writing) then are the mechanisms for executing communication. Language ability affects the pre-schooler's learning in all subject areas and about self. He/she is able to put information and understanding into symbolized form which expresses ideas, feelings, and needs. The acquisition of language is a most important aspect of the pre-schooler's intellectual development. Young children must determine, solely from the speech around them, the rules and conditions that govern language usage. A sequential, continuous pattern of language behavior, beginning at birth, is undertaken in the language arts curriculum to deal effectively with the refining, enhancing, and enriching of language skills which young children bring from home. The pre-school program can deal with these from the standpoint of teaching/learning language skills as the base for building efficiency and competency in reading, writing, speaking, and listening, as well as in the use of standard dialect. The young child is viewed as a special combination of inherited traits and influences of his/her environment. Therefore, the pre-school curriculum is designed to fulfill the role of language arts in providing

99

teaching and learning episodes in pre-reading experiences, speaking skills, listening skills, and writing skills.

WHAT ARE THE SUBJECT AREAS THAT COMPRISE THE LANGUAGE ARTS CURRICULUM IN PRE-SCHOOL?

The subject areas in the Language Arts Curriculum area: 1) Pre-Reading; 2) Speaking; 3) Listening; and 4) Writing. All of these areas are interrelated.

Pre-Reading is the state whereby young children are exposed to language arts experiences in the home and in the classroom/center that are designed to prepare them for learning to read. It is commonly referred to as "reading readiness" since young children are introduced to books, printed materials, show and tell activities, scribbling, records, storytelling and listening, performing tasks and following instructions, and others as will be discussed in this chapter. They will be involved in activities and experiences to develop skills in visual discrimination, auditory discrimination, directionality orientation, language development, listening comprehension, and handwriting.

Speaking is the process of giving verbal expression to meanings acquired through experiences. The language that young children hear in their homes will be used in the classroom/center. An atmosphere where talking is encouraged and expected is essential for helping pre-schoolers build speaking skills. Care must be taken to expand growth in language development through respect and empathetic understanding of each child's speaking patterns and problems. Providing many opportunities for young children to talk about themselves, their families, friends, events, and things will enhance the subject area of speaking.

Listening is a mental process calling for thought and reaction to hearing, recognizing, interpreting, and/or comprehending spoken language. It is an area that is too often taken for granted in the pre-school. Therefore, the pre-school curriculum must pay attention to "listening" as a vital subject area which joins "learning" as a closely related concept. The forms or types of listening are: 1) Passive or marginal listening; and 2) Active listening (Appreciative, Attentive and Analytical). The pre-school curriculum in language arts must provide information and materials to help caregivers to deal effectively with these types of listeners. This chapter will provide strategies to effect the necessary teaching and learning experiences for pre-schoolers.

Writing as a subject area in language arts for pre-schoolers is focused on "handwriting" which is called "manuscript" writing. Handwriting encompasses the physical basis of the development of small muscles and eye-hand coordination. The pre-school curriculum must provide activities and experiences to enhance handwriting through motor development and coordination, as well as through interest of the young children (labeling work) and opportunities for the caregiver to use handwriting (chalk board, charts, etc.). Specific activities and experiences will be offered in another part of this chapter.

WHAT ARE THE GOALS AND OBJECTIVES FOR TEACHING THE LANGUAGE ARTS?

The language arts/pre-reading curriculum integrates the communications processes of speaking, listening, reading and writing in an attempt to accomplish the following goals:

o   To develop the proficiency and enjoyment of the various forms of language and communications.

o   To develop growth in language development which encourages building speaking skills and understanding speaking patterns and problems.

o   To develop skills in purposeful listening and good habits of gaining and making use of information, thinking critically, evaluating ideas, enjoying and appreciating the experiences of others.

o   To develop readiness for skill subjects by gaining experiences in preliminary reading activities, recognizing likenesses and differences, recognizing and identifying sounds, using gross and fine motor coordination, and focusing on and responding to spoken language.

o   To develop skills in finger and hand dexterity, small muscles and eye-hand coordination in using writing tools.

o   To develop wholesome personal worth and confidence.

o   To develop an intellectual curiosity and capacity for critical thinking.

o   To develop abilities, attitudes, and knowledge in social sensitivity and effective participation in group life.

101

º To develop an appreciation for a rich, expressive vocabulary, ability to write creatively, and appreciate good literature.

Objectives for Speaking are:

To say the name of concrete objects.

To say the name of pictured objects.

To say the name of the parts of the body.

To show and tell about events in the environment.

To say the name of familiar people.

To imitate speech and develop good speech patterns.

To demonstrate the ability to repeat words and sentences.

To demonstrate the ability to speak clearly and distinctly.

To demonstrate the ability to wait a turn to speak.

To demonstrate courtesy in speaking by not talking while others are.

To demonstrate ability to speak in unison with others.

To demonstrate the ability towards good dramatization.

To provide an environment and atmosphere where talking is encouraged and required during activities.

Objectives for Listening are:

To develop skill in communicating feelings.

To develop skill and ability to discriminate speech sounds.

To develop skill and ability to listen to appreciate experience.

To develop skill and ability to listen for enjoyment.

To develop skill and ability to describe the sequence of ideas.

To develop skill and ability to identify rhyming elements.

To develop skill and ability to interpret what is heard in terms of personal experiences.

To develop thoughtful listening.

To develop purposeful listening in order to obtain information, details, directions, etc.

To experience singing as a means of listening and expressing sounds.

Objectives for Pre-Reading are:

(Visual Discrimination)
To develop ability to see likenesses and differences in objects, shapes, colors, and sizes.

To develop ability to distinguish among letter and word forms.

(Auditory Discrimination)
To identify sounds from surroundings.

To distinguish likenesses and differences in sounds.

To identify initial consonant sounds, words that rhyme, and associate letter names with letter sounds.

To develop skill and ability to understand the spoken language and use it commensurate with age and maturity.

To gain ability to focus on and respond to spoken language.

To develop directionality-orientation by using gross and fine motor coordination to develop left-to-right progression.

To develop ability to put things in sequence.

Objectives for Writing are:

To name and identify instruments used in writing (pencil, pen, crayon).

To develop ability to grasp writing instruments.

To develop skill and ability to trace simple objects, letters, numerals, and shapes.

To identify capital and small letters (lower case) of the alphabet.

To identify words in books and printed materials to denote capital and lower case letters.

To develop skill and ability to scribble on paper with writing instruments.

To develop skill and ability to cut paper and use cutting tool (scissors).

To gain experiences in coloring with crayons and covering paper and materials.

To gain experiences in pasting objects on paper.

To develop ideas about writing as a means of communication.

To develop experiences in using written materials for identification of personal belongings and identifying objects and materials (labeling).

Goals and objectives are important to the curriculum and teaching process. It is a basic concern that the pre-school program utilize the principle that there is a direct relationship between what is taught and the goals and objectives for teaching the subject matter. Individual differences of pre-schoolers must be taken into consideration as goals and objectives are implemented. The establishment of concepts in the subject areas are best identified through first-hand perceptual experiences and situations that pre-schoolers are best suited for and have experienced.

WHAT APPROACHES TO USE TO EXPAND/EXTEND CURRICULUM THEORY INTO TEACHING/LEARNING APPLICATIONS FOR THE LANGUAGE ARTS (PRE-READING EXPERIENCES)?

Pre-school curriculum and teaching entails three major components:

o   Learning theories (possible ways child learns various subjects)

° Theories of Instruction (best ways to teach children)

° Teaching/Learning Process (rationale, purpose, strategies, methods, techniques, assessment, and resources)

There are two approaches suggested to expand/extend curriculum theory into practical application. The first approach is "a strategy" for formulating a process of impartment (knowledges, skills, attitudes, and competencies) between the professor/instructor and the student (preservice teacher) in training or the practitioner (inservice teacher, parent). This approach characterizes "curriculum and instructional design." Concepts, methods, techniques, readily accessible information/ materials, and teaching expertise formulate the second approach. This approach characterizes "practical applications."

Curriculum and Instructional Design: A Strategy

A "three dimensional process of impartment" (between the professor/ instructor and the student in training or practitioner) is a strategy to enable caregivers to develop a systematic approach to learning curriculum and instructional design. The dimensionals "TO KNOW," " TO FEEL," and "TO DO" are formulated to show how curriculum theory (through personal competency) is expanded/extended into practical applications (Vance, 1973). See diagram in Figure 5.

TO KNOW	TO FEEL	TO DO
(Curriculum Theory)	(Personal Competency)	(Practical Application)
• How Children Learn • What Subjects To Teach	• Knowledgeable • Skilled	• Perform effectively in the helping process as caregiver (Utilizing relevant, appropriate, ample materials and resources)
• What Are The Purposes For Teaching	• Competent (in curriculum areas and acquisition of information	• Articulate planing, programming and evaluation in a diagnostic-prescriptive teaching/learning approach
• What Are The Goals For Teaching The Subjects	• Confident (in executing teaching and learning process)	• Implement instructional episodes in teaching/learning process
• What Appropriate Content To Teach	• Efficient (in curriculum theory, development and practice)	• Demonstrate competence in dealing with individual children and their families

Figure __5__ .   A Three Dimensional Process of Impartment

106

The Language Arts curriculum is composed of content (learning experiences) in speaking, listening, writing, and pre-reading as contained in previous parts of this chapter:

○ Introduction To Subject Areas and Role of the Language Arts

○ Subject Areas Comprising The Language Arts

○ Goals and Objectives For The Language Arts

This information provides the basis for curriculum theory. Since the goals and objectives set the premise for planning daily, weekly, monthly, and/or yearly curriculum, caregivers should "know" this theory. Mastery of curriculum theory enables the caregiver to "feel" competent in enhancing changes in pre-schoolers' behaviors at the end of effective instruction (do). The latter (instruction) is designed to be accomplished through efficient practical applications and ready access to materials, methods, and resources.

While all of the people involved in the education of the children play a role in curriculum development (through preparing and developing goals and objectives for pre-reading, speaking, listening, and writing), the caregiver is responsible for implementing instruction. This means that the caregiver must be capable of understanding, recognizing, and translating connections of "theory" into "practice." The practical application approach represents the strategy for consolidating curriculum theory and expanding/extending it into practice.

Practical applications: Expressive Arts Curriculum Concepts, Performance Outcomes, Activities, Teaching Methods and Resources

Social, emotional, physical, mental, and language development are acquired by pre-schoolers through the language arts and pre-reading experiences. Theory is expanded/extended into practice by the caregiver in order to help pre-schoolers to grow and develop holistically. The following procedures are suggested as an effective way of making this connection:

○ Interpret and consolidate goals and objectives for teaching the language arts in reference to desired behavior changes for pre-schoolers. This integrative thought process should result in condensed statements of purpose (CONCEPTS) for teaching each subject area (pre-reading, speaking, listening, and writing).

º Relate these <u>concepts</u> to <u>performance outcomes</u> for pre-schoolers and formulate <u>activities</u> to ensure desired learning behaviors in each subject area.

º Implement the <u>activities</u> by using a wide variety of instructional strategies (teaching methods, techniques, and resources) in the teaching/learning process.

<u>The Connecting method</u>

The simplest way to deal with the "connection of <u>theory</u> and <u>practice</u>" is to graphically show the process by using charts. The charts are designed to show a "flow" of information and materials (curriculum theory) being expanded/extended into teaching and learning episodes (practice) through a "connecting" relationship. Therefore, the chart includes curriculum categories (concepts, performance outcomes, activities, teaching methods and resources) for fostering the suggested procedures for effecting the connection between "theory" and "practice." A sample is shown in Figure <u>6.</u>

An explanation of the "connecting method" for using this chart is as follows.

º The Speaking CONCEPT, "Arrange for daily language periods for conversation and discussion" (has been condensed from goals and objectives) <u>flows</u> into

º PERFORMANCE OUTCOME, "Developed speaking skills and abilities to express self" (to be the desired behavior) <u>flows</u> into

º ACTIVITIES to help pre-schoolers develop this desired behavior (showing and telling about people, places, and things in their home environments, etc.) <u>flow</u> into

º TEACHING METHODS AND RESOURCES to be performed by the caregiver in order to implement the activities (children's performances) designed to accomplish the desired behavior (performance outcome) based on the concept (condensed goal/objective), "Prepare teaching/learning environment to foster a lot of talking (free expression and guided speaking)" is an example of the practical application.

CURRICULUM EXPERIENCES FOR TEACHING/LEARNING THE LANGUAGE ARTS

(Subject) CONCEPTS	PERFORMANCE OUTCOMES	CHILDREN'S ACTIVITIES	TEACHING METHODS AND RESOURCES
SPEAKING Arrange for daily language periods for conversation and discussion	Developed speaking skills and abilities to express self	-Showing and telling about people, places, and things in home environment	-Prepare teaching/learning environment to foster a lot of talking (free expression and guided speaking)

Figure 6 . Sample Chart of Curriculum Experiences for Teaching/Learning Language Arts (Pre-Reading Experiences)

The use of charts as herewith provided, then, is intended to provide systematic, functional (ease of accessibility to information) plans for connecting curriculum theory to practical application.

Caregivers must be prepared (training and experience) to implement teaching/learning experiences to foster creative potential in each of the pre-schoolers. Therefore, the curriculum must be planned and designed to impart information, concepts, methods, activities, and resources for developing experiences and opportunities for pre-schoolers to become free, independent, and creative thinkers, performers, and learners. Through language arts (pre-reading experiences) pre-schoolers begin to understand other people and other cultures. This is an excellent opportunity for them as they engage in the language arts and pre-reading activities, to view the world from another point of view. Experiences, then, in the language arts must be built around a well-planned, organized, sequenced, and relevant curriculum that is implemented by a competent caregiver. This caregiver must have acquired an understanding of the "three dimensional process of impartment" (to know, to feel, to do) and is capable of expanding/extending curriculum theory into practice by being able to:

° Describe or illustrate the desired behavior of children (concepts);

° Identify and plan performance outcomes and activities in relation to the desired behaviors;

° Execute teaching methods and resources to help children to acquire the desired behaviors and to make changes; and

° Recognize and assess the desired behaviors before, during, and after instruction.

These charts are constructed into a "curriculum model" that can be used as a written curriculum for a program. The value of this model depends, to a great degree, upon the users' understanding of its potentials and limitations. It is not to be used as a "packaged program" without care and consideration given to the particular needs and conditions of the local pre-school situation. The information and materials herewith contained are extensive, but not exhaustive, therefore requiring the caregivers (preservice teachers, inservice teachers, parents, and early childhood professionals) to add, use, and adapt the curriculum to the age, sex, race/culture, and special needs of the pre-schoolers.

This chapter is the model chapter for showing "the approaches to use to expand/extend curriculum theory into teaching/learning applications" for the other subject areas -- Social Living (Chapter 5); Expressive Arts (Chapter 6); Mathematics (Chapter 7); and Science (Chapter 8). Therefore, the text will refer the reader to Chapter 4 for procedures and concepts of information and materials if and when it may be necessary to "review" how to transfer "curriculum theory" into "practical application."

The following charts are provided to show "curriculum experiences for teaching/learning the language arts and pre-reading experiences" in the pre-school.

CURRICULUM EXPERIENCES FOR TEACHING/LEARNING LANGUAGE ARTS (PRE-READING)—CHART 6

(Subject) CONCEPTS	PERFORMANCE OUTCOMES	CHILDREN'S ACTIVITIES	TEACHING METHODS/RESOURCES
SPEAKING			
Self expression	Developed language	-Showing and telling about	-Provide materials for chil-
Articulation	and speaking skills	home and school events	dren to use in their act-
Show and Tell	and abilities	-Talking informally about	ivities, for example:
Self concept		ideas, things, people,	picture file of assorted
Projection		and places	pictures from magazines,
Confidence		-Playing guessing games	books, etc.; Empty boxes
Wait turn to		(what's in the box, bag,	of all sizes, mirrors,
to speak		etc.)	books, props for dramatic
Speak in unison		-Participating in dramatic	play (old clothes, toys,
Dramatization		play (puppetry, plays,	blocks, etc.), puppets,
Speaking patterns		etc.)	tape recorder, record play-
Speaking problems		-Playing game with mirror	er, assorted records of
Sound		(talking about self)	stories, songs, etc.;
Repeat words		-Playing with blocks	charts and posters, maga-
		-Playing in the house-	zines, and paper bags.
		keeping area	
		-Listening to stories	-Prepare atmosphere where
		and talking about what	talking is encouraged.
		happened in the story	
		-Talking about pictures	-Plan for daily language
		-Becoming aware of people	periods for conversations
		in families, other places,	and discussion (Show and
		and of many nationalities	tell).
		through reading materials	
		(books, stories, films;	-Have show and tell where
		filmstrips, movies, etc.)	children bring object/item
		-Practicing left-to-right	from home and talk about
		directionality	it.

(Subject) CONCEPTS	PERFORMANCE OUTCOMES	CHILDREN'S ACTIVITIES	TEACHING METHODS/RESOURCES
		- Activities are included in the "teaching methods/resources" and should be considered for children to perform.	-Provide acceptance of children's initial efforts to express themselves; encourage timid child to talk and help incessant talker to develop self-control.
			-Serve as model for correct speech (tone of voice, pronunciation, enunciation, and grammar).
			-Set atmosphere for free flow of spontaneous conversation.
			-Provide help to children in speaking clearly and in simple sentences.
			-Play guessing games (what's in the bag, box, etc.) to encourage talking.
			-Present dramatic play activities (plays, puppets, dramatization, etc.) to involve children in oral communication.
			-Present "mystery box" activity (a box with

CURRICULUM EXPERIENCES FOR TEACHING/LEARNING LANGUAGE ARTS (PRE-READING)—UNIT 6

(Subject) CONCEPTS	PERFORMANCE OUTCOMES	CHILDREN'S ACTIVITIES	TEACHING METHODS/RESOURCES
		- Activities are included in the "teaching methods/resources" and should be considered for children to perform.	assorted objects) whereby the child reaches in, feels one object and describe it. Supply descriptive words to help child, like, "is it hard, soft, etc." in order to have child learn vocabulary. -Play "mirror, mirror" where the child stands in front of the class and holds the mirror in front of him/her and tells about himself/ herself. -Use "snack time" as a speaking activity whereby children discuss the food in view of health and nutrition, like and dis- like, cultural value, etc. -Use "lunch" time for conversations, also. -Provide materials to facil- itate discussions, like: pictures of basic food groups, pictures of differ- ent groups of people

CURRICULUM EXPERIENCES FOR TEACHING/LEARNING LANGUAGE ARTS (PRE-READING) —CHART 6

(Subject) CONCEPTS	PERFORMANCE OUTCOMES	CHILDREN'S ACTIVITIES	TEACHING METHODS/RESOURCES
		- Activities are included in the "teaching methods/resources" and should be considered for children to perform.	(different nationalities), books, fingerplays, puppets, different colored objects, song books, records, tapes, filmstrips (farm, circus, holidays, sports events, etc.), word cards, labels for furniture and objects in the environment, art materials and supplies, (paper, paints, glue, paste, scissors, tape, etc.)
			-Provide in learning center a box of objects of various colors and have children name the colors.
			-Sing different songs appropriate for young children (substitute words and express actions whenever possible).
			-Read and tell stories to children. Talk about stories (words, phrases, actions).
			-Use play telephones and have children talk to each other (unstructured—about anything they desire;

CURRICULUM EXPERIENCES FOR TEACHING/LEARNING LANGUAGE ARTS (PRE-READING) —CHART 6

(Subject) CONCEPTS	PERFORMANCE OUTCOMES	CHILDREN'S ACTIVITIES	TEACHING METHODS/RESOURCES
		- Activities are included in the "teaching methods/resources" and should be considered for children to perform.	structured-about specific topics suggested by teacher). -Read jokes adn riddles to children which are absurd and have them correct the joke/riddle. -Have children close eyes and ask them to imagine seeing a picture of things that are named--circus, birthday party, holiday, sports events --and have them tell about "what they saw." -Provide real and vicarious experiences which require the use of words--supply precise words to convey correct meanings, explain words which children use but do not correctly understand, explain the meanings in terms of what the children already know, encourage the use of descriptive words, use vivid words when talking to children, and teach contrasting and opposite words. -Encourage using play materials that are high

116

(Subject) CONCEPTS	PERFORMANCE OUTCOMES	CHILDREN'S ACTIVITIES	TEACHING METHODS/RESOURCES
		– Activities are included in the "teaching methods/resources" and should be considered for children to perform.	in conversational value (dolls, toys for dramatic play, blocks, clay, pets, etc.). Materials needed include: dolls, blocks, art materials, junk items from the home, school, and community; space for play action, books, masks, flannel board, play telephones. –Present deeper meanings for words already known and show that the same words may have more than one meaning (belt – for conveying things and belt– an article of apparel; <u>hand</u>– part of the clock and <u>hand</u>– part of the body, etc.) –Reproduce (writing on chalkboard, charts, etc.) letters, messages, stories, personal experiences in order for children to discuss. –Have children engage in spontaneous dramatic play by: acting out their

117

(Subject) CONCEPTS	PERFORMANCE OUTCOMES	CHILDREN'S ACTIVITIES	TEACHING METHODS/RESOURCES
		- Activities are included in the "teaching methods/resources" and should be considered for children to perform.	experiences, telling incomplete stories and children make up different endings, etc.
			-Tell stories using a series of pictures and objects (puppets, toys, etc.)
			-Use teaching aids to portray stories, poems, plays (flannel boards, masks, puppets, pictures, films, etc.)
			-Evaluate activities on a daily basis and get verbal feedback from children.
			-Use activity times for solving problems through discussion (planning activities, social relationships, use of materials, evaluation of work, etc.).
			-Help the children learn information about themselves (play game, i.e., "I Am Lost, whereby children must know their names, addresses; phone numbers, parents' names,

(Subject) CONCEPTS	PERFORMANCE OUTCOMES	CHILDREN'S ACTIVITIES	TEACHING METHODS/RESOURCES
		- Activities are included in the "teaching methods/resources" and should be considered for children to perform.	and the like).

-Invite community persons to talk with children, i.e., friendly police person, fireman/woman, gardener, painter, etc.

-Provide materials to support activities for speech development, like: mirrors (full length and hand), liquid detergent for soap bubbles, drinking straws, pin wheels, sail boats, dried beans, peas for pea shooters, liquid beverages--water, juice, sodas, cool aid, milk, etc., hollow rollers from hand towels, toilet tissue, aluminum foil, etc., candles, raw vegetables--carrots, radishes, celery, etc., snack items --licorice, gum drops, raisins; use snack and lunch periods; records of sounds; pictures of faces, people, etc.; books and printed materials for reading and listening. |

CURRICULUM EXPERIENCES FOR TEACHING/LEARNING LANGUAGE ARTS (PRE-READING)—CHART 6

(Subject) CONCEPTS	PERFORMANCE OUTCOMES	CHILDREN'S ACTIVITIES	TEACHING METHODS/RESOURCES
Use good health rules in implementing activities in speech development		-Participating in activities to develop speech as presented in "teaching methods/resources."	-Stimulate speech development by exercising the speech muscles. Provide many blowing activities, like, blowing soap bubbles, blowing out candles, blowing pin wheels, blowing hot beverages and soups, imitating the sound of the wind, doing straw painting, blowing sail boats in containers of water, blowing horns made from hollow rollers, etc.; Provide activities that involve chewing movements, like, chewing raw vegetables, chewing meats well, chewing licorice and gum drops, playing chewing games from dramatizations—stories, poems, etc.; Provide activities that involve sucking liquids through a straw, swallowing liquids and solids during snack time, lunch time, etc.; and Providing activities to encourage lip exercises, like, imitating and making various sounds of animals, musical instruments, emergency vehicles, climatic

(Subject) CONCEPTS	PERFORMANCE OUTCOMES	CHILDREN'S ACTIVITIES	TEACHING METHODS/RESOURCES
			conditions, baby's cry, humming simple melodies, making funny faces, making happy faces, making sad faces, making angry faces, saying tongue twisters, etc.
LISTENING			
Purposeful listening	Developed skills in purposeful lsitening; good habits of obtaining and making use of information; abilities to think critically, to evaluate ideas, and to enjoy and appreciate experiences of others	-Listening to directions and instructions pertaining to activities	-Identify types of listeners among the children:
Good habits to attention		-Listening for different reasons as described in the methodologies	Marginal Listeners
Gain and make use of information			-Listen just enough to be vaguely aware of what is being said.
Critical thinking			
Evaluate ideas			-Help (marginal listeners) to increase attention span; increase repertoire of words to build oral language background; increase experiences to give emotional security (reinforce initial behavior in activity), change instances of play activity to cut down on long periods of involvement in the same activity, and work on helping child to concentrate on pleasant activity,
Enjoy and appreciate experiences of self and others			
Marginal listening			
Active listening			

CURRICULUM EXPERIENCES FOR TEACHING/LEARNING LANGUAGE ARTS (PRE-READING)-CHART 6

(Subject) CONCEPTS	PERFORMANCE OUTCOMES	CHILDREN'S ACTIVITIES	TEACHING METHODS/RESOURCES
		-Listening as described in the "teaching methods/resources" to be performed by children.	as well as be tolerant of unpleasant activity. Dwell on the fundamentals of "active" listening.

Active Listeners

-Listen with intentions of hearing with attention or purpose.

-Provide experiences to enhance appreciative listening (depicting books as sources of beauty and pleasure; developing good listening habits; listening for specific words and meanings; understanding and learning about others and their feelings).

-Provide experiences to enhance attentive listening (providing activities that require listening for directions, announcements, obtaining information, details).

-Provide experiences to enhance analytical listening (developing |

122

CURRICULUM EXPERIENCES FOR TEACHING/LEARNING LANGUAGE ARTS (PRE-READING) –CHART 6

(Subject) CONCEPTS	PERFORMANCE OUTCOMES	CHILDREN'S ACTIVITIES	TEACHING METHODS/RESOURCES
Developing good listening habits Look directly at the speaker Be courteous when others are speaking		-Participating in activities on individual and group bases as described in the "teaching methods/resources" for children to perform.	thoughtful listening, detailing information to specific terms of personal experiences). -Help children identify situations where good listening practices are important (doing assignments, chores, completing tasks in home environments, etc.) -Show alertness, courtesy, and attention in the environment as a model of good listening practices when dealing with children and adults. -Arrange environment to accomodate and accomplish good listening experiences (arrangement of furniture, space availability, ventilation, lighting, sound proof or less noisy areas for various activities). -Play the game "Simon says" whereby the teacher gives commands to the children

123

CURRICULUM EXPERIENCES FOR TEACHING/LEARNING LANGUAGE ARTS (PRE-READING) -CHART 6

(Subject) CONCEPTS	PERFORMANCE OUTCOMES	CHILDREN'S ACTIVITIES	TEACHING METHODS/RESOURCES
		-Extract activities from the "teaching methods/resources" as described fro children to perform.	who must listen to hear if "Simon" says do it. If "Simon" says do it, the child will comply; if "Simon" did not say do it, the child will not follow the command. The children are in a vertical line and are attempting to reach a point in the play area that has been designated as the "finish" line. The first one to reach this finish line is the winner.

-Have children guess familiar objects in the environment after you have described them.

-Have children play the game "Repeat and Add" whereby the child must repeat what he/she hears from the lead person and add something from the statement.

-Identify and commend quickly good listening practices in children. |

CURRICULUM EXPERIENCES FOR TEACHING/LEARNING LANGUAGE ARTS (PRE-READING)-CHART 6

(Subject) CONCEPTS	PERFORMANCE OUTCOMES	CHILDREN'S ACTIVITIES	TEACHING METHODS/RESOURCES
		-Use activities as described in "teaching methods/resources" for children to perform.	-Help children build standards of courtesy. -Prepare the environment for good listening habits by avoiding needless repetition, encouraging children that listening is a pleasant privilege, and specify how information learned should be used. -Examine needs of children and record (mentally) facts about each learner in view of needs, interests, assets, and problems. Provide for individual differences of children in listening ability, skill, and habit. -Plan a "Listening Center" in an area that is quiet and protected from traffic. -Provide good equipment and stimulating materials. For example: listening
A Listening Center facilitates developing good listening skills and abilities	Used materials and equipment to enhance good listening and performed well in activities	-Participating in activities assigned by the caregiver as described in the "teaching methods/resources" for children to perform.	

CURRICULUM EXPERIENCES FOR TEACHING/LEARNING LANGUAGE ARTS (PRE-READING)-CHART 6

(Subject) CONCEPTS	PERFORMANCE OUTCOMES	CHILDREN'S ACTIVITIES	TEACHING METHODS/RESOURCES
		-Participating in the activities as described in the "teaching methods/resources" for children to perform.	booths, classroom tables, book cases, wooden screens to afford privacy, record player, tape recorder, headset jacks for record player and tape recorder, set of headsets with audio-tronic box, tapes of stories, records of stories and songs, books to accompany tapes and records, also independent stories, space for one to six children, shelves for equipment, storage space, electrical outlets for equipment with covers for outlets not in use, hook boards or wall hooks to hang headsets, records (Holidays, Sounds Around Us, and Pre-School Themes)
			-Plan many positive experiences with the tape recorder and the record player.
			-Set the criteria for using the listening center and make sure each child understands the rules.

(Subject) CONCEPTS	PERFORMANCE OUTCOMES	CHILDREN'S ACTIVITIES	TEACHING METHODS/RESOURCES
		-Participating in the activities as described in the "teaching methods/resources" for children to perform.	-Interrelate the activities in the center with those in the environment. -Have children listen to stories, poems, riddles, songs, tapes, films and filmstrips. -Have children listen to and identify sounds in the environment (streets, nature, school, musical, common noises like running water, turning pages in books, ticking clocks, tearing paper, turning on the lights, blowing fan, electrical appliance, and others. -Have children listen to recordings for specific directions (things to do). -Inform children of automatic responses to certain signals in the environment (Bells, whistle blowing, telephone ring, alarm clock, etc.).

CURRICULUM EXPERIENCES FOR TEACHING/LEARNING LANGUAGE ARTS (PRE-READING)-CHART 6

(Subject) CONCEPTS	PERFORMANCE OUTCOMES	CHILDREN'S ACTIVITIES	TEACHING METHODS/RESOURCES
		-Participating in the activities as described in the "teaching methods/resources" for children to perform.	-Present sounds (honk of horn, ring a dinner bell, start a car, make animal sounds, etc.) and have children imitate them.
			-Have children listen to music to distinguish between music that is high and low, soft and loud, and fast and slow.
			-Have children imitate simple rhythms that are tapped out.
			-Have children identify speaking voices of persons on tape, out of sight, etc.
			-Bounce a ball and have children identify the number of times it was bounced.
			-Have children listen to weather reports on radio, television, etc. and repeat the information for others.

CURRICULUM EXPERIENCES FOR TEACHING/LEARNING LANGUAGE ARTS (PRE-READING)-CHART 6

(Subject) CONCEPTS	PERFORMANCE OUTCOMES	CHILDREN'S ACTIVITIES	TEACHING METHODS/RESOURCES
		-Participating in the activities as described in the "teaching methods/resources" for children to perform.	-Have children identify objects by the sound made on a tape. -Tap a stick on various objects in the environment and have children listen for the variation in sound. -Have children listen to short stories with a "thought" missing. The children should be given a chance to discuss what was missing and why they know that. The stories have to be ones that the children previously knew or had been exposed to. -Have children listen to and carry out various directions (go from simple to complex--put the book on the table to put the book on the left side of the table and bring the tape to me). -Have children respond to changes in tempo when certain songs are heard.

129

CURRICULUM EXPERIENCES FOR TEACHING/LEARNING LANGUAGE ARTS (PRE-READING)-CHART 6

(Subject) CONCEPTS	PERFORMANCE OUTCOMES	CHILDREN'S ACTIVITIES	TEACHING METHODS/RESOURCES
		-Participating in the activities as described in the "teaching methods/resources" for children to perform.	-Have children listen for long and short words when stories, poems, etc. are read or told.
			-Have children pick out words that sound alike in a poem, sotry, riddle, etc.
			-Have children supply a missing word to a poem, riddle, jingle, etc.
			-Bring in interesting resource persons to talk about their work (police-man/woman, postman/woman, crossing guard, doctor, lawyer, news reporter, etc.)
			-Play a word listening game with children (Which is an animal--a bear or a pear? Which is a tool-- a cake or a rake? Which is clothing--a boat or a coat?).
			-Play a game with the children whereby they identify the direction

CURRICULUM EXPERIENCES FOR TEACHING/LEARNING LANGUAGE ARTS (PRE-READING)—CHART 6

(Subject) CONCEPTS	PERFORMANCE OUTCOMES	CHILDREN'S ACTIVITIES	TEACHING METHODS/RESOURCES
		-Participating in the activities as described in the "teaching methods/resources" for children to perform.	in which a person is walking by listening to the footsteps behind a panel or portable wall divider (from floor up).
			-Use dolls as puppets to talk and children listen to drama.
			-Make a list of the daily listening activities and associate them with pleasant and interesting things learned and/or experienced.
WRITING			
Handwriting is a tool for written communication Communicate ideas in a written form that is legible and neat Mechanism for creating specific print markings	Showed achievement in readiness, body development and dexterity, and engaged in writing exercises	-Engaging in pre-writing skills activities like differentiating "left" from "right" -Playing games like Hokey Pokey -Putting puzzles together to distinguish parts, sizes, shapes, spatial relations, etc. -Recognizing sizes and shapes by using blocks	-Provide adequate and ample materials and tools for doing handwriting, like: fat pencils, fat crayons, paper (lined and unlined), pens, markers, typewriters, finger paint, tempora paint, scissors (round point), alphabet cards, books, chalk, writing strips (sentence strips), writing charts (lined and unlined),

131

CURRICULUM EXPERIENCES FOR TEACHING/LEARNING LANGUAGE ARTS (PRE-READING)-CHART 6

(Subject) CONCEPTS	PERFORMANCE OUTCOMES	CHILDREN'S ACTIVITIES	TEACHING METHODS/RESOURCES
Readiness for handwriting Development of small muscles and eye-hand coordination, grasp Printing names Drawing letters of the alphabet Functional use of manuscript writing for the teacher Relationship between sound and symbol Relationship between printed and spoken words Scribble Drawing Writing instruments (pen, pencil, crayon, etc.) The use of shape, lines, space, direction, and size		-Recognizing names of peers by observing name plates, closet markers, names on art work, and names on personal things -Cutting with scissors -Pasting with glue and paste on construction paper -Modeling clay -Hammering with wood and nails -Making collages by using pictures, scissors, clue, and paint -Playing on balance beams -Playing with toys (push, pull, roll, etc.) -Scribbling -Tracing -Drawing -Doing art work, like making cards, drawings, letters, notices of special events, etc.	sandpaper letters of the alphabet, portable chalk-board, magic slates, commercial and teacher made writing exercises, i.e., dotted letters from tracing, puzzles with numbers to be connected, dotted letters in name to be traced, and pictures, labels, and stories to be copied from printed materials; and Catalog - The Zaner-Bloser Company (The Guided Growth in Handwriting Series by Frank N. Freeman); Records - Penmanship Step by Step and Pocket Alphabet (Rosenbaum). -Make functional signs for the environment--captions, labels.

(Subject) CONCEPTS	PERFORMANCE OUTCOMES	CHILDREN'S ACTIVITIES	TEACHING METHODS/RESOURCES
PRE-READING			
Reading readiness skills and concepts Preparation for beginning reading instruction Maturational readiness--physical, emotional, psychological, experiential, social Physical maturation--development of normal speech patterns; ability do discriminate language sounds and phonemes; discriminate gross shapes of words and parts of words Emotional maturation--participates readily; have feelings of security	Developed abilities, skills, and attitudes that attributed to interest and aspiration for reading, language development, visual and auditory discrimination	-Engaging in activities that require using books, newspapers, magazines, and the printed page -Following directions in completing chores -Talking, listening, and writing as listed in the teaching methodologies -Using books and printed materials properly	-Show children how reading is fun by introducing new stories, poems, nursery rhymes, jingles, jokes, and others in an effort to prepare them for reading instruction. -Use reading experiences as the key to discussion about ideas, interests, places to visit, things that have happened, finding out about events, and others to make reading be seen as a thought-getting process and a fun activity. -Provide a well equipped classroom with relevant materials and human resources, book table, science table, nature walks, field trips, television, films, film-strips, books, parquetry blocks, mazes, puzzles, rough surface letters, cut pictures, magazines, flannel board, chalk board, workbooks, seat work, name

CURRICULUM EXPERIENCES FOR TEACHING/LEARNING LANGUAGE ARTS (PRE-READING)-CHART 6

(Subject) CONCEPTS	PERFORMANCE OUTCOMES	CHILDREN'S ACTIVITIES	TEACHING METHODS/RESOURCES
Psychological maturation-- understands reality; pos- sesses good self concept; sets and seeks goals Experiential maturation-- exposure to a variety of experiences in the environ- ment with books, stories, picture interpretation, letter forms, word forms, and sounds Social maturation --interactions with people and things and objects within the environ- ment which require speaking, listening, and writing		-Participating in the activities as described in the "teaching methods/resources" for children to perform.	cards, labeling strips, puppets, dress-up clothes, writing tools
Visual Discrimination -Recognizing like- nesses and differ- ences in gross forms -Recognizing like- nesses and differ-			-Provide an environment that is attractive and has eye-catching appeal with picture that can stimulate and have

134

CURRICULUM EXPERIENCES FOR TEACHING/LEARNING LANGUAGE ARTS (PRE-READING) —CHART 6

(Subject) CONCEPTS	PERFORMANCE OUTCOMES	CHILDREN'S ACTIVITIES	TEACHING METHODS/RESOURCES
ences in geo- metric and letter forms -Recognize and name letters of the alpha- bet in infor- mal situations -Recognize like- nesses and differences in word forms		-Participating in the activities as described in the "teaching methods/resources" for children to perform.	sufficient content, detail and action; objects of different sizes, shapes, and color. -Have various shapes of blocks, shapes of paper (square, circle, rectangle, triangle) and letter cut- outs placed on the boards (flannel, chalk) -- "A and H," "O and C." -Have children recognize and name letters of the alphabet in the environ- ment--letters on blocks, letters in names, letters in labels, letters in radio and television stations, letters on charts. -Have children identify words that are used in functional situations-- signs, labels, records, reports, titles of books, neames, bulletin boards. -Have children use games for individual choice

135

(Subject) CONCEPTS	PERFORMANCE OUTCOMES	CHILDREN'S ACTIVITIES	TEACHING METHODS/RESOURCES
		-Participating in the activities as described in the "teaching methods/resources" for children to perform.	during transition and work periods like dominoes, puzzles, lotto, etc.
			-Have children match shapes with colors--squares are red; rectangles are blue; circles are yellow; triangles are green.
			-Have children match pictures of animals that are similar--pictures of mother animals (bears) to pictures of baby animals (cubs); Cats to kittens, etc.
			-Have children recognize common objects in the environment and identify them by name and category.
			-Have children collect pictures from magazines and books and classify them according to category.
			-Have children select two like objects from an assorted group of objects.

(Subject) CONCEPTS	PERFORMANCE OUTCOMES	CHILDREN'S ACTIVITIES	TEACHING METHODS/RESOURCES
		-Participating in the activities as described in the "teaching methods/resources" for children to perform.	-Have children select pictures that fit into certain classifications from a group of pictures that represent a category --(from pictures of clothing, child selects clothes that represent winter).
			-Have children identify animals from pictures and have them make the sound that the animal makes.
			-Present a number of objects on a tray to children and have them recall the objects with the tray out of sight.
			-Have children name the object that has been removed from a group, or from a picture, and absent children.
			-Have children identify patterns like dots, solids, plaids, stripes.

137

CURRICULUM EXPERIENCES FOR TEACHING/LEARNING LANGUAGE ARTS (PRE-READING)—CHART 6

(Subject) CONCEPTS	PERFORMANCE OUTCOMES	CHILDREN'S ACTIVITIES	TEACHING METHODS/RESOURCES
Auditory Discrimination -Recognizing and identifying sounds -Recognizing likenesses and differences in sounds -Reproducing sounds that are heard -Understanding simple thoughts that are heard -Associating sounds, words, vocabulary,		-Participating in the activities as described in the "teaching methods/resources" for children to perform.	-Have children identify the change in position of certain objects in the environment. -Have children group articles in accord to color, shape, size, texture (pencils, bottles, jars, yarn, books, and junk items). -Have children recognize changes that happen in nature (seasons, growth of animals). -Prepare the environment to include a variety of experiences and activities involving sound—read stories, poems, riddles, jingles; play games like "rhyming" words, riddle games, and others that require the children to recognize, identify sounds in relation to objects, words, letters.

138

(Subject) CONCEPTS	PERFORMANCE OUTCOMES	CHILDREN'S ACTIVITIES	TEACHING METHODS/RESOURCES
experiences –identifying words that begin with the same sound and words that rhyme		–Participating in the activities as described in the "teaching methods/resources" for children to perform.	–Help the children to discriminate sounds of animals–listen to recordings and tapes of animal sounds which they identify and describe; take trip to the zoo and listen to the sounds of the animals and imitate them. –Use activities to discriminate various common household sounds––a toilet flushing; the garbage disposal; rattling of pots and pans, closing a door; using an electric mixer, tearing paper, stamping feet, clapping hands, setting the table (glasses, silver ware) whereby objects are brought together. –Have children identify sounds that are similar and different––have two each of a container (full and empty) and have children pair the ones together that have the same

139

CURRICULUM EXPERIENCES FOR TEACHING/LEARNING LANGUAGE ARTS (PRE-READING)-CHART 6

(Subject) CONCEPTS	PERFORMANCE OUTCOMES	CHILDREN'S ACTIVITIES	TEACHING METHODS/RESOURCES
Language Development -Using language as a tool -Understanding spoken language -Using words to relate to senses -Speaking in sentences -Asking questions for clarity and understanding		-Participating in the activities as described in the "teaching methods/resources" for children to perform.	sound when struck with an object. -Play rhyming games--read a sentence like "There was a mean old goat, who was dressed in a raggedy old _____. (coat) Use pictures of objects and discover rhyming words. -Have children identify letter names with letter sounds and initial consonant sounds--use letters like "p" with pictures (pot, ball, pail) to identify "p" sound. -Provide cooperative group experiences--show and tell, stories, singing games, talking about nature (seasons, insects, weather, animals, plants, etc.), discuss familiar things, expand on ideas growing out of discussions, use ideas of children for activities, assess children's health and performance characteristics --poor hearing, poor

140

(Subject) CONCEPTS	PERFORMANCE OUTCOMES	CHILDREN'S ACTIVITIES	TEACHING METHODS/RESOURCES
-Speaking clearly when communicating -Using basic vocabulary -Using listening comprehension		-Participating in the activities as described in the "teaching methods/resources" for children to perform.	vision, speech defects, adenoids, inappropriate diets, birth defects, etc., have children practice instant replays of short stories, poems, riddles, jiggles to remember sequencing and thought processes -Provide materials to be used, like: picture file, blocks, puppets, assorted books, word cards, old catalogs for cutting and pasting, play telephones, dress up clothes, tape recorder
Directionality/ Orientation -Use of gross and fine motor coordination -Left to right progression -Eye-hand coordination -Putting ideas and objects into sequence			-Provide activities that teach "left" and "right" --identifying body parts, playing games like the hokey-pokey, acting out directions, finding objects located in certain sides of the room, drawing lines from the left side of the paper to the right side; Have children develop motor skills by

141

CURRICULUM EXPERIENCES FOR TEACHING/LEARNING LANGUAGE ARTS (PRE-READING)-CHART 6

(Subject) CONCEPTS	PERFORMANCE OUTCOMES	CHILDREN'S ACTIVITIES	TEACHING METHODS/RESOURCES
		-Participating in the activities as described in the "teaching methods/resources" for children to perform.	working with building tools, writing tools, and by manipulating and handling objects in the environment; Have children pantomime various stories recalling times, places, and order of events; Have children act out directions, draw figures, lines, circles, etc.; Have children do puzzles, nesting blocks, peg board activities.

-Provide materials to be used, like: picture file, games, puzzles, blocks, crayons, paints, drawing paper, old magazines, tools--hammer, nails, pieces of wood. |

HOW IS EVALUATION CONDUCTED IN THE
LANGUAGE ARTS CURRICULUM?

Pre- and post- assessment of the pre-schoolers are best made through sensitive observations by the caregivers. The children's behaviors are exhibited through their work and play in the environment, therefore, the caregivers can evaluate their learning through direct listening and observing their performances. The strategies/methods/techniques/ activities should be presented in a manner that provides a built-in "assessment" process. That is, the tasks should be stated behaviorally (show, point to, pick out, put, take away, identify, match, etc.) to give immediate feedback as to the quality of the performance. So, as the caregiver listens, observes, and directs the activity, he/she is capable of making a decision about the performance. If the child performed satisfactorily, the caregiver should make a note (mentally or written) and expand the experiences; if the child does not perform well, the caregiver will either make a note (mentally or written) and plan to work with the child in mastering the task, or the caregiver should deal with the correction on the spot. This might mean having the child perform the task in a developmental manner (step-by-step), having the child repeat the correct form after the caregiver, or showing the child the mistake and have him/her correct it, with or without the help of the caregiver.

Along with informal observation and listening during the children's work and play experiences to assess their learning, the caregiver might use checklists, recordkeeping notes, and other tools to remember specific details about each child's strengths and weaknesses. This is an excellent idea as the day's activities can sometimes be trying and caregivers have a tendency to forget some details of the teaching/ learning process. Many informal assessment tools (pre- and post-) can be developed by the caregiver. Many are already developed by early childhood specialists and professionals that can be used in the teaching/learning environments.

Another evaluation method for appraising the learning of the pre-schoolers is that of standardized/commercial-made tests. There are several tests available for use in the curriculum to pre-and post-test the performances of children. They need to be reviewed by the caregiver to make sure that they can benefit the child and the caregiver in obtaining the type of assessment information needed for specific teaching and learning. The caregiver should become oriented on the types of tests available at the program, or the types available for use and obtain them as their programs plan to make use of them

143

in their curriculum. These tests should be used as an action guide for the caregiver to evaluate teaching and learning and not as work tools for the children. The diagnostic-prescriptive approach to teaching and learning can best be implemented through the use of tests and sound planning, programming, and instructing.

Parents are direct sources of evaluation for their children in the pre-school programs. Pre- and post- assessment procedures, informal checklists, and standardized tests should be communicated to parents in view of what the purposes and desired outcomes will yield. Parents should be expected to assist caregivers in the continuous appraisal of their children. Therefore, they will have a first-hand knowledge of their children's levels of competencies in the language arts. They should help caregivers to understand cultural differences, specific health and handicapping conditions of the children, language development and usage, and other pertinent factors to enhance the evaluation of the children's speech, listening, pre-reading, and language abilities and disabilities.

The language arts curriculum is a show, tell, do, feel type of teaching/learning process that involves the children's total growth and development--socially, physically, mentally, and emotionally. Therefore, the caregivers can expect to perform continuous, comprehensive evaluation during the execution of teaching and learning by them and the children in a realistic manner.

HOW DO THE LANGUAGE ARTS CORRELATE WITH THE TOTAL PRE-SCHOOL CURRICULUM?

The Language Arts Curriculum for pre-schoolers includes pre-reading experiences, listening skills, speaking skills, and writing skills. These are the basic subject areas for learning and bear kinship to all other curriculum areas (mathematics, science, expressive arts, play, social studies). The caregiver should use every possible opportunity to integrate teaching/learning in language arts with other curriculum areas for the sake of motivation, interest, stimulation, appreciation, and understanding of language and communications.

In expressive arts, experiences in language and communications include remembering words, expressing emotions through songs and singing, comprehending lyrics, communicating feelings, reading notes, words, and voice and speech. Language and communications are used in visual arts when learning various names and meanings of art mediums, materials, supplies, and tools for drawing, painting, collages, paper

144

mache, easels, brushes, primary colors, secondary colors, and so forth. The development of language and communications skills is enhanced in drama through voice and speech exercises, expressions, feelings and emotions. Vocabulary is built, creative expression is encouraged, poems are learned by memory, scripts and speeches are read and are learned by memory, pre-reading skills are built through listening, speaking, and creative writing--story telling, making-up poems, riddles, show and tell activities, puppetry, and so forth.

In mathematics there are experiences in reading number concepts, numerals, and worded problems. In listening and speaking activities the children are experiencing number concepts of quality in pitch and volume of sound; and in literature, through poems, stories, and show and tell, the children come in contact with mathematics--how many, what size, what distance, and so forth.

In science, labeling plants and animals and saying names of plants, animals, and objects utilizes language and communications. Recording results of experiments on the chalkboard, charts, posters by teachers, storytelling and story reading about weather, seasons, people, the solar system, clothing, plants, animals, and things implicate language and communications. Listening skills and speaking skills are needed in science as experiences and activities are implemented in the teaching/learning process.

In social studies, children are provided an excellent resource through language and communications for showing, telling, discussing, and dramatizing aspects of social living. They imitate various roles and responsibilities of people in their environments; they can tell stories about families, friends, neighbors, and others in their environment; they can write and listen to stories about people, places, and things in their social world; and they can learn to spell, identify, and relate to specific concepts about group living, cooperative play, culture, and heritage.

ACTIVITIES FOR STUDY AND DISCUSSION

1. Develop a list of suggestions for "developing good listening habits," identifying the role of the caregiver in each one.

2. Plan an area for a "Listening Center" in a quiet location protected from center/classroom traffic, with good equipment and stimulating, ample materials. Develop a design showing: purposes, arrangement of booths, equipment needed, activities and materials.

3. Develop a list of suggestions for "developing good speaking ability," identifying the role of the caregiver in each one.

4. Plan a "pre-reading program," identifying the skills which the children now possess and the skills to be developed. List the factors that contribute to general readiness and those contributing to the skills needed for reading. Plan activities to cover the areas of "visual discrimination," "auditory discrimination," and "preliminary reading activities."

5. Make a "reading" display in the center/classroom giving the children easy accessibility and use of many books. Set criteria for developing the display--provision of/for books; selection process and procedures for borrowing; caregiver's role and responsibility; children's role and responsibility, and so forth.

6. Review and discuss research reports on pre-reading programs and activities for pre-schoolers.

7. Review and discuss research reports on language development in pre-schoolers and the roles played by the home and school in fostering speech and language use in pre-schoolers.

8. Review research reports and discuss the importance of "handwriting" in the pre-school curriculum. What factors are involved in fostering this task and what activities to use in the teaching/learning process are important aspects for discussion. Make a list of opportunities for the caregiver to use "manuscript writing" in the pre-school.

9. Discuss the significance of "creative writing" to the growth and development of the pre-schooler in fostering language/speech development.

10. Show how speaking, listening, writing, speech/language development, and exposure to books and reading materials correlate to set the basis for pre-reading development. Discuss the role of language arts in the pre-school curriculum.

REFERENCES

Allen, Roach V. and C. Allen, **Language Experience Activities.** Boston: Houghton Mifflin Company, 1976.

Anderson, Paul, **Language Skills in Elementary Education.** New York: Macmillan Publishing Company, Inc., 1972.

Auckerman, Robert C., **Approaches To Beginning Reading.** New York: John Wiley and Sons, 1984.

Auckerman, Robert C., **How Do I Teach Reading?** New York: John Wiley and Sons, 1981.

Bootchurch, Ellen, **Learning Things: Games That Make Learning Fun for Children 3-8 Years Old.** California: Pitman Learning Inc., 1982.

Broman, Betty and Paul Burns. **The Language Arts in Childhood Education.** Boston: Houghton Mifflin Co., 1983.

Carrillo, Lawrence W., **Teaching Reading.** New York: St. Martin's Press, Inc., 1976.

Collier, Mary Jo, **Kids' Stuff.** Nashville, Tennessee: Incentive Publications, Inc., 1969.

Dial Books for young Readers, Dutton Children's Books, Lodestar Books, Sven Bergh, Andre Deutsch. 2 Park Avenue, New York, New York 10016 (212/725-1818), 1986.

Earyl, Margaret, **Look, Listen and Learn.** New York: Harcourt Brace Jovanovich, Inc., 1974.

Flood, James, **Language and the Language Arts.** Englewood Cliffs: Prentice-Hall, Inc., 1984.

Greene, Harry and Walter Petty, **Developing Language Skills in the Elementary School.** New York: Macmillan Publishing Company, 1984.

148

Hankerson, Henry E. and Dolores Dickerson, "A Study on the Perceptions and Attitudes of Parents, Teachers, and Students Regarding Teaching Reading to Pre-Schoolers, Ages 3 to 5," (University Sponsored Research Grant, Howard University), 1979.

Hankerson, Henry E., "Intervention Strategies Are The Key To Relevant Curriculum and Effective Instruction in Early Childhood Education," **The Journal of Early Child Development and Care**, Volume 8, Number 1 (1982), pp. 31-43.

Hendrick, Joanne, **Total Learning for the Whole Child**. (Second Edition). Columbus: Merrill Publishing Company, 1986.

Herr, Selma E., **Learning Activities for Reading**. Dubuque, Iowa: Wm. C. Brown Company Publishers, 1982.

Hillerich, Robert L., **Reading Fundamentals for Pre-School and Primary Children**. Columbus, Ohio: Bell and Howell Company, 1977.

Jaffe, Elsa, **Teachers Guide to Readiness Experiences and In the City and People Read**. New York: The Macmillan Company, 1967.

Lemlech, Johanna, **Curriculum and Instructional Methods for the Elementary School**. Boston: Allyn and Bacon, 1975.

Machado, Jeanne, **Early Childhood Experiences in Language Arts**. New York: Delmar Publishers Inc., 1980.

Reeke, Angela S. and James L. Laffey, **Pathways to Imagination: Language Arts Learning Centers and Activities for Grades K - 7**. Pacific Palisades, California: Goodyear Publishing Company, Inc., 1979.

Rubin, Dorothy, **Teaching Elementary Language Arts.** New York: Holt, Rinehart and Winston, 1975.

Schaff, Joanne, **The Language Arts Idea Book** (Classroom Activities for Children). Pacific Palisades, California: Goodyear Publishing Company, Inc., 1976.

Vance, Barbara, **Teaching the Pre-Kindergarten Child: Instructional Design and Curriculum**. Monterey, California: Brooks/Cole Publishing Co., (A Division of Wadsworth Publishing Company, Inc.), 1973.

Wortham, Sue C., **Organizing Instruction in Early Childhood** (A Handbook of Assessments and Activities). Boston: Allyn and Bacon, Inc., 1984.

CHAPTER FIVE

SOCIAL LIVING EXPERIENCES

COOPERATIVE GROUP LIVING, FAMILY IN SOCIETY, HERITAGE
AND CULTURE, VALUES-CUSTOMS-TRADITIONS, AND HEALTH
AND CHILD WELFARE

CHAPTER 5

SOCIAL LIVING EXPERIENCES

- WHAT ARE THE PURPOSES OF SOCIAL LIVING EXPERIENCES?: AN INTRODUCTION

- WHAT ARE THE GOALS AND OBJECTIVES FOR TEACHING SOCIAL STUDIES?

- WHAT ARE THE MAJOR SUB-AREAS IN THE SOCIAL STUDIES CURRICULUM?

- WHAT APPROACHES TO USE TO EXPAND/EXTEND CURRICULUM THEORY INTO TEACHING/LEARNING APPLICATIONS FOR SOCIAL LIVING EXPERIENCES?

- HOW WILL THE TEACHING/LEARNING BE EVALUATED?

- HOW DOES SOCIAL STUDIES CORRELATE WITH THE TOTAL PRE-SCHOOL CURRICULUM?

- ACTIVITIES FOR STUDY AND DISCUSSION

- REFERENCES

152

WHAT ARE THE PURPOSES OF SOCIAL LIVING EXPERIENCES: AN INTRODUCTION

Social living experiences for pre-schoolers should be geared toward helping them to work and play with others and to become more aware of the world around them. Planned activities in social studies help young children to grow in their attitudes, skills, and abilities to make adjustments within themselves as well as their peers, siblings, parents, and caregivers in home and school environments. The curriculum should make provisions for developing interaction techniques that bring positive responses from within and outside of the family unit. Helping the child to find acceptance of self and to give acceptance of others are vital ingredients to the development of social skills. Social living experiences are the key to helping young children develop positive and effective group living competencies.

Experiences in the social environment help to develop concepts in group living. In group settings all members of the group take turns, share materials, learn to respect self and others, respect property, respect property rights of others, adjust to adults who are not parents, and learn to appreciate and utilize school as valuable places for learning (Philadelphia Head Start, 1965-67). Since young children are basically egocentric, experiences in social living are dire to helping them to become interdependent-beings.

WHAT ARE THE GOALS AND OBJECTIVES FOR TEACHING SOCIAL STUDIES?

The goals and objectives for teaching social studies provide a curricular guide for the instructional program to help pre-schoolers to understand self and their world. Some of the goals and objectives for teaching social studies are as follows:

º   Goal: To teach pre-schoolers that people are interdependent.

    º   Objectives:
    To study man and society in reference to making a living in order to have the main necessities of life: food, clothing, and shelter.

    To examine the relationship of man's involvement with one another in order to obtain the basic needs: food, clothing, and shelter.

To become aware of the states of dependence and independence as they relate to getting along with people in the social environments.

° Goal: To teach pre-schoolers the art of cooperation.

   ° Objectives:
   To be involved in experiences that teach one to work together in small and large groups.

   To participate in activities that encourage courtesy and attentiveness in group efforts.

   To show appreciation for the contributions of others in the social setting by exercising the principles of listening, responding, and utilizing ideas as suggested.

   To execute the act of sharing and taking turns.

° Goal: To teach pre-schoolers to develop an inquiring mind.

   ° Objectives:
   To use observation of children's behavior to obtain their interests and aptitudes.

   To identify problems, issues, and concern in the social environment and provide avenues for solutions and resolutions by children.

   To stimulate and evoke questioning about the environment and interaction processes.

° Goal: To teach pre-schoolers how to work effectively within the school, home, and community.

   ° To instill within the child a sense of purpose; responsibility.

   To provide opportunities for planning, implementing, following through, setting goals, purposes, limits, rules and procedures for developing good work habits.

   To provide avenues for self-attainment, direction, and acceptance of work performance through built-in motivation systems (intrinsic and extrinsic).

o   Goal: To teach pre-schoolers how to make provisions for using the process of democracy in social environments.

  o   Objectives:
      To model democratic principles in the teaching/learning process.

      To teach the chain of command in group functioning (family--parents, siblings, others; school--teacher, principal, peers, others; community--church, business, recreation--purposes, responsibilities, respect, fairness, etc.)

      To role play situations of social interactions for the purpose of teaching conflict resolution.

o   Goal: To teach pre-schoolers the purposes and functioning of their community and civil affiliates.

  o   Objectives:
      To expose children to the classification system of community, city, state, region, nation, world.

      To teach civil responsibility--good citizen, roles and responsibilities--through practical experiences in the learning environment.

o   Goal: To teach pre-schoolers to deal effectively with child abuse and neglect.

  o   Objectives:
      To expose children to the concepts of abuse and neglect through visual representations, i.e., pictures of abused children, pictures of neglected children, and signs and notices.

      To help children become aware of abuse and neglect through verbal representation, i.e., television, radio, reading articles from the newspapers, magazines, etc.

      To help children perceive the concepts of abuse and neglect through role-playing and socio-dramatic play.

WHAT ARE MAJOR SUB-AREAS IN THE SOCIAL STUDIES CURRICULUM?

For the purpose of this book in pre-school curriculum, five main areas of social studies will be presented. These are: (1) Cooperative Group Living; (2) Family in Society; (3) Heritage and Culture; (4) Values, Customs and Traditions; and (5) Health and Child Welfare.

Cooperative Group Living

As one of the five main areas of social studies, cooperative group living has the following objectives: 1) to help children to develop feelings of self-worth and dignity; 2) to help children understand the personal and property rights of each individual; 3) to help children see the worth and dignity of others; 4) to help children understand that the community living demands that individuals assume responsibility for their own behavior; 5) to help children understand that human emotion can be expressed in acceptable ways; and 6) to help children learn responsibility.

Family In Society

There are many objectives for teaching "family in society" in the pre-school curriculum. Some of them are: 1) to help children to understand the different types of family structures; 2) to help children to develop an awareness of the need for rules in communal living; 3) to help children understand that all families are unique, yet there are many similarities and commonalities; 4) to help children realize that family members are interdependent; 5) to help children to realize the basic needs of the family, and to distinguish between "needs" and "wants;" 6) to help children understand that in order to satisfy needs and wants, people produce and consume goods and services; 7) to help children understand the basics of our economic system; 8) to help children understand the means of communication and transportation and how they bring people together; 9) to help children realize that people live and work in the community together for mutual protection, help, and convenience; 10) to help children become aware of community rules for living, composition of their and other communities, and the wide range of work roles and their contributions to the community.

Heritage and Culture

The derivatives of people from many cultures are diverse, unique, and related. The personal history and the importance of heritage of people are important topics for the pre-school curriculum. In order to combine the cultural diversity and heritage, several objectives for teaching this as a part of the social studies curriculum are formulated. They are: 1) to help children understand the variety of people in the world; 2) to help children understand the development of the countries in the world; 3) to help children understand the development of the countries; 4) to help children to learn about the people of these countries in reference to skin color, languages, body structures, and so forth; 5) to help children to respect all people regardless to where they are from or how they look; 6) to help children to recognize key people in their country; 7) to help children to understand and appreciate their family history and culture; and 8) to help children to recognize heritage and culture as important aspects to social living.

Values, Customs, and Traditions

Some objectives for teaching values, customs, and traditions in the social studies curriculum are: 1) to help children understand the meaning of values; 2) to help children learn the values in their home and in their school; 3) to help children to learn to respect the values of other people in their country and in other countries; 4) to help children to learn the customs of their homes and schools; 5) to help children to demonstrate some of the traditions of their country and of other countries; and 6) to help children learn customs and traditions of other people and compare and contrast theirs.

Health and Child Welfare

Young children are experiencing many health hazards that are imposed upon them through ills of society, like alcoholism, drug addiction, abuse, neglect, family violence, hunger, incest and other means of exploiting their rights. The pre-school curriculum must provide an audio-visual and verbal mechanism to teach children how to deal with the practices of harm being done to them by unscrupulous, uncaring, confused, and mentally ill adults.

Information and materials designed to protect children from physical and mental harm must be afforded and practiced by caregivers, parents and others in the community. The psychological, physical, emotional, and social effects that health hazards can have on young children are overwhelmingly high and many. All precautions should be used and taken to curtail any and all of them.

These five sub-topic areas of the social studies curriculum are important to the development of wholesome attitudes, proper social skills, and competencies of the pre-schoolers. The activities and resources contained in the next section are necessary to implement the social studies curriculum in the five sub-topic areas as previously discussed.

WHAT APPROACHES TO USE TO EXPAND/EXTEND CURRICULUM THEORY INTO TEACHING/LEARNING APPLICATIONS FOR SOCIAL LIVING EXPERIENCES?

Pre-school curriculum and teaching entails three major components:

- ° Learning Theories (possible ways children learn various subjects)

- ° Theories of Instruction (best ways to teach children)

- ° Teaching / Learning Process (rationale, purpose, strategies, methods, techniques, assessment, and resources)

The approaches suggested to expand/extend curriculum theory into practical application have been discussed in a comprehensive manner (diagrams, figures, strategies, etc.) in Chapter Four, "Language Arts Curriculum - Pre-Reading Experiences." The reader is directed to refer to the information and materials contained in that chapter (Four) if and when study and review are necessary.

The following charts, constructed into a "curriculum model" that can be used as a written curriculum for pre-school programs, are provided to show "curriculum experiences for teaching/learning social living encounters in the pre-school.

CURRICULUM EXPERIENCES FOR TEACHING/LEARNING SOCIAL LIVING—CHART 7

(Subject) CONCEPTS	PERFORMANCE OUTCOMES	CHILDREN'S ACTIVITIES	TEACHING METHODS/RESOURCES
GROUP LIVING			
Encourage feelings of self-worth, pride, dignity, and respect for self and others	Cooperated in group experiences as a dynamic self with respect for the contributions of others	-Sharing materials, ideas, and experiences -Taking turns -Following rules set for the environment -Following directions for performing experiences in social living (identify classmates, teachers, parents, etc. by playing games, singing games, ring plays, dramatizations, etc.) -Tracing selves on large pieces of butcher paper--color pictures and display on the wall, "This Is Me" -Reading and listening to stories (picture books, word books, etc.)	-Provide an atmosphere of warmth and acceptance whereby children and parents can feel wanted. -Make sure each child is greeted individually each day and expect a response. -Set up an orientation program so that each child can explore and become familiar with the environment (work areas, materials and equipment, physical plant, etc.) -Call children by names whenever interacting verbally. -Print the names of the children on their work and display. -Provide a mirror in the classroom where children can view themselves and become aware of appearances, actions, and characteristics. -Take photographs of each child and use them in many activities--bulletin board for birthdays, news bulletins, posters, etc.

CURRICULUM EXPERIENCES FOR TEACHING/LEARNING SOCIAL LIVING--CHART 7

(Subject) CONCEPTS	PERFORMANCE OUTCOMES	CHILDREN'S ACTIVITIES	TEACHING METHODS/RESOURCES
Individual rights and responsibilities are key elements to effective group living Accepting, handling, and dealing with individual emotions in healthy ways are essential to group living	Developed a sense of responsibility and participated in the activities of the group as a "team member"	-Participating in group experiences (storytime, show and tell, doing errands, maintaining work and living areas, etc.) -Cooperating with peers in keeping the work space organized and tidy, in keeping personal space--desk, lockers, and activity space--in order -Sharing family events and personal adventures with the group -Listening to experiences of others in the group -Planning a class field trip to places in the community with the caregiver -Participating in the routine of class time (being assigned chores, selecting helpers, organizing materials, storing materials, etc.)	-Read books to children--Everyone Has A Name, Your Eyes and Mine, and Your Skin and Mine by Paul Showers, and others. -Include children in work of the center--helping to prepare snacks, watering plants, feeding pets, cleaning chalkboards, etc. -Make the routines of the school day an integral part of teaching and learning--assigning chores, selecting helpers, etc. -Assign spaces to individuals and set rules for maintaining that space--put materials away, clean off desk, table, etc. when its time for work, etc. -Set rules for keeping center or work space clean and tidy--after and before play. -Play games with children where they have to express their feelings about issues--"I think that..." -Collect pictures of people expressing various emotions--sad, happy, angry, afraid, excited,

CURRICULUM EXPERIENCES FOR TEACHING/LEARNING SOCIAL LIVING – CHART 7

(Subject) CONCEPTS	PERFORMANCE OUTCOMES	CHILDREN'S ACTIVITIES	TEACHING METHODS/RESOURCES
			etc.--and conduct discussions with them in an effort to teach dealing with and handling feelings. Bring real situations into the discussions.
			-Read, tell stories, dramatize, and see films about 'feelings'. --A Letter To Amy; Curious George; Snowy Day; are examples of books to be read.
			-Record conversations and creative stories told by children. Play them to children and call attention to their feelings, voice, etc.
			-Use dramatic play, socio-dramatic play, pantomime to have children act out various roles--dress up clothes, housekeeping materials and equipment, doll house stuff, makeup kits, etc.--about group living experiences, right and wrong ideas.
FAMILY IN SOCIETY Children should be able to iden- tify with differ- ent family structures	Showed an awareness, understanding, and appreciation for family life through positive involve- ment, responses,	-Showing and telling about family events and func- tions -Working with pictures of families and family mem- bers in grouping and	-Provide opportunities for chil- dren and adults to listen to each other in discussions about family--use pictures of various family groupings, i.e., mother/ father/children; and so forth

161

CURRICULUM EXPERIENCES FOR TEACHING/LEARNING SOCIAL LIVING—CHART 7

(Subject) CONCEPTS	PERFORMANCE OUTCOMES	CHILDREN'S ACTIVITIES	TEACHING METHODS/RESOURCES
	and participation in activities	regrouping to form families	breaking them into various groups
All families are unique, yet there are many similarities and commonalities		—Working with pictures of animals to group into families —Discussing families and how they work together to make living positive for each other	—Use pictures of family life of different ethnic groups--visual aids and discussion purposes.
Family life is not only exercised by human beings, but animals are classified and associated with "family"		—Making posters about families —Drawing pictures of families —Painting, coloring, cutting-out, and pasting pictures of families	—Use pictures of different family groups of animals. —Make scrap books, photo albums, posters, displays about families of children in center of school--discuss survival mechanisms--work, food, shelter, clothing, responsibilities, etc.
Family is a form of communal living where each one cooperates to take care of basic needs		—Listening to stories about families (people and animals--Three Bears, One Morning in Maine, etc.) —Using puppets to tell stories	—Use pictures to discuss the differences in needs and wants--foods, clothing, shelter, cars, diamonds, candy, medicine, drugs, etc.
People are interdependent and must work together to yield protection, care of basic needs, mutuality, etc.		—Using dramatization and pantomime to tell about family experiences —Sing songs about community helpers, family members, etc.	—Make charts or posters of pictures showing production and consumption of goods and services; include those of community workers
People travel in various ways and utilize transportation modes for exchanging goods		—Taking field trips and excursions in the neighborhood —Copying letters to send to friends, families, and pen pals	—Have children cut out pictures from magazines, newspapers, etc. to demonstrate people working together--use flannel board to visually describe discussions, make collages, posters, etc.

CURRICULUM EXPERIENCES FOR TEACHING/LEARNING SOCIAL LIVING-CHART 7

(Subject) CONCEPTS	PERFORMANCE OUTCOMES	CHILDREN'S ACTIVITIES	TEACHING METHODS/RESOURCES
and services, and for communication as a means of bringing "families" and "people" together People live in communities for mutual benefits		-Working as postal service workers in a play "post office" -Listening to the radio and television news -Pretending to be news reporters -Talking on the telephone to friends, family, and community service people -Dressing up as community helpers -Making a community using boxes, pictures, manipulatives, etc.-- houses, stores, schools, people, and animals -Looking at maps (home, school, neighborhood, city, state, U.S., world, etc.) -Practicing safety rules in the home, school, community -Practicing rules to obey the law and discussing purposes and why these rules bring order to the system of people working together as a family (group)	-Have dress-up clothes of the various community helpers-- nurses, doctors, firemen, telephones repairmen, etc.-- use dramatizations. -Play games with rules to depict concepts of community living in families--role playing of mother, father, sister, insurance man, etc.; red light - green light; Mother May I?. -Set up a supermarket in the classroom and have children play roles as workers and customers. -Take neighborhood walks to businesses--grocery stores, laundry mats, construction sites, farms and gardens, police station, fire station, etc. -Make a display of "ways families travel together" to meet their basic needs--goods and services, recreation, modes of communication, i.e., letters, packages. Use cars, trucks, airplanes, buses, trains, boats--pictures, models, books, etc.

163

CURRICULUM EXPERIENCES FOR TEACHING/LEARNING SOCIAL LIVING—CHART 7

(Subject) CONCEPTS	PERFORMANCE OUTCOMES	CHILDREN'S ACTIVITIES	TEACHING METHODS/RESOURCES
			—Have a letterwriting project. Set up a post office in the classroom for sending letters, packages, etc. to children within and outside of the classroom.
			—Make a telephone display. Let children practice dialing and talking on the telephones. Emphasize numbers and words to use in emergencies, and for contacting family members for emergencies and when lost.
			—Take a few minutes during the day to let children listen to the radio or television or read the newspaper to them about news items. Children can be taught to construct these things for dramatic play situations in the classroom.
			—Construct a dimensional model of a neighborhood. Use small boxes and objects to represent houses, businesses, cars, trucks, trees, people, etc. Have children use this model to learn and share about their neighborhood—where they live; where their parents work; etc.

164

(Subject) CONCEPTS	PERFORMANCE OUTCOMES	CHILDREN'S ACTIVITIES	TEACHING METHODS/RESOURCES
			-Use maps for teaching about the neighborhood. Have children make maps and use commercial ones.
			-Make a chart of rules. Equate these rules to show a relationship of rules in the classroom with the rules in the home. Expand these rules to traffic rules and safety rules.
			-Use pictures to discuss civic responsibilities--protection of property, safety and protection laws, voting, group participation, etc.
CULTURAL HERITAGE AND DIVERSITY			
People come from different places in the world with individual and common differences	Showed interest in all children in the environment, and shared willingly in experiences involving songs, stories, dances, speaking, and listening	-Looking at pictures of people from various places in the world -Comparing pictures with others in the environment -Listening to stories about different people in the world -Looking at films, filmstrips, and slides about different people -Dressing up like different people in the world	-Display pictures and objects from different countries. -Show films about different cultures. -Set up visits to art museums and galleries in the community. -Make bulletin boards about different people and their roles in life. Do specific topics as they relate to the children in
People have different and important lives that have shaped culture and heritage in the past, present, and in the future	Showed interest in self and reasons for		

CURRICULUM EXPERIENCES FOR TEACHING/LEARNING SOCIAL LIVING—CHART 7

(Subject) CONCEPTS	PERFORMANCE OUTCOMES	CHILDREN'S ACTIVITIES	TEACHING METHODS/RESOURCES
	being as "I am" and why I respond to and ascribe to a certain social identity	-Sharing pictures and objects that come from different places in the world -Taking trips to art museums and galleries in the community -Listening to music from different places in the world -Dancing and moving to music and songs by and from different people throughout the world -Participating in activities sponsored by community people to share their cultural heritage (art, music, dance, clothing, foods, literature, etc.)	the present environments, i.e., Blacks, Indians, Latinos, etc. -Have birthday celebrations of children in the classroom. Relate these birthdays with different people in history by dates, months, etc. Make a display or bulletin board of the children's birthdays as well as others who come in the same month. -Have forums where people from the community as well as relatives of children can come and share various experiences of the past—games played, foods, clothings, etc.
VALUES, CUSTOMS AND TRADITIONS			
Children form many values through family and friends	Developed certain value constructs and beliefs about self, family, and others that are free of biases	-Purchasing articles from "play" store using "play" money -Discussing "likes" and "dislikes" and the reasons during group time	-Set up a store in the classroom and have children make purchases. Talk about likes and dislikes and why children bought what they bought.

CURRICULUM EXPERIENCES FOR TEACHING/LEARNING SOCIAL LIVING—CHART 7

(Subject) CONCEPTS	PERFORMANCE OUTCOMES	CHILDREN'S ACTIVITIES	TEACHING METHODS/RESOURCES
Children understand customs and traditions based on historical events and experiences	Developed an interest for historical continuity in cultural knowledge (through storytelling, reading about different families and people, etc.)	-Talking about differences of children's families, costumes, foods, etc. through looking at pictures, films, filmstrips, etc. -Listening to stories about their culture (customs and traditions) and about the culture of others -Discussing holidays and their origins -Using dolls and other objects to show customs, traditions of self and others -Using puppets -Participating with community people in presenting their customs and traditions through the arts, foods, holidays, and other events -Dramatizing ways of various people	-Read stories to the children and have them draw conclusions based on their experiences. -Use situations in the classroom where children have experienced conflicts--fights, arguments, etc. -Display materials to represent different holidays. Discuss reasons for celebrating. Use pictures, books, foods, songs, etc. -Display pictures of costumes from different countries. Use dolls, films, filmstrips, also. -Use people in the community to share experiences with children in a variety of ways --pictures, slides, objects, clothes, foods, etc.
HEALTH AND CHILD WELFARE Children must understand concept of neglect and	Developed a sense of awareness of people's behaviors and actions	-Listening to announcements about child abuse and neglect on radio, television	-Join in and reinforce public awareness projects on health and child welfare hazards.

167

CURRICULUM EXPERIENCES FOR TEACHING/LEARNING SOCIAL LIVING—CHART 7

(Subject) CONCEPTS	PERFORMANCE OUTCOMES	CHILDREN'S ACTIVITIES	TEACHING METHODS/RESOURCES
abuse through vicarious exper- iences	that are different from those taught as "normal" Developed the ability to talk about the care and actions taken in the home and the community for reward and punishment Developed ability to recognize peo- ple and things in the environment that are unhealthy, unsafe, and unnat- ural in their environment	and public programs (church, boys' and girls' clubs, boy and girl scout, etc.) -Looking at films, filmstrips, and slides about abuse and neglect -Discussing pictures about abuse and neglect (signs to look for on body, appearance of children, signs to look for in adult --alcohol, drugs, etc.) -Making collages out of pic- tures from grocery bags; and information on grocery bags can be used to make charts and posters -Attending sessions on child abuse and neglect with parents at school, church, and community meetings -Using the telephone to call the emergency number (911) -Acting out situations of danger in dramatization	-Use pictures of missing chil- dren on milk cartons, flyers, grocery bags, etc. to bring attention to the problem with the children. -Focus attention on messages, announcements, etc. on tele- vision, radio, posters, signs and alerts given at social and community events. -Specify a plan of action with children to help protect them: (Talk with them about behaviors of alcoholics, drug addicts, sexual perverts, etc. on a very basic scale using basic terms and showing many typical actions to describe behaviors of these people. -Check out the home environ- ment and community (signs of troubled parents, route to school or from school, church, park, etc.) and call attention to spots or areas that could present a hazard or danger like, alleyways, vacant lots, condemned houses, wooded areas, dark areas, etc. Give advise to children as to "what to do, if...".

168

HOW WILL THE TEACHING/LEARNING BE EVALUATED?

An on-going evaluation system must be utilized in the teaching-learning process of social studies in order to see whether or not children are growing in their abilities to make wholesome adjustments to one another, to new personalities, and to the world in which they live. As social living experiences are appraised through unit teaching and planning, both whole group and the individual assessment must be made. The various subject topics will determine the particular method(s) of evaluation. For example, performances of the children will be used as a method; observation of the children as they perform and the effect that the experiences bring in setting and guiding their attitudes about the activity and other children is another method; checklist of skills may be used to appraise the amount of learning taking place; measurements of attainments may be obtained through both standardized and teacher made tests; and using behavioral objectives for each assigned task is a sure method of evaluating children's learning and progress.

The learning that takes place in social living experiences should be measured in reference to the goals, objectives, and teaching task as planned and programmed by the caregivers. Socio-dramatic, dramatic, role playing, and other teaching/learning methods of a social interaction nature are excellent tools for evaluation. Giving information to parents and getting feedback from parents about the behaviors and experiences of the children are other ways to evaluate. Children must be aware of their own progress and needs through conferences, interviews, and discussions.

Evaluation of the teaching/learning process is continuous and must provide information to direct change in the subject matter content, methods of teaching, goals/objectives formation, and children's levels of performances. All of these changes must be directed to the purpose and role of teaching social studies.

HOW DOES SOCIAL STUDIES CORRELATE WITH THE TOTAL PRE-SCHOOL CURRICULUM?

The learning environment and atmosphere must be of such that children can learn social skills in an acceptable and consistent manner. The curriculum must be structured in a way that all subject matter areas yield a broad spectrum of experiences in social living encounters. These experiences can be obtained through adventures in both the classroom and the community. Therefore, all subject areas will utilize the social living concepts of developing wider interest through field trips, neighborhood walks, and visitors. More specifically, social studies can be integrated with other aspects of the curriculum as follows.

Language Arts inclusive of reading can provide an excellent resource for the social studies as children are provided opportunities to show, tell, discuss, and dramatize aspects of social living. They can imitate various roles and responsibilities of people in their environments; they can write and listen to stories about people, places, and things in their social world; and they can learn to spell, identify, and relate to specific concepts about group living, cooperative play, culture, and heritage.

Mathematics can be correlated with social studies in the pre-school program because children are in direct contact with quantities: numbers of children in families, sizes and shapes of homes, money and the value of coins and bills, and so forth. Acting as consumers of goods and services involves counting, valuating, buying, and being thrifty. All of these are directly related to social studies and mathematics.

Science is another subject area which bears a direct correlation with social studies. As the children deal with foods, seasons, the weather, the atmosphere, holidays, living things--plants and animals, and using scientific concepts in reasoning, understanding, and making decisions, the subject areas of social studies and science are definitely correlated.

Creative Arts as a subject area, including visual arts and music, is a correlate of social studies. Various paintings about different people, their lives, and customs depict social learning experiences. Ethnic music/songs, crafts, stories, and poetry have important places in the creative arts and are directly correlated with social living experiences. Attitudes and feelings are shared and understood through different forms of creative expressions about various people, places, and cultures. Values are formed and morals are developed through interacting with the arts--drawings, paintings, poems, songs, stories, and folk tales. These are directly related to the language arts, also.

Social studies cuts across all areas of the curriculum and can be used as a medium through which other areas as previously described may be taught. Social studies must be seen as an important vehicle for children to use in understanding self, others, and the physical, cultural, and political world around them.

ACTIVITIES FOR STUDY AND DISCUSSION

Through social living experiences in the pre-school environment, children are expected to develop security and self-confidence. The children should be accepted as they are and provisions must be made to expose them to knowledges, skills, and abilities as they encounter experiences in cooperative group living, families in society, heritage and culture, and values, customs and traditions. Activities which are teacher-oriented will help to give a broader perspective to the curriculum area of social studies.

1. Read and study the "role of social studies in pre-school education" as it relates to the broad concepts of social living experiences in education.

2. Organize and present a conceptual approach to the social studies since factual knowledge is one aspect of the curriculum that must be recognized, taught, and tested.

3. Discuss the inquiry approach and its relationship to conceptual learning in the social studies.

4. Expand on the concept in social studies of helping pre-schoolers to "discover the wider world" through activities and experiences about home, school, neighborhood, community, communication, transportation, living things, holidays, and civic responsibilities.

5. Plan and organize trips and walks as direct experiences for children. Take into consideration the factors of pre-planning, on the spot discussions, and follow-up.

6. Organize and develop a resource manual for utilizing people, places, and things in the neighborhood, community, and school.

7. Develop a resource unit for the pre-school program. From this resource unit, extract a teaching unit. Take the teaching unit and develop several lessons to cover the topic of the social learning experiences.

8. Plan and implement several teaching demonstrations with peers and with children in the area of social studies.

REFERENCES

Books For Caregivers

Day, Barbara, **Early Childhood Education: Creative Learning Activities** (Second Edition). New York: Macmillan Publishing Co., Inc., 1983.

Flemming, Bonnie M., and D.S. Hamilton, **Resources for Creative Teaching in Early Childhood Education.** New York: Harcourt Brace Javanovich, Inc., 1977.

Frankson, Carl, and K. Benson, **Crafts Activities.** New York: Parker Publishing Company, Inc., 1970.

Hendrick, Joanne, **Total Learning: Curriculum for the Young Child** (Second Edition). Columbus: Merrill Publishing Company, 1986.

Hildebrand, Verna, **Introduction to Early Childhood Education** (Fourth Edition). New York: Macmillan Publishing Co., Inc., 1986.

Malehorn, Hal, **Encyclopedia of Activities for Teaching Grades.** New York: Parker Publishing Company, Inc., 1970.

Marbach, Ellen, **Creative Curriculum: Kindergarten Through Grade Three.** Provo, Utah: Brigham Young University Press, 1977.

Massialas, Byron G., and Joseph B. Hurst, **Social Studies In A New Era** (Seventh Edition). New York: Longman, Inc., 1978.

Michaelis, John U., **Social Studies for Children: A Guide to Basic Instruction** (Eighth Edition). Englewood Cliffs, New Jersey: Prentice-Hall, Inc., 1985.

Oxley, Mary Boone, **Illustrated Guide to Individualized Kindergarten Instruction.** New York: Parker Publishing Company, Inc., 1976.

Schickendanz, Judith, et. al., **Strategies for Teaching Young Children** (Second Edition). Englewood Cliffs, New Jersey: Prentice-Hall, Inc., 1983.

Skeel, Dorothy, **The Challenge of Teaching Social Studies in the Elementary School.** Pacific Palisades, California: Goodyear Publishing Company, Inc., 1970.

Wortham, Sue C., **Organizing Instruction in Early Childhood: A Handbook of Assessment and Activities.** Boston: Allyn and Bacon, Inc., 1984.

Books For Children

Berger, T. **I Have Feelings.** New York: Behavioral Publications, Inc., 1971.

Brown, M.W. **The Little Fireman.** New York: Young Scott Books, 1952.

Brown, M.W. **The Little Farmer.** New York: Young Scott Books, 1948.

Buckley, H.E. **Grandfather and I.** New York: Lothrop, Lee and Shepard, 1961.

Buckley, H.E. **Grandmother and I.** New York: Lothrop, Lee and Shepard, 1961.

Clure, B., and Ramsey, H. **Me.** Glendale, Calif.: Bowman Publishers, 1968.

Clure, B., and Ramsey, H. **Where is Home?** Glendale, Calif.: Bowman Publishers, 1971.

Delton, J. **Two Good Friends.** New York: Crown Publications, 1974.

Ets, M.H. **Just Me.** New York: The Vikings Press, Inc., 1937.

Francoise, A. **The Things I Like.** New York: Charles Scribner's Sons, 1957.

Green, M. McB. **Everybody Has a House.** New York: Charles Scribner's Sons, 1957.

Green, M. McB. **Everybody Has a House and Everybody Eats.** New York: Young Scott Books, 1961.

174

Hoban, R. **A Baby Sister For Francis.** New York: Harper and Row, Publishers, 1964.

Kaufman, C. **My First Book of Trucks.** Bronx, N.Y.: The Platt and Munk Co., Inc., 1954.

Kessler, E., and Kessler, L. **Big Red Bus.** New York: Doubleday and Co., Inc., 1954.

Krata, S. **Hi, New Baby.** New York: Simon and Schuster, Inc., 1970.

Lenski, L. **The Little Sailboat.** New York: Oxford University Press, Inc., 1940.

Lenski, L. **The Little Train.** New York: Oxford University Press, Inc., 1940.

Lenski, L. **The Little Fire Engine.** New York: Oxford University Press, Inc., 1946.

Lenski, L. **The Little Airplane.** New York: Oxford University Press, Inc., 1950.

Lenski, L. **The Little Auto.** New York: Oxford University Press, Inc., 1956.

Merriam, E. **Mommies at Work.** New York: Alfred and Knopf Inc., 1955.

Oppenheim, J. **Have You Seen Roads?** Reading Mass.: Addison-Wesley Publishing Co., Inc., 1969.

Oppenheim, J. **Have You Seen Boats?** Reading Mass.: Addison-Wesley Publishing Co., Inc., 1971.

Schlein, M. **The Way Mothers Are.** Chicago: Albert Whitman and Co., 1963.

Seuss, Dr. **Happy Birthday To You!** New York: Random House, Inc., 1959.

Slobodkin, L. **One is Good, But Two Are Better.** New York: Vanguard Press, 1955.

Thompson, V. **Sad Day, Glad Day**. New York: Holiday House, 1961.

Tresselt, A. **A Day Without Daddy**. New York: Lothrop, Lee and Shepard Co., 1953.

Zolotow, C. **Big Brother**. New York: Harper and Row, Publishers, 1960.

Zolotow, C. **Big Sister and Little Sister**. New York: Harper and Row, Publishers, 1966.

Audio-Visuals

(F=Film   FS=Filmstrip)

"The Five Senses." FS. Set of 5 filmstrips, David C. Cook. Elgin, Ill., 60102.

"Just Me." FS. Weston Woods Studios, Inc., Weston, Conn., 96880.

"They Need Me." FS. Set of 4 filmstrips, David C. Cook. Elgin, Ill., 60120.

"The Little Engine That Could." F. Coronet Films, Inc., Chicato, Ill., 1963.

Records

Concept Records, Basic Songs for Exceptional Children--a section entitled "Body Concepts and Self-Identity" includes "What's Inside Me," "My Body," "Knees, Knees, Knees."

Bowmar Records, Glendale, Calif., "Fun and Fitness for Primary Children," B2057.

Children's Record Guild, New York (7-inch records), includes "I Wish I Were," "Let's Be Firemen," "Me, Myself and I."

"What Are You Wearing?" "What Is Your Name?" on learning Basic Skills Through Music, vol. I, AR514.

"Feeling," "Left and Right," "Be My Friend," on Getting to Know Myself, AR543.

Marlo Thomas and Friends, Bell Records, a division of Bowmar Records, Glendale, California.

"More Singing Fun," Alb. I. (Examples include "Big Black Train," "Fire Truck," "Chug, Chug, Chug," "I Can Fly.")

Folkways Records and Service Corp., Englewood Cliffs, N.J. 97632.

Pictures

David C. Cook. Elgin, Ill. 60120
   Transportation (30635)
David C. Cook, Elgin, Ill. 60120
   Health and Cleanliness (24224)
   Home and Community Helpers (97203)
   Learning About Careers (74450)
   Learning About Values (68544)
   Moods and Emotions (49916)
   My Community (24232)
   Safety (07013)
   Social Development (2457)
   Also available are several sets on ethnic groups and children around
   the world
Society for Visual Education (SVE), Inc., Chicago, Ill. 60614
   Police Department Helpers
   Fire Department Helpers
   Postal Helpers
   Dairy Helpers
   Supermarket Helpers
   Hospital Helpers
Children's World, Elgin, Ill. 60120
   Moods and Emotions
   People Who Come to My House (foldout)
   People in the Neighborhood (foldout)
   Children of America
   Children Around the World

Afro-American Educational Materials
   Toys and Games
   Puzzles

Teaching Aids
Posters
Display and Study Prints
Plays
Coloring Books
Comic Books
Records and Cassettes
Filmstrips
Video Cassettes
Story Books
History Books
Paperback and R-I-F Collections
Library Collections

(AFRO-AM Distributing Company, 819 South Wabash Avenue, Chicago, Illinois 60605

CHAPTER SIX

EXPERIENCES IN THE EXPRESSIVE ARTS

MUSIC, VISUAL ARTS, DRAMA, DANCE AND MOVEMENT

CHAPTER 6

EXPERIENCES IN THE EXPRESSIVE ARTS

- WHAT ARE THE SUBJECTS TO BE TAUGHT IN THE PRE-SCHOOL CURRICULUM IN THE EXPRESSIVE ARTS?: AN INTRODUCTION

    - MUSIC, VISUAL ARTS, DRAMA, DANCE AND MOVEMENT

- WHAT ARE THE PURPOSES, GOALS AND OBJECTIVES FOR TEACHING THE EXPRESSIVE ARTS?

- WHAT APPROACHES TO USE TO EXPAND/EXTEND CURRICULUM THEORY INTO TEACHING/LEARNING APPLICATIONS FOR THE EXPRESSIVE ARTS CURRICULUM?

- HOW CAN THE EXPRESSIVE ARTS BE EVALUATED IN REFERENCE TO TEACHING/LEARNING?

- HOW DO THE EXPRESSIVE ARTS CORRELATE WITH THE TOTAL PRE-SCHOOL CURRICULUM?

- ACTIVITIES FOR STUDY AND DISCUSSION

- REFERENCES

WHAT ARE THE SUBJECTS TO BE TAUGHT IN EXPRESSIVE ARTS IN THE PRE-SCHOOL CURRICULUM?: AN INTRODUCTION

The Expressive Arts Curriculum in the Pre-School covers, for the most part, the subjects of music, visual arts, drama, and dance and movement. Expressive Arts activities foster individual thinking and creativity in the pre-schooler, and enhance all areas of development--social, emotional-personal, physical, and intellectual. This is a valuable medium through which values, heritage, customs and traditions of groups of people can be transmitted. Therefore, the pre-school curriculum must include the expressive arts as an integral part of its teaching/learning process.

Every culture has some form of music and shares a fundamental place in the educated minds of people. Music is considered a universal language, because regardless of the language a person speaks or where in the world a person lives or is from, he/she can respond to rhythms and melodies of any form or style of music. It is a subject area that pre-schoolers participate in with little or no effort from adults. Music experiences become an integral part of learning for pre-schoolers. Music fits into their lives very early and is often felt to be like a breath of fresh air, natural, but yet magical. Music is a part of creativity and must be offered early in the pre-school curriculum (Haines, 1984).

Visual Arts is a part of the Expressive Arts curriculum in the pre-school program. Through this medium, the pre-schoolers are allowed opportunities to manipulate, touch, feel, squeeze, pull, pinch, scribble with and on, and transform materials. The area of physical--fine and gross motor coordination--development is being exercised in visual arts activities. Opportunities are thereby provided for heightening sensitivity to the physical world, bringing into existence a visible token of imagination and feeling, and introducing order into the sense impressions. All of these opportunities help to increase the pre-schoolers capacities to use their senses in experiencing their environments.

The use of various materials help pre-schoolers to create representations of objects, and to express feelings or emotions that are hard or improbable to express in words. Visual arts--drawing, painting, coloring, scribbling, sculpturing, using clay for modeling and ceramics, weaving macrame, carving wood, and others--allow pre-schoolers to develop originality, sensitivity, fluency, and flexibility. It is a necessary component of the pre-school expressive arts curriculum.

Drama offers pre-schoolers many and unusual opportunities to develop their communication potential through the use of the body, their problem-solving abilities, their abilities to analyze and appreciate drama and theatre as enrichment of the human condition rather than just passive entertainment, and their interests in their cultural heritage as reflected in creative dramatics. The pre-school curriculum in Expressive Arts uses this area to teach and help pre-schoolers to develop abilities to sequence, organize, portray roles, and use language. They are engaged in role-playing and games of make-believe which magnify the natural instincts of pre-schoolers.

Motivation is often increased through drama experiences. The human emotions are stimulated and provide a rehearsal of life for pre-schoolers. Both language and communications skills are fostered through drama.

Dance and movement go hand-in-hand as dance is described as an art of rhythmic bodily movement having an ordered sequence of moving visual patterns of line, solid shape, and color. Movement, on the other hand, is depicted by Mimi Chenfield (1976) as being as natural to learning as breathing is to living, further connoting that movement is synonymous with the growing child. Dance involves the pre-schoolers in learning to control and to move freely parts of their bodies or their entire bodies which enhances physical growth and development. This utilizes both fine and gross motor skills. Movement helps pre-schoolers to become aware of the great potential of their bodies and fosters control of the body through balance and coordination. Successful mastery of movement, hopping, skipping, jumping, stretching, etc., helps pre-schoolers to grow psychologically and physically. Whenever a dance idea is presented or introduced, the process of movement has to intervene, like thinking about the idea to discover steps or ways to express the action in order for the dance to be characteristic of rhythmic bodily movements, using part and/or all of the body is a systematic order of expression.

Through the Expressive Arts experiences in the pre-school curriculum, there are opportunities for pre-schoolers to:

1) feel free to, and about the ways they, communicate:

2) express their ideas and thoughts creatively (individually);

3) gain the abilities to develop aesthetic appreciation;

4) develop acceptable ways to relieve tension;

5) increase perception and concept development;

6) appreciate their, and others', cultural heritage; and

7) experience the enjoyment of art activity for its own sake.

WHAT ARE THE PURPOSES, GOALS, AND OBJECTIVES FOR TEACHING THE EXPRESSIVE ARTS?

<u>Purposes</u>

The Expressive Arts--music, visual arts, drama, dance and movement-- are important to the pre-school curriculum for the purposes of enhancing growth and development. Through the expressive arts, the needs and individual differences of pre-schoolers are addressed socially, emotionally, personally, physically, and intellectually. The pre-schoolers have opportunities to express themselves freely and naturally for both self-fulfillment as well as making a contribution to the lives of others. The Expressive Arts develop within pre-schoolers the feeling of self worth and contribute to their personal growth as they are engaged in creative play. They (pre-schoolers) are encouraged to listen with purpose and understanding, to deal with abstractions, fantasy, and real life situations by making decisions of resolution and expressing each.

The Expressive Arts are needed in the pre-school curriculum as a vehicle for helping pre-schoolers to understand and appreciate their culture and the cultures of others. This is achieved by their exploring, developing, and expressing their own uniqueness and creativity. Also, implied in the exposing of pre-schoolers to the expressive arts is the influence of their career choices, social values, and life styles. The emotions that pre-schoolers find difficult to express in words can be revealed through self-expressions in the arts activities.

The Expressive Arts provide a broad field of study which cuts across all subject matter areas and are sure ways of motivating academic performances. The learning endeavor is thereby more vivid and memorable, as ideas are united and relationships are shown in actions to portray the theoretical concepts. For pre-schoolers with special needs, the Expressive Arts serve as therapy in enriching their experiences. The curriculum in pre-school is much richer in quality when, and only when, the Expressive Arts are an integral part of it.

Goals and Objectives

The Expressive Arts encompass many goals which can be sub-divided into objectives for each content area. The goals are:

- To serve as a planned means of expressions and communications.

- To develop and enhance aesthetic senses and appreciations.

- To support concepts and skills development, as well as perception.

- To provide opportunities for natural self-expression in an atmosphere of freedom and trust where divergent and creative interpretation is encouraged.

- To serve as acceptable ways fore relieving tension and expressing emotions.

- To provide avenues for pleasure and enjoyment of the arts for its own sake.

- To expose and teach pre-schoolers to appreciate cultures of self and other people.

- To encourage the use of the body and its parts in social, emotional, physical, and intellectual growth and development through creative and spontaneous activities and experiences.

- To support and strengthen learning in all subject and content areas of the curriculum.

- To provide experiences in exploring both natural and man-made objects from many sources.

Objectives for Music are:

- To help pre-schoolers to gain/develop a sense of music appreciation through exposure to various musical experiences.

- To help pre-schoolers to recognize sounds and to discriminate sounds.

184

° To provide experiences in singing songs.

° To provide opportunities to become familiar with and to play instruments.

° To provide opportunities and experiences in listening skills.

° To give pre-schoolers opportunities to create and perform musical tasks.

° To develop and extend voice ranges.

° To promote growth in motor control.

° To encourage and develop pre-schooler's sense of mastery, creativity, and self-esteem.

° To develop auditory-memory skills and reinforce language development.

° To support concepts and skills in the development of social understanding.

Objectives for Visual Arts Are:

° To experience art materials and processes to determine their effectiveness for achieving personal expressive form.

° To provide opportunities for pre-schoolers to express ideas and create things.

° To provide opportunities for individual ideas and feeling through utilization of a variety of art media suited to the manipulative abilities and expressive needs of the pre-schoolers.

° To provide experiences to work with materials appropriate to the abilities of pre-schoolers in order to develop manipulative skills needed for satisfying aesthetic expression.

° To help pre-schoolers to develop self-awareness, self-direction, self-confidence and a sense of being responsible.

° To encourage the visualizing of ideas, thoughts, and feelings in original expressions.

° To develop an understanding of shape, color, size, and texture.

° To help pre-schoolers develop pride in craftsmanship.

° To provide experiences in observing artist's work and working through studio visits, exhibits, art shows, and audiovisuals.

° To provide opportunities for pre-schoolers to exhibit art work.

° To help pre-schoolers develop self-confidence and satisfaction in production and accomplishment of original ideas.

° To foster the development of eye-hand coordination and other motor skills and abilities.

Objectives for Drama are:

° To use dramatic play as a means for pre-schoolers to verbalize their thoughts and feelings through body actions (pantomime) and with words (dramatize) in both planned and unplanned situations.

° To provide experiences in assuming roles of characters from stories and other media.

° To provide opportunities of recall memorization--actions of a sequence in a story, and for working in cooperation with others--dramatization of a story.

° To help pre-schoolers gain skills in meaningful physical movement.

186

o   To provide opportunities for pre-schoolers with special needs to use viable forms of self-expression in front of others.

o   To help pre-schoolers turn their fantasies into enriching learning experiences in the context of the real world.

o   To develop competencies in self-expression and problem solving techniques through play roles.

o   To develop respect for the worth and contributions of others.

o   To understand and gain an appreciation of the principles which drama shares with other art forms and how drama facilitates learning in other subject areas.

o   To provide experiences in a variety of creative dramatic activities--socio-dramatic play, finger plays, puppetry, and dramatization.

o   To develop psycho-motor skills, abilities and attitudes.

Objectives for Dance and Movement are:

o   To develop motor skills.

o   To help foster locomotive and sustained movements.

o   To develop a sense of rhythm through mastery and creativity of body movement.

o   To develop awareness, balance, coordination, and control of bodily movements with and without musical elements.

o   To provide opportunities for participation in individual and group activities for the purposes of expressing thoughts, feelings, and ideas about self, others, and life.

o   To provide experiences to show the great potential of the body and its parts in coordinating the mind, emotions, feelings, and movement in an identifiable form.

° To show expressions of ideas and emotions through dance.

° To show a correlation of dance and movement to other subject areas by using materials and concepts as themes (folk dancing, tapping, etc.) from cultural heritages, and so forth.

WHAT APPROACHES TO USE TO EXPAND/EXTEND CURRICULUM THEORY INTO TEACHING/LEARNING APPLICATIONS FOR THE EXPRESSIVE ARTS CURRICULUM?

Pre-school curriculum and teaching entails three major components:

° Learning Theories (possible ways child learns various subjects);

° Theories of Instruction (best ways to teach children); and

° Teaching/Learning Process (rationale, purpose, strategies, methods, techniques, assessment, and resources).

Expanding/extending curriculum theory into practical application has been discussed in Chapter Four of the text. The reader is directed to refer to that chapter in the case he/she needs study and review to make the transfer. The following charts are constructed into a "curriculum model" as a guide to show "curriculum experiences for teaching/learning the Expressive Arts--visual arts, music, drama, dance and movement--in the pre-school."

CURRICULUM EXPERIENCES FOR TEACHING/LEARNING EXPRESSIVE ARTS-CHART 8

(Subject) CONCEPTS	PERFORMANCE OUTCOMES	CHILDREN'S ACTIVITIES	TEACHING METHODS/RESOURCES
MUSIC			

Expose pre-school-ers to a variety of music exper-iences	Developed a sense of music apprecia-tion, pleasure, and enjoyment	-Singing songs in groups
		-Listening to various songs and types of music
		-Singing along with records and tapes
		-Responding freely to music by using bodies and body parts to perform many functions and expressions
		-Hearing a variety of music representing types and cultures
		-Participating in sing along games
		-Attending assembly programs, concerts, recitals
		-Watching television to see musicians perform
		-Listening to radio
		-Taking field trips to the record stores
		-Making simple musical in-struments out of art materials and junk found in and around the home, school, and community - round cereal boxes for tom-toms, cylinders from aluminum foil, paper towels, toilet tissue
			-Arrange teaching/learning environment to have a music atmosphere by:
			  Providing song books, record player, records, tape recorder, tapes, piano; pictures of musicians, music groups, and instruments; classroom musical instruments - drums, bells, tambourines, triangle, auto-harp, etc.; sing along games - Six little ducks, Clap hands with me, If you're happy, etc.;
			
			  Providing a wide repetoire of songs - nursery rhyme songs, action songs, number songs, seasonal songs, nature songs, folk songs, patriotic songs, animal songs, plant songs, holiday songs, religious songs, etc.
			
			-Engage children in activities to help them become involved in musical expressions with

CURRICULUM EXPERIENCES FOR TEACHING/LEARNING EXPRESSIVE ARTS –CHART 8

(Subject) CONCEPTS	PERFORMANCE OUTCOMES	CHILDREN'S ACTIVITIES	TEACHING METHODS/RESOURCES
		for horns, soda tops nailed to pieces of wood to make tambourines, etc.	their bodies and body parts for fun (to the music of the piano, recordings, rhythm instruments – clapping, swaying, walking, running, galloping, marching, rocking, etc.)
			-Invite local musicians, singers, and groups to perform for the children during special assembly programs (holidays, Black History Month, career fairs, cultural experiences of people in the neighborhood and/or community).
Musical experiences are attained through sound	Recognized and discriminated sounds and enhanced listening skills	-listening to environmental sounds (siren of emergency vehicles, rain on windows, wind blowing through the trees, etc.)	-Bring to the attention of the children environmental sounds (i.e., "it is raining hard, let's listen to the sound it is making;" "can anyone make a sound like a fire engine? a police car? an ambulance? an ice cream truck? etc.)
		-Hearing differences in sounds of various rhythm instruments (cymbals, drum, rhythm sticks, etc.) and notes on piano.	
		-Noting how different children in the class sound when singing songs, singing without accompaniment, supplementing words in songs with words to fit certain occasions and situations	-Provide rhythm instruments and engage children in group activity whereby they identify sounds and differences in sounds (high-low, loud-soft, etc.)
			-Provide opportunities for children to sing (Present new

190

CURRICULUM EXPERIENCES FOR TEACHING/LEARNING EXPRESSIVE ARTS—CHART 8

(Subject) CONCEPTS	PERFORMANCE OUTCOMES	CHILDREN'S ACTIVITIES	TEACHING METHODS/RESOURCES
		-Listening for change of rhythm -Listening to music for relaxation (snack time, lunch, sleep and rest period) for short durations -Listening to recorded songs	songs, for example: <u>intro-duce a song to them</u> - "I know a song about one of our community helpers, the policeman. Listen and find out what it says;" sing the song for them using little or no instrumentation so they may hear the words and the tune; sing the song again and encourage children to join in with you; play the song using an instrument - piano, xylophone, bells, etc.- and sing along; the children will join in as they become familiar with the song.) It is necessary that the care-giver knows the words, rhythm, and spirit of songs. -Engage children in playing matching-tone games to help them find their "singing voices" - the echo game, sing their names, tooting like a train, etc.
Experiences in sing-ing songs provide many musical impli-cations (direction: up, down, forward backward; dynamics: soft and loud;	Enjoyed singing as a means of expression and singing spon-taneously	-Singing short action songs -Singing informally at work and play -Playing tone-matching games (imitating birds and animal calls-cuckoo, owl, duck; imitating echoes; etc.)	-Engage children in singing by presenting short, melodic and rhythmic songs--use song books, musical rhythm instruments--drum, xylophone, bells, etc., piano, record player, records, tape, recorder, tapes, etc.

191

CURRICULUM EXPERIENCES FOR TEACHING/LEARNING EXPRESSIVE ARTS—CHART 8

(Subject) CONCEPTS	PERFORMANCE OUTCOMES	CHILDREN'S ACTIVITIES	TEACHING METHODS/RESOURCES
movement: jumping, swinging, etc.; melody: repeating tones; tone accented and loud; tempo: fast and slow; rhythm: pulse or beat; pitch: high and low	Responded physically to rhythms to enhance motor coordination and to provide for emotional release	-Singing with light, natural voices a wide repertoire of songs -Singing along with recorded songs -Dramatizing songs and acting out song-stories -Becoming familiar with and using rhythmic instruments for matching sounds, hearing sounds, moving to music by walking, hopping, skipping, swaying, marching; for recognizing melody, tones, and tempos -Imitating environmental sounds and engaging in dramatic play (flying birds, swaying elephants, hopping bunnies, dancing bears) with music as the basis of the activities -Relating music experiences to vocabulary and meanings of basic elements (melody--movement of tones; rhythm--movement of beats; tone color--sound of voices; dynamics--degree and attacks of volume; tempo--the speed of the movement of the musical composition	-Set up a music corner or table in the environment and display instruments, books, records, and other materials. -Prepare the environment to accommodate freedom of body movement (space and simple props--scarves, hats, feathers). -Encourage exploration and utilization of rhythmic instruments in the environment-- rattlers, maracas, tambourines. -Invite musicians and singers to visit with the children (talk and discuss) to arouse interest in music and singing -Call children's attention to rhythms in the environment, i.e., patter of feet, ticking of clock, motions of the swings, seesaw, etc. and have them dramatize them.
Musical experiences enhance social skills and development; auditory-memory skills and language; creativity, mastery, and self-esteem			-Conduct simple singing games, dances and action songs (Punchinello, The Farmer in the Dell, Ten Little Indians, and others:

CURRICULUM EXPERIENCES FOR TEACHING/LEARNING EXPRESSIVE ARTS--CHART 8

(Subject) CONCEPTS	PERFORMANCE OUTCOMES	CHILDREN'S ACTIVITIES	TEACHING METHODS/RESOURCES
		-Striking objects that produce different sounds (with eyes closed) to identify the object -Playing guessing games--identifying voices of classmates who are not in-sight; naming song titles from memory, etc. -Moving bodies in rhythmic patterns in time to music	Musical stories--Tubby the Tuba, Sparky the Talking Piano, Peter and the Wolf, and the Nutcracker music; records of a wide variety: Afican Songs and Rhythms for Children (Folkways), Tom Glazier's Music for Ones and Twos (CMS), Woodie Guthrie Songs to Grow On: Nursery Days - vol. 1 (Folkways), Burl Ives' Little White Duck (Decca), Ella Jenkins' Song, Rhymes and Chants for the Dance (Folkways), Carole King's Really Rosie (Ode), Little Marches by Great Masters (Philips), Frank Luther's Mother Goose Songs (Decca), Alan Mills' Folk Songs for Young Folk: Animals vol. 1 (Folkways), Carl Orff's Music for Children (Angel), Hap Palmer's Creative Movement and Rhythmic Expression (Activity) Nancy Raven's Wee Songs for Wee Folk (Elektra)
VISUAL ARTS			
Art exists around us in many forms **Variety plays a major role in art** **Common materials can be made**	Achieved personal expressive form from ideas and creating things	-Taking nature walks and get first hand experiences in observation, ideas, and communication about the beauty of objects in the environment--color, shapes, etc.:	-Take trips within the neighborhood, to art centers, orchards, woods, and so forth -Provide a variety of art materials, supplies, etc.:

193

CURRICULUM EXPERIENCES FOR TEACHING/LEARNING EXPRESSIVE ARTS —CHART 8

(Subject) CONCEPTS	PERFORMANCE OUTCOMES	CHILDREN'S ACTIVITIES	TEACHING METHODS/RESOURCES
Lines have certain properties such as defining space, having direction, and having character-istics	Utilized a variety of art media for gaining skills in manipulating and in satisfying aesthetic expres-sion	forms, textures, size and space -Painting with a variety of colors -Doing blot printing -Doing finger painting -Doing sponge painting -Making constructions--three dimensional designs, box sculptures, wood sculptures, junk sculpture, paper bag puppets, paper mache designs and sculptures -Demonstrating length, size, or shape with lines	magazines, displays, films, variety of colors--construction paper, crayons, markers, etc--orange, blue, black, red, white, brown, purple, yellow, brown; finger paints, finger painting paper, chalk, scrap material box, baby food jars, dish washing detergent, straws, strings, newspaper, pieces of old sponges, manila paper--small and large sheets, real art objects, different size boxes, wood pieces, different size paper bags, clay, blocks, records, drawing paper, rulers and yardsticks
	Developed self-awareness, self-direction, self-confidence and a sense of respon-sibility		
	Developed an under-standing of shape, color, size, and texture	-Drawing lines which move in different directions like down, over, across, -Drawing lines which are fat, thin, winding, climbing, and so forth -Drawing pictures of objects, persons, places, shapes and scenery	
	Developed pride in craftsmanship		-Delineate space where children sit on floor for activities by painting shapes for each child -Play games with art and music as activities

194

CURRICULUM EXPERIENCES FOR TEACHING/LEARNING EXPRESSIVE ARTS--CHART 8

(Subject) CONCEPTS	PERFORMANCE OUTCOMES	CHILDREN'S ACTIVITIES	TEACHING METHODS/RESOURCES
Primary colors can be mixed to make secondary colors Fine motor development is enhanced through art Gross motor development is enhanced through art Coordination is enhanced through art	Experienced the opportunity to see what "to create" means Enhanced eye-hand coordination and other motor skills and abilities	-Mixing primary colors to make secondary colors-- red and yellow (orange); yellow and blue (green); red and blue (purple) -Introduce children to various art media and the appropriate tools -Using free movement with crayons by doodling, coloring in time to music, scribbling -Painting pictures on easel, table surface using small and large paint brushes -Cutting paper for experience and experimenting-- make confetti, cut shapes from big to small, cut on lines--straight, curved, zig-zag	-Provide books--Art and Visual Perception (Arnheim), Little Blue and Little Yellow (also film); Shapes (Schlein), Art from Scrap (Davis), Creating with Paper (Johnson), Sesame Street Book of Shapes (Time World), Square Is a Shape (Lerner), Harold and His Purple Crayon (Johnson). -Supply different primary colors, baby food jars, sticks for stirrers; different sizes of crayons; tempera paint, water paint, easels, different size brushes, manila paper, butcher paper, scissors--blunt ends, sharp ends, and different sizes; wall paper, glazed shelf paper, paste, liquid starch, Elmer's glue, tissue paper, gloss polymer-medium, plasticene clay, pottery clay, play dough (3 cups flour, 1 cup salt, 1 tbs. olive oil, and vegetable food coloring), containers for clay, plastic cloth -Provide books--Who's Seen the Scissors (Krahn), A Picture Has a Special Look (Borten)

195

(Subject) CONCEPTS	PERFORMANCE OUTCOMES	CHILDREN'S ACTIVITIES	TEACHING METHODS/RESOURCES
		-Cutting pictures from magazines and newspapers -Tearing paper -Pasting paper pictures and objects to make forms, figures, designs, on flat surfaces -Making collages -Making constructions using food items--rice, macaroni, seeds -Making art items to be used in their homes from junk materials--paper plates, aluminum plates, etc. -Modeling objects from clay, dough, soap where they have to pound, pull, push, twist, pinch, carve, cut and strip	-Make displays of children's work (bulletin boards, exhibits, etc.) -Invite artists to talk with children, demonstrate and display their art work

DRAMA

Creative drama builds awareness and confidence of creative abilities and awareness of the environment	Encouraged turning fantasies into enrichening learning experiences in the context of the real world Gained skills in meaningful physical movement	-Acting out personal experiences -Acting out simple stories -Making up situations and acting out -Acting out objects in the environment--flower, wind, animals, people, etc. -Playing in the housekeeping area of the environment -Listening to stories, poems, plays, operettas	-Facilitate a free interchange of conversation among children during "show and tell," story-telling time, free play, snack and lunch time, etc. -Prepare a housekeeping area with dramatic play materials -Set up a storytelling area and other materials for role-playing and make-believe games--rug, mats, musical instruments--drums,

CURRICULUM EXPERIENCES FOR TEACHING/LEARNING EXPRESSIVE ARTS—CHART 8

(Subject) CONCEPTS	PERFORMANCE OUTCOMES	CHILDREN'S ACTIVITIES	TEACHING METHODS/RESOURCES
Creative drama involves movement	Communicated thoughts and feelings through body actions (pantomime) and with words	-Acting out situations with bodies and body parts to portray the character of mother, father, doctor, dancer, fireman, cook, nurse, and storybook characters	rhythm sticks, bells, cymbals, and tambourine; dresses, pants, shirts, aprons, hats, shoes, boots, pocket books, and the like; pictures, books--Little Miss Muffet, The Three Bears, The Three Pigs, Little Red Riding Hood, Cinderella, Snow White and the Seven Dwarfs,
Role playing and games of make-believe are natural to children	(dramatize) in both planned and unplanned situations	-Moving bodies and body parts to rhythms--drum beat, music, handclapping, tambourines	Caps for Sale (Slobodkin), Jack and The Beanstalk, Three Billy Goats Gruff, Ask Mr. Bear
Creative drama involves verbal and/or non-verbal communications through the use of the body, voice and interest	Developed recall memorization and dramatization of a story	-Playing action games that require movement of body and body parts--finger plays, puppetry, story games	(Flack), Nursery Rhymes; films --The red Balloon finger plays --The Alphabet Son, Right Hand, Left Hand; Ten Little Fingers, Days of the Week,
Creative drama helps children develop their problem-solving abilities	Developed respect for the contributions and worth of others	-Doing pantomime activities --act out being in various locations (elevator, circus, haunted house, desert island, car, boat, etc.)	-Plan many experiences to help children express themselves creatively--group activity, programs, make believe tele-
Creative drama helps children to sequence and organize, to take on roles, and to use language	Developed psychomotor skills, abilities, and attitudes	-Doing pantomime activities using only sounds of things and not talking--act out being a car, bus, plane, sewing machine, etc.	vision shows, radio shows, puppet shows
	Experienced a variety of creative drama activities which enhanced learnings in other subject areas, also	-Listening to part of a story, then tell about the ending in their own words and thoughts	-Make penny theatre

-Provide a "stage" in the environment--an area raised by thick boards/bricks for children to perform their actions |
| | | -Acting out a story that has been told and narrate each scene | |

CURRICULUM EXPERIENCES FOR TEACHING/LEARNING EXPRESSIVE ARTS—CHART 8

(Subject) CONCEPTS	PERFORMANCE OUTCOMES	CHILDREN'S ACTIVITIES	TEACHING METHODS/RESOURCES
	Developed competencies in self-expression and problem solving techniques	-Making and using hand puppets and creating own stories -Listening to stories, poems for the purpose of dramatizing (acting out) and using words, events, and resolutions (socio-dramatic episodes)	-Have children dramatize nursery rhymes--using effects to show actions--cymbals, drums, music, and furniture
DANCE AND MOVE-MENT			
Dance enhances rhythmic bodily movement Dance and movement go hand-in-hand with an ordered sequence of moving visual patterns of line, solid, shape, and color Children should learn to move for the reason that "man has always had to move in order to satisfy a need"	Developed motor skills Developed a sense of rhythm through mastery and creativity of body movement--awareness, coordination, and control Showed expressions of ideas and emotions, expressed thoughts, feelings and movement in an identifiable form	-Expressing thoughts, feelings, and ideas through moving bodies to music -Performing axil movements and shapes such as twist, stretch, bend, curve, or one-legged -Feeling a straight shape by moving and feeling like a robot, an umbrella -Feeling a bent shape by moving and feeling like cracking ice, a worm, etc. -Using bodies to feel and move in form to develop a sense of space, like growing like a flower, stretching limbs by reaching and kicking, etc.	-Play music or tap drum and get children to pretend to be animals, planes, ragdolls, etc. -Have children experience various movements: finger movements--pinching, tickling, touching; leg and foot movements--kicking, tapping toes, hills, stamping, etc.; ways in which to move--slowly, quietly, quickly, joyfully; directions in which to move--up, down, in a circle, the other way, sideways, between, etc. -Provide records: Music for Young Americans, Whipped Cream, Dance a Story Series; Singing songs: Ring-Around the Rosey,

(Subject) CONCEPTS	PERFORMANCE OUTCOMES	CHILDREN'S ACTIVITIES	TEACHING METHODS/RESOURCES
Dance enhances the ability to control and move freely parts of the body or the entire body Dance and movement enhance the physical growth and development		-Moving bodies to demonstrate time, space, and mood (rhythmically by reaching up, down, to the side, to the front, to the back, making self small, big, etc.) -Moving bodies to various types of music in the way that the music makes people feel (happy, sad, wild, etc.)	-London Bridge, The Farmer in the Dell; Thumbkin, Jack and Jill, Five Little Fishies; -Provide rhythm instruments: castanets, bongo drums, cymbals, clappers, drums, rhythm bells, rhythm sticks, sand blocks, tambourine, triangle, maracas; cassettes, piano, record player, adequate space--indoors or outdoors--for performing activities.
Moving to rhythms is categorized as locomotor movements, body movements, and a combination of movements	Fostered locomotive and sustained movements to music/ rhythms and without music/rhythms	-Doing locomotor movements-- walking, hopping, jumping, running, and leaping; body movements--bending, twisting originating from a stationary position of the body; combination of movements-- using hands, feet, body, etc. -Performing activities like "moving to rhythm"--popcorn game, grasshopper song, jack be nimble game, kalamazoo the kangaroo; "jumping and leaping"--little grasshopper, skipping songs, skip to my Lou, gallop and gallop my pony, galloping horses, the bear; "creeping on all fours"-- spiders, crabs; "walking"-- baby, little man, big man game, the gentle giant, dinosaur, elephant game, the	-Invite dancers to talk with children about dancing for physical and mental satisfactions, as well as for a career choice. -Take children to dance recitals. Put on dance recitals in the school or community facility.

199

CURRICULUM EXPERIENCES FOR TEACHING/LEARNING EXPRESSIVE ARTS –CHART 8

(Subject) CONCEPTS	PERFORMANCE OUTCOMES	CHILDREN'S ACTIVITIES	TEACHING METHODS/RESOURCES
		cat on the fence, the high wire walker; "posture and balance"--hokey pokey, bow, bow, bow, Belinda, puncinello, with my hands I clap, clap, clap, Johnny works with one hammer	

HOW CAN THE EXPRESSIVE ARTS BE EVALUATED IN REFERENCE TO TEACHING/LEARNING?

The expressive arts--music, visual arts, drama, dance and movement-- are teaching-learning experiences that are spontaneous, joyful, structured, unstructured, natural, original and contain elements of creativity. Therefore, evaluation should be done in ways that do not infringe upon these creative aspects of performance. Observation is the best method of evaluation. The best tools for evaluation are records and performance.

A record should be kept on each child on a regular basis. The task(s) that the child is expected to perform in each expressive arts area should be listed. Also, behaviors that occur naturally in each area should be indexed to show references to audiovisuals, tapes, videotapes, etc. The records should be kept to show ongoing as well as past performance to note progress.

The child's performance of a task is the greatest proof of teaching and learning in the expressive arts. Observation and listening of/to a child's performance constitute an evaluation procedure. The evaluator (caregiver) will be able to see how well the child mastered the material as instructed; uses the concepts and elements learned through the teaching activities--music, art, drama, dance and movement. The appraisal should be recorded for future planning, teaching, and learning experiences.

The evaluator (caregiver) should always give constructive feedback to the child about the quality of his/her work, performance, and so forth. Comments should be made on specific elements so as to encourage continued efforts of improvement and growth. Evaluation is a method of examining the teaching-learning process to obtain its effectiveness and, therefore, must be done positively. Commenting on the elements of performance that were "good" is a constructive way to get at what needs to be done to make it better. By focusing on the "bad," the risk of discouraging the child is too great. Use evaluation as an integral part of the teaching/learning process so that pre-schoolers view it as a developmental step that is necessary for their mastery of a task (objective activity, etc.).

HOW DO THE EXPRESSIVE ARTS CORRELATE WITH THE TOTAL PRE-SCHOOL CURRICULUM?

The Expressive Arts provide an adventurous and aesthetically pleasing method to teaching and reinforcing concepts in other curriculum areas.

In mathematics--the rhythmic beats in music allow children to count, match rhythm on an instrument, keep time; visual arts entail measuring the size of objects, paper for drawing; dealing with amounts of paint; number of crayons, colors, tools--brushes, easels, tables, dimensions of objects in terms of distance--near, far away and pictorial representation for putting thoughts into graphic symbols; drama deals with concepts of space, size, shape--how big, small, bent, round; keeping time to music as the body is moved in various directions entails dance and movement. Counting, using space, size, shapes--rhythmic coordination with gross and fine motor movements with hands-reaching, feet-moving up, down, high, low, over, out, and body swaying-left, right, around, squarely, bent, and so forth.

In language arts--music encounters remembering words, expressing emotions through songs and singing, comprehending lyrics, communicating feelings, reading notes, words, and voice and speech; learning names and meanings of various art mediums, materials, supplies, and tools--drawings, paintings, collages, paper mache, easels, brushes, primary colors, secondary colors, and so forth--constitute visual arts in language and communication; drama enhances the development of language and communication skills, exercises voice and speech, expression, feelings and emotions, builds vocabulary, encourages creative expression, learning of poems, scripts and speeches by memory; reading, listening to, and telling stories; dance and movement help expression of body to communicate feelings.

In science--the parts of the body are learned which are used in musical exercises, making sounds, distinguishing and identifying sounds and their sources are music activities that have scientific implications; mixing primary colors to create secondary colors is a visual arts activity that deals with chemistry; drawing and painting pictures using various materials and capturing different scenes such as water, air, wind, rain and so forth--entails science--paper from wood from trees, light and dark shades implying day, night, sunshine, moon; using various mediums for art work implies scientific actions--straw painting (blowing wind), using lines (movement in different directions); dance and movement involve scientific concepts as far as the use of the body, space, and distance utilized by the body.

In social studies--music is an excellent way to teach about people, places, and how people work and play together; visual arts products depict seasons, scenes of people, places, concepts of living in a community, costumes, holidays and other cultural aspects of people; <u>drama</u> demonstrates the actions of various cultural groups, living styles, and ways of communicating and socializing in groups; <u>dance and movement</u> are ways to express the heritage of groups of people, customs and traditions; and all of the expressive arts portray values, heritage, beliefs and basic givens of people and their birth places vividly and colorfully.

ACTIVITIES FOR STUDY AND DISCUSSION

1. Develop field trips in each of the Expressive Arts areas. Tell the purpose, the place, contracts, concepts to be developed, list possible questions to be asked, and follow-up activities.

2. Collect materials and resources in each of the expressive arts areas: 1) to be kept in the classroom, 2) to be found in materials center or library; 3) to be visited, and 4) to be invited to visit with group.

3. Make a list of places to be visited in your school community and share with others in your school/center.

4. Make a plan to show specific environmental arrangements needed to conduct certain activities in each of the expressive arts areas.

5. Make a card file of activities and resources (songs, books, plays, etc.) to be used in each expressive arts area.

6. Plan activities in each of the expressive arts areas for play, assemblies, and presentations to coincide with special occasions, holidays, celebrations, and events pertaining to study themes.

7. Make a "penny theatre" and put on puppet shows of several types (storytelling, finger plays, special events--fire prevention, safety tips, etc.).

8. Make a television out of a large cardboard box (refrigerator, stove) and produce shows (talent shows, game shows, talk shows) as a way to enhance dramatic play.

9. Design a dramatic play project whereby "commercials" are made. Use the influence of the expressive arts to enhance your project.

REFERENCES

Bayless, K. and M. Ramsey, **Music: A Way of Life for the Young Child.** St. Louis: The C.V. Mosby Company, 1982.

Brittain, W. Lambert, **Creativity, Art, and The Young Child.** New York: Macmillan Publishing Co., Inc., 1979.

Chandler, Bessie W., **Music in Early Learning Experiences.** Dansville, N.Y.: The Instructor Publications, Inc., 1970.

Chenfield, Mimi B., **Creative Activities for Young Children.** New York: Harcourt Brace Javanovich, Inc., 1983.

Cratty, Bryant J., **Active Learning.** Englewood Cliffs, N.J.: Prentice-Hall, Inc., 1971.

Daniels, Elva, **Creative Rhythms for Your Class.** Danville, New York: F.A. Owen Publishing Co., 1965.

Eliason, C. and L. Jenkins, **A Practice Guide to Early Childhood Curriculum.** Second Edition, St. Louis: The C.V. Mosby Company, 1981.

Froebel, Friedrich, **Education of Man.** New York: D. Appleton & Company, 1887.

Ginott, Haim, **Teacher and Child.** New York: The Macmillan Company, 1972.

Green, Marjorie M. and Elizabeth L. Woods, **A Nursery School Handbook for Teachers and Parents.** Sierra Madre, California: Sierra Madre Community Nursery School Association, 1972.

Greenberg, Pearl, **Art and Ideas for Young People.** New York: Van Nostrant Bun Reinhold Co., 1970.

Haines, Joan E. and Linda Gerber, **Leading Young Children to Music: A Resource Book for Teachers.** Second Edition, Columbus: Merrill Publishing Co., 1984.

Hendrick, Joanne, **Total Learning: Curriculum for the Young Child.** Columbus: Merrill Publishing Co., 1986.

Herberholz, Barbara, **Early Childhood Art.** Sacramento, California: William C. Brown Company Publishers, 1974.

Hildebrand, Verna, **Introduction to Early Childhood Education** (Fourth Edition). New York: The Macmillan Company, 1986.

Hoover, F. Louis, **Art Activities for the Very Young.** Worchester, Mass.: Davis Publications, 1961.

Klonsky, Ruth L., **Art Lessons that Mirror the Child's World.** West Nyack, N.Y.: Parker Publishing Company, Inc., 1975.

Kuhn, Jacqueline, **Thirty-three Rhythms for Children.** New York: Bregman, Vocco, and Conn, Inc., 1956.

Lament, Marylee M., **Music in Elementary Education.** New York: Macmillan Co., Inc., 1976.

Landeck, Beatrice, **Songs to Grow On.** New York: Edward B. Marks Music Corp. and William Sloane Assoc., Inc., 1950.

Lark-Horovitz, Betty, Hilda Lewis, and Mark Luca, **Understanding Children's Art for Better Teaching.** Columbus, Ohio: Charles E. Merrill Books, Inc., 1967.

Leeper, Sarah and others, **Good Schools for Young Children** (Fourth Edition). New York: Macmillan Company, 1979.

Maynard, Olga. **Children and Dance and Music.** New York: Charles Scribner's Sons, 1968.

McCartney, Laura. **Songs for the Nursery School.** Cincinnati, Ohio: Willis Music Co., 1937.

McDonald, Dorothy T., **Music In Our Lives: The Early Years.** Washington, D.C.: National Association for the Education of Young Children, 1979.

Raposo, Joe and Jeffrey Moss, **The Sesame Street Song Book.** New York: Simon and Schuster/Children's Television Workshop, Inc., 1971.

Read, Katherine, The Nursery School (Human Relationships and Learning). Philadelphia: W.B. Saunders Company, 1976.

Rudolph, Marguerita. **From Hand to Head.** New York: Webster Division, McGraw-Hill Book Company, 1973.

Schickedanz, Judith A., Mary E. York, Ida Santos Stewart, and Doris White, **Strategies for Teaching Young Children.** Englewood Cliffs, N.J.: Prentice-Hall, Inc., 1983.

Simmons, Gene, "A Rationale for Early Training in Music." Education, 99:257-264, Spring, 1979.

Southwest Educational Development Laboratory. **Bilingual Early Childhood Program.** Austin, Texas: National Educational Laboratory Publishers, Inc., 1974.

Spodek, Bernard, **Teaching in the Early Years.** Englewood Cliffs: Prentice-Hall, Inc., 1972.

Tuch, Barbara, and Harriet Judy, **How To Teach Children to Draw, Paint and Use Color.** West Nyack, N.Y.: Pap Parker Publishing Company, Inc., 1975.

Wadsworth, Barry J., **Piaget's Theory of Cognitive Development.** New York: David McKay Company, Inc., 1971.

Werner, Peter and Elsie Burton, **Learning Through Movement,** St. Louis: The C.V. Mosby Company, 1979.

Winn, Marie and Allan Miller, **The Fireside Book of Children's Songs.** New York: Simon and Schuster, 1966.

CHAPTER SEVEN

MATHEMATICAL EXPERIENCES

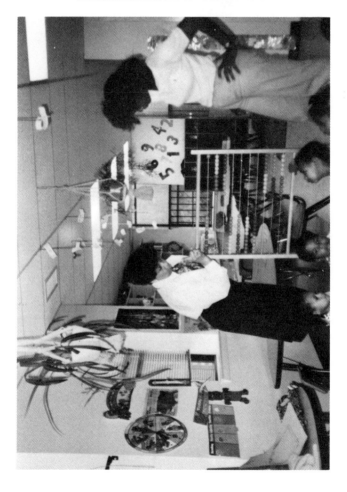

NUMBERS, NUMERATION, MEASUREMENT, AND GEOMETRY

CHAPTER 7

MATHEMATICAL EXPERIENCES

- WHY MUST MATHEMATICS BE EMPHASIZED AS A SEPARATE SUBJECT IN THE PRE-SCHOOL CURRICULUM?: AN INTRODUCTION

- WHAT ARE THE GOALS AND OBJECTIVES FOR TEACHING MATHEMATICS?

- WHAT IS THE COMPOSITION OF THE PRE-SCHOOL MATHEMATICS CURRICULUM?

- WHAT APPROACHES TO USE TO EXPAND/EXTEND CURRICULUM THEORY INTO TEACHING/LEARNING APPLICATIONS FOR EXPERIENCES IN MATHEMATICS?

- HOW DOES MATHEMATICS CORRELATE WITH THE TOTAL PRE-SCHOOL CURRICULUM?

- WHAT REFERENCES ARE HELPFUL TO THE PRE-SCHOOL MATHEMATICS CURRICULUM?

- WHAT IS THE EXTENT OF USING REFERENCES IN THE PRE-SCHOOL MATHEMATICS CURRICULUM FOR THE CAREGIVERS AND THE CHILD?

- ACTIVITIES FOR STUDY AND DISCUSSION

- REFERENCES

WHY MUST MATHEMATICS BE EMPHASIZED AS A SEPARATE SUBJECT IN THE PRE-SCHOOL CURRICULUM?: AN INTRODUCTION

The need for a greater supply of people with good foundations in the basic skills of mathematics has grown tremendously in the 1980's. Due to the large number of people in the United States who have not had the opportunity to attain this mathematical foundation, poor achievement results of our high school graduates have reflected a serious deficit in the curriculum. The plea for "going back to the basics" became, and still is, very popular. This educational deficit in mathematics learnings (skills, attitudes and abilities) has handicapped these people from the standpoint of (1) not being able to get challenging employment, and (2) not having very positive feelings about themselves and their personal worth. It is with this circumstance that community expectations have risen to the level of requesting more basic competencies in mathematics. Therefore, early childhood education is the first step in building this foundation for developing mathematical competencies.

There are many ideas and theories about teaching mathematics as a formal or separate subject in pre-school. Some suggest, on the one hand, never to teach "mathematics" alone, but in conjunction with the other major subject areas due to the complexities of the abstract nature of mathematics. On the other hand, early childhood educators and others promote mathematics as a subject area worthy of individual approach. Mathematics is an integral part of the young child's life. Everyday living situations require basic and sometimes complex knowledges of numbers and numeration, measurements, geometry, algebra, and statistics and probability estimations. Being able to identify a numeral and to understand a number concept, like a telephone number--emergency--and how to dial it, can make the difference in a life or death situation. The child's world is full of experiences where he/she will have to make decisions about weight, size, and/or location. Being able to tell someone where you live or how to find your house or what your house number is could mean the difference in getting home safely or being lost or having an abundance of frustrations and anxieties, for both young children and parents. For some young children, the differences in the size of a piece of cake or candy bar can mean pure joy or sadness or sickness--as some parents might view it. A more subtle knowledge of shapes may be indicated when a child builds something or describes a toy or picture. Also, a young child may no longer be as content with a big nickel in the 1980's as some were in the 1960's, especially when they know that very little--or no candy or cookies--can be purchased with less than a dime.

While many mathematics competencies are taught incidentally through other subject area, there are numerous other mathematical operations and concepts that are absolutely essential for participation in our society today. Such concepts and operations like: conservation of quantity, quality, length; correspondence of sets, seriation, number facts, and so forth, are too important to the mathematics basic skills foundation to leave to incidental or accidental teaching. Therefore, pre-school mathematics must be taught as a separate subject using as many hands-on and concrete experiences as possible. According to Piaget, the pre-school child will deal with mathematics through intuition rather than logic as a rule. However, the concepts and operations in mathematics can be learned if and when taught through a concrete, manipulative approach.

WHAT ARE THE GOALS AND OBJECTIVES FOR TEACHING PRE-SCHOOL MATHEMATICS?

Pre-school mathematics is taught whenever the learner gives evidence of "readiness" through his/her everyday participation in the teaching/learning process. Therefore, the goals and objectives for teaching pre-school mathematics are somewhat individually oriented to the instructional program. These represent a continuum of progress in an unordered sequence rather than an ordered one.

Some "goals" for teaching pre-school mathematics are:

1. To inspire children to enjoy the study of mathematics and to develop positive attitudes towards the subject.

2. To lead young children to recognize the importance of mathematics in an increasingly technological society.

3. To prepare young children to handle mathematical concepts and operations through the functions of number-numeration, measurements and geometry.

Some "objectives" for teaching pre-school mathematics in the sub-topic area are:

Numbers and Numeration:

1. To help children develop competence in classification.

2. To help children develop competence in matching one to one.

3. To help children develop competence in recognizing and naming sets, and in counting.

4. To help children develop competence in reading numerals and associating them with the numbers they represent.

5. To help children gain competence in combining and separating sets.

6. To help children gain competence in working with base ten.

7. To help children develop competence in addition, subtraction, multiplication, and division facts.

8. To help children gain competence in using place value.

Measurement:

1. To help children develop competence in investigating length.

2. To help children develop competence in investigating weight.

3. To help children develop competence in measuring area.

4. To help children develop competence in measuring volume.

5. To help children understand that time is not controlled by actions.

6. To help children understand that time is independent of the measuring device.

7. To help children learn to recognize and name common coins and bills.

8. To help children understand the value of each piece of money.

9. To help children understand the exchange rates of various pieces of money.

Geometry:

1. To help children develop competencies in identifying geometric solids and shapes.

2. To help children develop competence constructing geometric shapes and solids.

3. To help children develop an awareness of geometric shapes and solids in connection with the environment.

WHAT IS THE COMPOSITION OF THE PRE-SCHOOL MATHEMATICS CURRICULUM?

Teaching methodology, concepts, performance objectives in the form of activities, and resources formulate the curriculum format for the pre-school mathematics curriculum. These elements play an important part in establishing "instructional strategies" as a rational, conceptual, and systematic approach to implementing curriculum. The teaching learning process relies heavily on the proper functioning of the caregiver, the learner (child), and the instrument for evaluating the outcomes of their efforts. The "teaching methodologies/activities" as presented in this curriculum guide format help to weld together the concept of comprehensiveness of teaching and learning the sub-categories of number-numeration, measurement and geometry.

"Number" is the first sequence of the sub-category. Although it is abstract in nature, a multiplicity of pre-operational experiences set the stage for examing and organizing the concept of number into logical relationships. The greatest aspect of the "number sequence" is manipulation of objects. This will enable the pre-school child to explore the "concept of number" through the means of creative interactions to build "number readiness."

The scope and sequence of "Numeration" are provided through an extension of the number sequence when greater mathematical meaning is derived through understanding written number symbols, theory, value and operations.

"Number-Numeration of the Pre-School Mathematics Curriculum" gives a comprehensive teaching-learning approach to the curriculum guide format for operationalizing involvements in classification, ordering, counting, number meaning, base ten, place value, addition, subtraction, multiplication, and division. Implicit in these operations are fractional numbers; algebra and probability and statistics.

The "pre-school mathematics curriculum" utilizes the concept of "measurement" as a practical hands-on approach to teaching and learning mathematics. A wealth of materials provided for the learner ensures greater participation and more in-depth involvement with a wide range of experiences in concepts of measurement. It is important that each child experiences the concrete tasks individually in order to become competent in measurement skills and abilities.

The teaching/learning approach to the curriculum guide format is arranged to present a holistic conceptualization of the measurement sequence which include: (1) geometric measures like linear, area, and volume; and (2) non-geometric measures like time, money, temperature, weight, and liquid. The essence of the "metric" system is evident in the array of practical activities for teaching and learning.

The "Pre-School Mathematics Curriculum" addresses the fact that the world is composed of shapes, forms, relations, and locations. Experiences in geometric concepts prepare the child for living, surviving and operating in this dimensionally-perceptive world. The activities included in the curriculum will serve to give the child many experiences relevant to motivational and background knowledges of his/her environment.

The teaching/learning approach to the curriculum guide format suggests many opportunities to manipulate, identify, reproduce, match, and utilize geometric forms. The teaching/learning process in the pre-school mathematics sub-category of geometry will include the aforementioned opportunities as well as avenues for discussion of properties and generalizations of problematic outcomes.

A mathematics "vocabulary" is necessary in the pre-school mathematics curriculum. The major purpose is to give the young child a series of words to verbalize mathematical concepts in everyday living, since living is dictated by numbers. Getting up in the morning, going to bed at night, taking a break, going to lunch, completing a chore or task, making a phone call, keeping healthy by checking diet (calories) and weight, weigh-in at birth, speed limit, distance between places and people, family members, school promotions, years in college, dressing according to the temperature, purchasing food, clothing and shelter, and an infinite array of living activities are controlled by "numbers" and quantitative measures. Therefore, it is imperative that young children have "words" to develop their thought processes by drawing mathematical conclusions, expressing mathematical concepts, and comparing and contrasting mathematical learnings and experiences.

The pre-school mathematics curriculum is not complete unless mathematics vocabulary is an integral part of its format. It is as important to mathematics learning as the reading vocabulary is to the subject of "reading." The mathematics experiences of manipulation, oral communication, sight vocabulary learning, and basic understanding of computational activities.

The pre-school mathematics curriculum is based upon practical, hands-on, and manipulative experiences. Therefore, most of the supplies, materials, and field excursions are instructional in nature. A wide variety of instructional resources must be selected and/or produced for its usage in the pre-school mathematics curriculum. The importance of resources is high since pre-schoolers are relying on their psychomotor skills to gain mathematical concepts and understandings. These instructional materials provide "concrete" experiences for setting mathematics readiness and for extending mathematics operations.

In keeping the Pre-School Mathematics Curriculum as comprehensible as possible, an assortment of supplies, materials and places to strengthen the teaching learning process is provided.

WHAT APPROACHES TO USE TO EXPAND/EXTEND CURRICULUM THEORY INTO TEACHING/LEARNING APPLICATIONS FOR MATHEMATICAL EXPERIENCES?

Pre-school curriculum and teaching/learning entails three major components:

o   Learning Theories (possible ways children learn various subjects)

o   Theories of Instruction (best ways to teach children)

o   Teaching/Learning Process (rationale, purpose, strategies, methods, techniques, assessment, and resources)

Information and materials to show approaches suggested to expand/extend curriculum theory into practical application are found in Chapter Four of the text. The reader is directed to refer to that chapter if and when it is necessary to review or study the transfer. Curriculum experiences for teaching/learning "mathematics" in the pre-school are formulated into the following charts to be used as a written curriculum model.

(Subject) CONCEPTS	PERFORMANCE OUTCOMES	CHILDREN'S ACTIVITIES	TEACHING METHODS/RESOURCES
NUMBER-NUMERATION Materials are classified in accord to attributes Objects are ordered by relationships into sets	Developed a sense of mathematical operations in dealing with numbers and counting in everyday functions	-Showing and telling -Watching films, filmstrips and slides of number-numeration concepts -Matching objects that are alike -Matching objects that are different -Sorting objects that are the same color -Recognizing objects that are the same size -Recognizign objects that are the same shape -Placing objects in various positions (up, down, under, over, behind, etc.) -Identifying objects that are different in size -Identifying objects that are different in color -Identifying objects that are different in shape -Selecting objects and materials that are the same texture (soft, hard, rough, smooth, etc.) -Selecting objects and materials that are of different textures -Sorting objects and materials that are the same patterns	-Set up mathematics learning center to include assorted objects as specified in activities. -Give directions for performing the task or activity. -Construct materials for activities. -Perform the teacher-directed tasks by individual child or by group of children by explaining the object of the task. For example, say, "watch me" or "listen" then demonstrate; now say, "you do it with me," then say, "let's do the play or song." After the task(s) is (are) completed, say, "you did a good job," or "I like how you sing, listen, talk, etc." or other comments or praise. -Prepare the learning environment to include assorted activities on a scheduled basis per your teaching plans.

217

CURRICULUM EXPERIENCES FOR TEACHING/LEARNING MATHEMATICS—CHART 9

(Subject) CONCEPTS	PERFORMANCE OUTCOMES	CHILDREN'S ACTIVITIES	TEACHING METHODS/RESOURCES
			-Be thoroughly familiar with activities and explain "how" and "why" for each in a step by step fashion; demonstrate readily.

-Provide resources to include: Counting frame (abacus), flash cards (numerals), flannel board with objects, crayons, macaroni, checkers, bottle tops, colored buttons, beads (different sizes), balls, blocks, construction paper, (different sizes and colors), puzzles, games, dolls, jacks, material pieces (different textures), pictures, number cards, game and playing cards, dominoes, patterns of shapes, straws, nesting cups, peg boards, toy soldiers, toy cars, toy trucks, colored yarn, books, number lines, popsicle sticks, tongue depressors, tooth picks, charts, tile floors, brick walls, counting discs, plastic and wooden chips, finger plays, story books using mathematical concepts |

CURRICULUM EXPERIENCES FOR TEACHING/LEARNING MATHEMATICS—CHART 9

(Subject) CONCEPTS	PERFORMANCE OUTCOMES	CHILDREN'S ACTIVITIES	TEACHING METHODS/RESOURCES
			--Count and Cee (Hoban), Number of Things (Oxenbury), Numbers (Reiss), Count With Me (Witt), Best Counting Book Ever (Scarry), Norman Rockwell's Counting Book (Taborin), musical records that use counting concepts, empty spools, rulers, yardsticks, calendars, clock faces, index cards, pots, pans, bowls, cups, string, yarn, sundial, alarm clock, stop watch, unit blocks, hollow blocks, tape measure, scales (bathroom, doctor's, spring), thermometers, graph paper, furniture, flowers, dowel rods, cylinders (paper rolls, aluminum foil rolls, etc.), spoons for measuring, different size cotnainers (empty milk cartons, juice cartons, condiment bottles, etc.), picture books--It's About Time (Schlein), House for Willie: A Story Bout Time (Britten), Think Metric (Branley), block building assesories, block bin, or block cart, lego blocks

CURRICULUM EXPERIENCES FOR TEACHING/LEARNING MATHEMATICS—CHART 9

(Subject) CONCEPTS	PERFORMANCE OUTCOMES	CHILDREN'S ACTIVITIES	TEACHING METHODS/RESOURCES
Numbers use base ten and place values Mathematics operations include adding, subtracting, multiplying, and dividing		-Recognizing and naming properties in sets of ones, tens, hundreds -Regrouping sets in tens (eleven means, one group of ten and one group of one, etc.) -Regrouping sets to expand counting to larger numbers (forty-seven means, four groups of ten and seven groups of ones) -Putting together objects that will increase the size of the set: (●) + (●) means (1) + (1) up to less than ten objects	for connections, assortment of coins and bills--pennies, nickels, dimes, quarters, bills (use play money), story books--Jimmy Potter Buys A Lollipop (Hellsing), Last Sunday I Had A Dollar (Viorst), play cash register, piggy banks, classroom store, trips to grocery store, bank, lumber yard, construction sites, etc. -Provide resources for accompanying activities, like, checkers, chairs, counting discs, fraction plates and cards, design cubes, place value chart, abacus, counting frame, peg board and pegs, toys, balls, string, holding trays; sets of objects--fruits, sticks, balls, shoes, boxes, pictures, symbols; Match-Mate Puzzles, Peabody Kit, number cut-outs, numeral cards, wall charts showing children's heights, books--The Very Tall Little Girl (Krasilovsky); filmstrip, etc.

(Subject) CONCEPTS	PERFORMANCE OUTCOMES	CHILDREN'S ACTIVITIES	TEACHING METHODS/RESOURCES
		-Taking away objects from the set to show how many are left (●●●●●●● = 6); If two (2) of the objects are removed (taken away) how many will be left in the set?	

Therefore, ●●●●●● - ●● = ●●●● (6)   (2) = (4)

-Grouping objects and counting the totals in multiplying numbers (one set of one = 1 x 1 = 1; two sets of one's = 2 x 1 = 2; three sets of one's = 3 x 1 = 3). A repeated addition equation (2 fours = 8; 4 + 4 = 8; 2 x 4 = 8)

-Finding out how many groups of certain objects can be found in a set in dividing numbers (how many one's are in a set of three?)

(●●) (●●) (●●) 3 ÷ 1 = 3; how many two's are in a set of six?

(●●) (●●) (●●) 6 ÷ 2 = 3

(Subject) CONCEPTS	PERFORMANCE OUTCOMES	CHILDREN'S ACTIVITIES	TEACHING METHODS/RESOURCES
		-Sorting objects and materials that are of different patterns	Number fingerplays, counting books--Number: A First Counting Book (Allen), One Snail and Me (McLeod), Chicken Little Count To Ten (Friskey and Evans), Ten Apples Up On Top (LeSieg), Number of Things (Oxenbury), Ten Black Dots (Crews), Count on Calico Cat (Charles), dot cards, small and large objects, numeral cards, word cards.
		-Combining and separating sets of objects to formulate the concepts of "equal," "more than," "less than."	
		-Arranging objects into sets in accord to attributes (biggest to smallest; full to empty; dark to light; shortest to tallest, etc.)	
Counting and number meanings are necessary operations		-Saying number words (by audio-rote counting) in order (one, two, three, four, five...ten)	
		-Counting objects, singing counting songs, playing counting games, and using books	
		-Identifying the number symbol (numerals) (1, 2, 3, 4, 5, ... 10)	
		-Matching the number symbol *numerals) and number word (by audio-sight) (one – 1; two – 2; three – 3; four – 4; five – 5; .... ten – 10)	
		-Recognizing the number word (by audio-sight) with the number symbol (numeral) and with objects to understand what the number is	

(Subject) CONCEPTS	PERFORMANCE OUTCOMES	CHILDREN'S ACTIVITIES	TEACHING METHODS/RESOURCES
		(one – 1 – ●; two – 2 – ●●; three – 3 – ●●●; four – 4 – ●●●●; five – 5 – ●●●●●..ten – 10 – ●●●●●●●●●●)	
MEASUREMENT			
Geometric measurements including linear, area, and volume are used daily	Developed an awareness and understanding of geometric measures through everyday functions and planned exercises	–Identifying the length of objects –Identifying the height of objects –Identifying the weight of objects –Identifying the size of objects and areas –Recognizing the differences in length, height, weight and size of objects and areas –Using linear non-standard units to measure distance (i.e., pencils, books, parts of the body, etc.) –Using linear standard units to measure areas in inches, feet, yards, etc. –Using metric instruments to measure areas in meters, centimeters, etc. –Using objects to represent arbitrary measuring units in order to approximate	–Provide resources to facilitate activities, like standard units of measure-- (English and metric systems) rulers, yardsticks, centi- meter sticks, scales, drawing space, drawing instruments like pencils, crayons, paper, markers, chalk; unit blocks, hollow blocks, sand box, water table, different size and shape containers, leaves, and other objects.

(Subject) CONCEPTS	PERFORMANCE OUTCOMES	CHILDREN'S ACTIVITIES	TEACHING METHODS/RESOURCES
		the area of a region in terms of units (i.e, tile, blocks, designs, patterns, and so forth) -Placing objects in various containers and spaces to see how much and how many they will hold and compare sizes -Buildign figures with blocks to see how many are contained within -Counting the number of cubic units (volume) contained in a box -Comparing volumes by using containers of sand, water, rice, etc. -Naming the number of units contained in a drawing of a rectangular solid divided into units	
Non-geometric measures includ-ing time, money, temperature, weight, and liquid are used daily	Developed an aware-ness and understand-ing of non-geometric measures through hands-on experiences and everyday func-tions	-Using a show and tell approach -Identifying the days of the week -Identifying the months of the year -Identifying the parts of the clock -Using the face of a clock to name the numerals for hours -Pointing out the hour (short) and the minute hand (long)	-Provide teaching-learning resources: clocks, ther-mometers; play money--coins (pennies, nickels, dimes, quarters, fifty cents piece, silver dollar), bills (one dollar, five dollars, ten dollars, twenty dollars, fifty dollars, one hundred dollars, and two dollars),

224

CURRICULUM EXPERIENCES FOR TEACHING/LEARNING MATHEMATICS —CHART 9

(Subject) CONCEPTS	PERFORMANCE OUTCOMES	CHILDREN'S ACTIVITIES	TEACHING METHODS/RESOURCES
		-Telling how many hours in a day -Telling time orally in whole hours, half-hours, quarter hours, minute intervals -Stating the number of minutes in an hour -Recognizing denominations of coins and bills -Using money vocabulary (coins, cents, dollars) -Comparing and order coins for identification -Practicing exercises to understand likenesses and differences in value by matching sets and forming sub-sets (penny = 1 cent; a nickel = 5 pennies = 5 cents and so forth) -Solving problems related to using money to buy items and make change (simple addition, subtraction, etc.) -Identifying a thermometer as the instrument for measuring temperature -Recognizing the different types of thermometers (oral, rectal, house, food, etc.)	play cash register, scales, assorted containers of all sizes, shapes, and volumes; watches; story books-- Jimmy Potter Buys A Lollipop (Helsing), Last Sunday I Had A Dollar (Viorst), piggy banks, classroom store, trips to grocery store, lumber yards, construction sites; check books, fraction plates and cards, geo-boards, nesting blocks, parquetry blocks.

CURRICULUM EXPERIENCES FOR TEACHING/LEARNING MATHEMATICS—CHART 9

(Subject) CONCEPTS	PERFORMANCE OUTCOMES	CHILDREN'S ACTIVITIES	TEACHING METHODS/RESOURCES
		-Naming the numerals on the thermometer and recognize the meaning of them as far as temperature is concerned (hot, cold, high, low, etc.) -Using temperature vocabulary (Fahrenheit, centigrade, freezing, boiling, etc.) -Investigating weights of objects by using scales (bathroom, doctor's, pan balance, spring balance) -Recognizing units of measurements as pounds, ounces, kilograms, grams, etc. -Solving problems pertaining to weight of objects -Using liquids to obtain measurements -Recognizing liquid measurement vocabulary (ounce, pound, cup, pint, quart, gallon, etc.) -Solving problems of conversion by using water to fill containers and get certain liquid measures (4 ounces = 1 cup, 16 ounces = 1 pint, 2 pints = 1 quart, 4 quarts = 1 gallon, etc.)	-Provide human resources-- weather men and women, doctors, nurses, surveyors, teachers, to visit school or to be visited by children on field trips.

(Subject) CONCEPTS	PERFORMANCE OUTCOMES	CHILDREN'S ACTIVITIES	TEACHING METHODS/RESOURCES
GEOMETRY Geometric shapes and relations are necessary operations	Gained a basic knowledge of geometry to implement and perform tasks involving shapes and solids.	-Identifying four geometric shapes--circle, square, triangle, and rectangle -Providing models of shapes and solids for tracing on paper, boards, etc. -Labeling the shapes and solids by names -Giving simple, yet explicit directions and examples for performing problem-solving tasks -Making models of shapes that are "sensorial" designed out of felt, sandpaper, etc. for feeling -Making models of solids that are "dimensional" designed out of corrugated cardboard, construction paper, etc. -Matching shapes and solids -Finding geometric shapes in objects in the room, books, and in magazines -Identifying shapes in foods (crackers, sandwiches, cups, napkins, etc.) and materials for snacks and lunch	-Provide story books--Circles, Triangles, Squares (Hoban), Shapes (Reiss), My Very First Book of Shapes (Quarles), Shapes (Schlein), Squares Are Not Bad (Salazar), A Kiss Is Round (Budney), TRY Series, magazines, food items for snacks and lunch, containers, flannel boards, flannel material, sand paper, cooking utensils, drawing paper, crayons, paint, easels, brushes, water, large wrapping paper, filmstrips, assorted objects.

CURRICULUM EXPERIENCES FOR TEACHING/LEARNING MATHEMATICS –CHART 9

(Subject) CONCEPTS	PERFORMANCE OUTCOMES	CHILDREN'S ACTIVITIES	TEACHING METHODS/RESOURCES
Geometric solids are used daily		-Identifying solids as being flat or curbed -Identifying solids by naming cubes, pyramids, cones, spheres and cylinders -Making solids by drawing, sorting and collecting models -Matching objects and pictures of solids	-Provide empty spools, rolls from tissue paper, aluminum foil, etc.; blocks, wooden figurines of solid shapes, puzzles, objects found in the environment.
VOCABULARY			
Number-numeration has specific vocabulary	Developed a vocabulary to enhance understanding of content	-Using vocabulary as an integral part of learning: match, sort, set, object, alike, different, same color--red, blue, green, white, black, purple, yellow, orange, brown; size, shape, quantity, quality, texture--hard, smooth, rough, soft; pattern, equal, not equal, less, empty, number, numeral, one, two, three..., zero, base, value, group, algorithm, operation,	-Provide wall charts, word lists, books, chalk board, chalk, posters, word cards, sentence strips, and labels.

(Subject) CONCEPTS	PERFORMANCE OUTCOMES	CHILDREN'S ACTIVITIES	TEACHING METHODS/RESOURCES
		add(ition), subtract(ion), multiply(ication), divide, division, plus, minus, time, count, order, rote, equation, fact, algebra, statistics, probability, belong...	
Measure has specific vocabulary		-Using vocabulary as an integral part of learning: linear, measure, measurement, geometry, geometric, area, length, height, weight, long, short, unit, compare, ruler, yardstick, metric, feet, inch, yard, volume, container, estimate, cubic, square, dimension, non-geometric, calendar, clock, time, day, week, month, year, minute, hour, hand, long, short, value, money, cent, coin, bill, dime, nickel, quarter, fifty cents, half dollar, dollar, sign, symbol, change, difference, scale, pound, ounce, Fahrenheit, centigrade, thermometer, freezing, boiling, balance, weigh, liquid, water, capacity, pint, quart, galion, cup, degree...	-Implement methods and provide resources as suggested above.

CURRICULUM EXPERIENCES FOR TEACHING/LEARNING MATHEMATICS—GRADE 9

(Subject) CONCEPTS	PERFORMANCE OUTCOMES	CHILDREN'S ACTIVITIES	TEACHING METHODS/RESOURCES
Geometry has specific vocabulary		-Using vocabulary as an integral part of learning: shapes, circle, square, triangle, rectangle, solid, cube, sphere, cylinder, cone, block, flat curve, round, model, build, construct, geometry, relation, operations, problem, solve, match...	-Implement methods and provide resources as suggested previously in "vocabulary" learning.

HOW DOES PRE-SCHOOL MATHEMATICS CORRELATE WITH
THE TOTAL PRE-SCHOOL CURRICULUM?

The major streams of the pre-school curriculum are flavored with mathematics. Mathematics in the pre-school correlates with: (1) the expressive arts--drawing, painting, dancing, singing; (2) the language arts--reading, listening, oral communication and written communication; (3) the social studies--family, geography, history, society and communicty; and (4) science--plants, animals and chemicals. Mathematics is an exact, yet abstract, science (a square will always have four equal sides and the square root of a negative number is imaginary) which is given substance by the aforementioned subject areas, on the one hand, while on the other hand, it contributes to the meaningfulness of the other subject areas.

In the expressive arts, for example, a song differs from the sentences it is comprised of because the syllables and/or words of the sentence are assigned symbols with specific values. A quarter note is worth one count in a four-four time signature, which means one fourth ($\frac{1}{4}$) of a whole number (fraction). When learning a particular dance or movement, one has to know and recognize number properties in order to move to a step cadence. For painting, volume of mixtures is necessary; the size of the paper, or picture is helpful; and numerous other activities require the use of mathematics as children engage in creative or expressive arts. Also, art includes various forms, figures and designs akin to shapes and solids.

There is a correlation between the language arts and mathematics as children experience activities in reading numerals, number concepts, and worded problems; in listening and speaking activities, the children are experiencing number concepts of quality in pitch and volume of sound; and in literature, through poems, stories, and show-and-tell experience, the children come in contact with mathematics; like, how many? what size? what distance? and so forth.

Science concepts and mathematics operations and concepts are closely correlated. The concepts of measurement, exactness, time, space and weight are appropriate for both subject areas.

The social studies areas of family, community, history, society, culture, and geography incorporate the area of mathematics as these topics are studied: weather, distance, population; the number of states, islands, lakes; and rotation and revolution.

This correlation as pinpointed here helps to reinforce the need for mathematics to be a separate, hands-on and manipulative course in the pre-school curriculum.

Teachable Moments for Purposeful Counting

1. When children are preparing for snack time, they are asked to count the napkins, individual cups of juice, crackers, and chairs that have to be set out for each child in the group.

2. When children collect books that they have been using during the period, they are asked to count the total number.

3. When boxes of crayon are collected after children have used them, the children are asked to count them.

4. When the teacher has collected money from the children for a gift, the class counts the money together.

5. When pencils are distributed or returned, they are counted by the group.

6. As the teacher counts out the number of sheets of paper the children need in order to do their work, the class counts them with the teacher.

7. When attendance is taken, the teacher asks the children to count the number of children who are absent.

Teachable Moments for Purposeful Measuring

1. Children measure their own height.

2. Children measure the growth of a plant.

3. Children measure their own shoe size.

4. Children measure the length of their fingers and compare them to their peers.

5. Children measure the height of the bookshelf.

6. Children measure the height of a block structure they have made.

232

7. Children measure their playhouse area.

Teachable Moments for Purposeful Weighing

1. Children can balance weights on a scale--heavy and light.

2. Children can weigh heavy articles, metal, nails, and other heavy metal objects.

3. Children can weigh light articles that are familiar to them.

4. Children can weigh sand, sugar, salt, or flour in small plastic packages.

5. Children can weigh something they brought to school, i.e., their lunch, a toy case, or a book.

6. Children can weigh packages of grocery objects, such as jello, cereal, or rice.

7. Children can weigh beans before they are cooked and afterwards to compare differences in weight.

8. Children can weigh packages that the teacher has prepared to mail to someone as a gift. Reasons for the post office having to charge by the ounce and pounds may be discussed at this point.

Teachable Moments for Purposeful Calculating

1. Children can add three more places at the table to accommodate three more children.

2. Children can count the number of people who need cookies and have not been served.

3. Children can decide how many paint brushes are needed for five cans of paint and place them where they belong.

4. Children can decide how many sponges are needed to be used by five children.

5. Children can decide if a child who has 23 pieces of candy has enough for 25 children; they can be asked if 23 is more or less than 25.

WHAT REFERENCES ARE HELPFUL TO THE PRE-SCHOOL MATHEMATICS CURRICULUM THAT SET STANDARDS FOR NUMBER-NUMERATIONS, MEASUREMENTS, AND GEOMETRY?

Standards are set through conversion tables that are integral parts of the subject area of mathematics. In the Pre-School Mathematics Curriculum, "Conversion Tables" should not be taught as an approach to learning mathematics. The information given from these tables should be used by the caregivers to direct the mathematical experiences in a natural way for the child. There are many "primary" versions of conversion tables that are available to the pre-school caregiver (The Instructor Aids). These tables/charts may be displayed in the child's environment for reinforcement referrals by the caregivers.

Some "examples" of using the conversion tables (standards) in natural learning approaches are:

o   Counting the number of days in a week, a month, and a year in accord to birthdays of children, holidays, seasons, and so forth.

o   Noting that weights and measures are used in daily living through weighing and measuring the children and making comparisons, through talking about the weather and the temperature, through playing "store" and using various containers for groceries--milk cartons, empty egg cartons, dried beans, rice, and cereal, by the pound, etc.

o   Using the clock daily in the child's play by making the child aware of the time, tell the time and show the time.

o   Showing and telling about trips and the mileage traveled, the distances from home to school and other places in the community and neighborhood.

o   Involving children in activities where they exchange money for goods and services; put together different coins to make a certain sum; and make change when a purchase is made.

o   Visiting the supermarket, clothing stores, and other places to experience mathematical concepts.

234

For the purpose of teaching pre-school mathematics, the following conversion scales are offered to assist the caregiver and the child as primary references. The caregiver may expand this information by utilizing other reference materials for additional and more precise conversion tables.

NUMERATION

Arabic	Roman
1	I
2	II
3	III
4	IV
5	V
6	VI
7	VII
8	VIII
9	IX
10	X
20	XX
30	XXX
40	XL
50	L
100	C
500	D
1000	M

TIME

60 seconds	=	1 minute
60 minutes	=	1 hour
24 hours	=	1 day
7 days	=	1 week
28-31 days	=	1 month
12 months	=	1 year
365 days	=	1 year
366 days	=	1 leap year

MONEY

1 penny	=	1 cent
5 pennies	=	5 cents (nickel)
10 pennies	=	10 cents (dime)
25 pennies	=	25 cents (quarter)
50 pennies	=	50 cents (½ dollar)
100 pennies	=	1 dollar

cent (¢)   dollar ($)

LINEAR MEASURE

1 mil	=	0.00 inch	(0.0254 millimeter)
1 inch	=	1,000 mils	(2.54 centimeters)
12 inches	=	1 foot	(0.3048 meter)
3 feet	=	1 yard	(0.9144 meter)
5½ yards	=	1 rod	(5.029 meters)
16½ feet	=	1 rod	(5.029 meters)
40 rods	=	1 furlong	(201.168 meters)
8 furlongs	=	1 mile	(1.6093 kilometers)
1,760 yards	=	1 mile	(1.6093 kilometers)
5,280 feet	=	1 mile	(1.6093 kilometers)
3 miles	=	1 league	(4.83 kilometers)

SQUARE MEASURE

1 square inch			(6.452 sq. centimeters)
144 square inches	=	1 sq. foot	(929.03 sq. centimeters)
9 square feet	=	1 sq. yard	(0.8361 sq. meter)
30½ square yards	=	1 sq. rod	(25.292 sq. meters)
160 square rods	=	1 acre	(0.4047 hectare)
4,840 sq. yards	=	1 acre	(0.4047 hectare)
43,560 sq. feet	=	1 acre	(0.4047 hectare)
640 acres	=	1 sq. mile	(2.590 sq. kilometers)

CUBIC MEASURE

1 cubic inch		(16.387 cu. centimeters)
1,728 cubic inches	=	(0.0283 cubic meter)
27 cubic feet	=	(0.7646 cubic meter)
16 cubic feet	=	(0.453 cubic meter)
128 cubic feet	=	(3.625 cubic meters)
8 cord feet	=	(3.625 cubic meters)

LIQUID MEASURE		Standard		Metric
1 teaspoon (tsp.)	=	1/6 ounce (oz.)	=	4.9 milligrams
1 tablespoon (tbsp.)	=	1/2 ounce	=	14.8 milligrams
1 cup	=	8 ounces	=	2.25 deciliters
1 pint	=	16 ounces	=	4.5 deciliters
4 1/3 cups	=	35 1/6 ounces	=	1 liter (10 deciliters)
1 gill	=	4 fluid ounces	=	0.1183 liter
4 gills	=	1 pint	=	0.4732 liter
2 pints	=	1 quart	=	0.9464 liter
4 quarts	=	1 gallon	=	3.7854 liter

DRY MEASURE				
1 pint	=	16 ounces (oz.)	=	0.5506 liter
2 pints	=	1 quart (qt.)	=	1.1012 liters
8 quarts	=	1 peck (pk.)	=	8.8098 liters
4 pecks	=	1 bushel (bu.)	=	35.23900 liters

METRIC SYSTEM

(Measurement Based on the Decimal System)

Basic Unit of Measure

METER   (linear measurement--inches, feet, yards)

GRAM   (weight--ounces, pounds)

LITER   (liquid volume--pints, quarts, gallons)

DEGREE CELSIUS (temperature--Fahrenheit)

A meter is longer than a yard (about 3-1/3 inches. It takes about 28-1/3 grams to make an ounce. A liter is a bit smaller than a quart.

Metric Units

Prefixes:	Deci (.1) 1/10 Centi (.01) 1/100
	Milli (.001) 1/1000 Deka (10 times)
	Hecto (100 times) Kilo (1,000 times)
Meters:	1 meter = 10 decimeter, 100 centimeters,
	1000 millimeters
	10 meters = 1 dekameter
	100 meters = 1 hectometer
	1000 meters = 1 kilometer

WHAT IS THE EXTENT OF USING REFERENCES IN THE PRE-SCHOOL MATHEMATICS CURRICULUM FOR THE CAREGIVERS AND THE CHILD?

Both caregiver and child references in the form of books, audio-visuals, program systems, periodicals, and numerous others are needed and used widely in the implementation of the pre-school mathematics curriculum. Since mathematics learning depends upon an enriched environment of materials for manipulation, the caregiver and the child must have more than adequate sources for obtaining, maintaining, and producing instructional and learning tools. Using references then is vital to curriculum implementation.

The curriculum guide format includes "REFERENCES" as a component area for providing a comprehensive curriculum in pre-school mathematics. This area will change and grow tremendously and will, therefore, need constant and regular updating and upgrading.

The references listed here, however, are books and materials to be used by the caregivers. The component on "Resources" in this chapter provides references for the child. (See the Curriculum Charts under the heading "Teaching Methods/Resources).

ACTIVITIES FOR STUDY AND DISCUSSION

Your own approach to teaching pre-school mathematics will be inherent in not only what you learn from this chapter, but will include other learning experiences. Complete the following exercises in an effort to strengthen your skills, knowledges, and teaching competencies in mathematics.

1. Discuss the relevance of teaching pre-school mathematics as a separate subject. Use as much research and references as possible in your presentation.

2. List goals and objectives of teaching pre-school mathematics.

3. Identify teaching areas within each of the sub-topic areas of mathematics and state teaching/learning concepts.

4. Take one of the sub-topic areas of mathematics and plan a teaching unit and/or lesson plan and demonstrate to peers or use in a classroom with children.

5. Research Piaget's and other theorists' conceptualizations on mathematics readiness stages and implications for teaching.

6. Construct mathematics learning centers and demonstrate their usages.

7. Relate personal likes and dislikes for mathematics as a subject area and discuss what this means to enhancing and/or hindering the teaching/learning process.

REFERENCES

Andrews, F.E., **Numbers Please.** Boston: Little, Brown, and Co., 1961.

Bell, Max S., Karen C. Fuson, and R. A. Lesh, **Algebraic and Arithmetic Structures: A Concrete Approach for Elementary School Teachers.** New York: The Free Press, 1976.

Benbrook, Joyce, C. Forester and James F. Shea, **Working With Numbers.** Austin, Texas: Steck-Vaughn Company, 1973.

Broman, Betty L., **The Early Years in Childhood Education.** Chicago: Rand McNally College Publishing Company, 1978.

Bureau of Curriculum Development-Board of Education, **Pre-Kindergarten and Kindergarten Curriculum Guide.** Brooklyn, New York: Board of Education of the City of New York, 1970.

Corle, Clyde G., **Skills Games for Mathematics.** Dansville, New York: The Instructor Publications, Inc., 1968.

Day, Barbara, **Early Childhood Education: Creative Learning Activities** (Second Edition). New York: Macmillan Publishing Co., Inc., 1983.

Deans, Edwina, McMun and Rathenia M. Jackson, **New Steps in Mathematics.** New York: American Book Company, 1969.

DeVaries, Rheta and Constance Kamil, **Piaget, Children, and Numbers.** Washington, D.C.: The National Association for the Education of Young Children, 1976.

DeVault, M. Vere, Rober Osborn and Beverly Truehardt, **Discovering Mathematics.** Columbus, Ohio: Merrill Books, Inc., 1965.

Dumas, Enoch and E.W. Schmike, **Mathematics Activities for Child Involvement.** Boston: Allyn and Bacon, Inc., 1977.

Eliason, Claudia F. and Loa T. Jenkins, **A Practical Guide to Early Childhood Curriculum**. St. Louis: C.V. Mosby Company, 1977.

Hendrick, Joanne, **Total Learning: Curriculum for the Young Child** (Second Edition). Columbus: Merrill Publishing Co., 1986.

Hildebrand, Verna, **Introduction to Early Childhood Education** (Fourth Edition). New York: Macmillan Publishing Co., Inc., 1986.

Howard, Charles F. and Enoch Dumas, **Basic Procedures in Teaching Arithmetic**. Boston: D.C. Heath and Company, 1963.

Instructor (The) Magazine, Arithmetic Vocabulary Charts for Primary Grades, Modern Mathematics Vocabulary Charts for Primary Grades, and Measurement Concept Charts for Primary Grades, (designed by Cynthia Amrine); and The Metric System. Dansville, New York: The Instructor Publications, Inc., 1972.

Kamii, Constance, **Number in Preschool and Kindergarten**. Washington, D.C.: The National Association for the Education of Young Children, 1982.

Kennedy, Leonard, **Guiding Children to Mathematical Discovery**. Belmont, Ca.: Wadsworth Publishing Company, Inc., 1977.

Lorton, Mary Baratta, **Mathematics Their Way**. Manto Park, California: Addison-Wesley Publishing Company, 1976.

Marglin, Edythe, **Young Children: Their Curriculum and Learning Processes**. New York: Macmillan Publishing Company, 1976.

McDonald, Blanche, Leslie Nelson and Ronald L. Brown, **Methods That Teach**. Dubuque, Iowa: Wm. C. Brown Publishing Company, 1972.

Robinson, Helen F., and Syndney L. Schwartz, **Learning At An Early Age**. (Volume Two), Englewood Cliffs, New Jersey: Prentice-Hall, Inc., 1972.

Schickedanz, Judith A., Mary E. York, Ida Santos Stewart, and Doris White, **Strategies for Teaching Young Children** (Second Edition). Englewood Cliffs, New Jersey: Prentice-Hall, Inc., 1983.

Seefeldt, Carol, **A Curriculum for Child Care Centers.** Columbus, Ohio: Merrill Publishing Company, 1974.

Spodek, Bernard, **Teaching in the Early Years.** Englewood Cliffs, New Jersey: Prentice-Hall, Inc., 1978.

Trencher, Barbara R., **Child's Play: An Activities and Materials Handbook.** Atlanta: Humanistics Limited, 1976.

Vance, Barbara, **Teaching the Pre-Kindergarten Child: Instructional Design and Curriculum.** Monterey, California: Brooks/Cole Publishing Company, 1973.

Wortham, Sue C., **Organizing Instruction in Early Childhood: A Handbook of Assessment and Activities.** Boston: Allyn and Bacon, Inc., 1984.

Zaslavsky, C., **Preparing Young Children for Math: A Book of Games.** New York: Schocken Books, 1981.

CHAPTER EIGHT

EXPERIENCES IN SCIENCE

LIVING THINGS, ASTRONOMY, EARTH, MATTER AND ENERGY,
CHEMISTRY

CHAPTER 8

EXPERIENCES IN SCIENCE

- WHY IS SCIENCE AN IMPORTANT PART OF THE PRE-SCHOOL CURRICULUM?: AN INTRODUCTION

- WHAT ARE THE GOALS AND OBJECTIVES FOR TEACHING SCIENCE?

- WHAT ARE MAJOR SUB-AREAS IN THE SCIENCE CURRICULUM?

- WHAT ARE THE PROVISIONS FOR HAVING AN EFFECTIVE SCIENCE CURRICULUM IN THE PRE-SCHOOL?

- WHAT APPROACHES TO USE TO EXPAND/EXTEND CURRICULUM THEORY INTO TEACHING/LEARNING APPLICATIONS FOR EXPERIENCES IN SCIENCE?

- HOW DOES SCIENCE CORRELATE WITH THE TOTAL PRE-SCHOOL CURRICULUM?

- ACTIVITIES FOR STUDY AND DISCUSSION

- REFERENCES

WHY IS SCIENCE AN IMPORTANT PART OF THE PRE-SCHOOL CURRICULUM?: AN INTRODUCTION

As young children grow and develop, physically, mentally, emotionally, and socially, learning occurs as the results of the interactions between the individuals and the world around them. All of the personalities, behaviors, objects, and events within the child's environment lay the foundation for "finding out" and "understanding" concepts and facts about nature and the interaction between matter. The subject area of the pre-school curriculum that provides the basis for acquiring knowledges, skills, and attitudes to explain the operations and functions of animate and inanimate aspects of the physical world is science.

From the point of conception, the human being begins to learn about the surroundings based on the human anatomy. At birth the infant's natural senses are activated to respond to the environment. The baby is eager to learn or find out about the happenings in the world around him/her. This exploration is the key to building the "psycho-motor" or "sensori-motor" stage of development. All of the perceptions formed out of this curiosity to gain concepts about the physical world are embedded in the young child's natural or innate knowledge. Science grows out of observations that are processed through scientific operations, hypotheses, experiments, inventions, discoveries, discussions, questions, and measurements of outcomes (Croft and Hess, 1974).

The caregiver, then, should motivate, stimulate, and capitalize on the young child's natural response or curiosity to his/her environment by providing many deliberately planned experiences in science. Moreover, if the pre-school curriculum is to remain true to its purpose of generating activity-sorts for every category of life's experiences, then, there must be a subject area to primarily consist of activities and experiences which are designed and planned to help develop critical thinking through observations, analyses, and many direct, first-hand involvements.

Including science as an important part of the pre-school curriculum insures a holistic approach to teaching and learning. Scientific study encourages young children to find out for themselves, rather than merely repeating events as revealed by others. Experiences in science that are planned as an integral part of the curriculum help the child to learn more in-depth knowledge from the process. This does not, however, alleviate the need and inclusion of "incidental" experiences in science. The latter can be a good indicator for the caregiver to gear experiences and activities in science to the interest and maturation of the young children. The pre-school curriculum includes science as the subject area which satisfies the requirement in the growth, development, and learning process for helping children to satisfy their curiosity and to comprehend the necessity of, and for, "order" and "relationships" within the environment (Croft and Hess, 1974).

Croft and Hess (1974) further substantiated science as a vital part of the pre-school curriculum because scientific operations (as directed by the caregiver) help the young child to inquire and develop skills to investigate and note independently: (1) Causal relationships--what makes/made something happen?; and (2) Predictability of results--what will happen if certain action is taken?

Other pre-school educators as specified in the "references" as well as child development theorists like Piaget, Bruner, Gagne, etc., provide evidences for including and keeping science as an integral part of the pre-school curriculum. This serves as the means for exercising "scientific operations" in the psycho-motor, cognitive, and affective domains. The teaching/learning process should provide experiences in science that will ensure the caregivers that the learners will be guided to perform in a thorough and systematic manner.

WHAT ARE THE GOALS AND OBJECTIVES FOR TEACHING SCIENCE?

Teaching science to pre-schoolers is a means for capitalizing on their curiosities by providing enriching, deliberately planned experiences. The major goal for teaching science is to help children develop thorough, critical, and systematic thinking through observations, inquiries, experiments, analyses and direct, first-hand experiences. Other goals for teaching science are: (1) to help children gain knowledge about the world around us; (2) to help children to be able to interpret the environment in reference to properties of objects and basic "laws" on which science is based; (3) to help children develop an interest and an appreciation for the animate and inanimate aspects of the physical world; (4) to help children become knowledgeable and skillful in understanding and portraying significant roles and responsibilities in the world around us; and (5) to help children acquire and use vocabulary germane to scientific thinking and performance.

Objectives for teaching science to young children are more specifically related to sub-topic areas of the broad topic of science. For teaching science in relation to physics and chemistry (matter and energy), some objectives are: (1) to develop an awareness of the properties and uses of air; (2) to become aware of the properties and uses of water; (3) to understand and become familiar with the properties and functions of light, heat, and fire; (4) to develop an awareness of sound and how it is used and produced; and (5) to become familiar with the use and operation of machinery. For teaching science in relation to biology (living things) some objectives are: (1) to become aware of the characteristics of plants and animals; (2) to understand the relationship of living things to one another; (3) to understand the needs and capabilities of plants and animals; and (4) to develop skills to investigate and understand the function of man as a living thing within the environment. For teaching science in relation to earth science and astronomy, some objectives are: (1) to become aware of the earth's constituents and habitants; (2) to understand the composition and function of the universe; (3) to develop knowledge and awareness of the different seasons; (4) to become aware of various atmospheric conditions and their cause and effect; and (5) to develop an appreciation and understanding of the world in reference to ecological principles. Objectives must be planned and designed by caregivers to include a broad range of scientific topics. Included in this range are (1) color; (2) shape; (3) texture; (4) odor; (5) position; (6) quantity; (7) size; and many others.

WHAT ARE MAJOR SUB-AREAS IN THE PRE-SCHOOL SCIENCE CURRICULUM?

There are three major sub-areas to the curriculum area of science. The pre-school science curriculum includes: (1) Living Things (biology)--which deals with the plants, animals, man (people), insects, bacteria, and other aspects of organisms, (2) Astronomy and Earth Science--which deals with the earth, the atmosphere (sky, weather, etc.), the environment, geology, seasons, and the universe (planets, stars, gravity, sun, moon, etc.), (3) Physics and Chemistry (matter and energy--which deals with air, water, fire, sound, magnetism, odor, quantity and so forth.

Caregivers are encouraged to be very resourceful in utilizing a wide array of science experiences in each of the sub-areas. The sub-topics might appear to be advanced subject areas, i.e., biology, physics, and so forth, however, the activities must be selected and designed to include concepts and mental/physical operations which young children are capable of understanding and performing. Examples of such experiences are presented in the next section of this chapter. The sub-area information is to benefit the caregivers in planning, developing and implementing science experiences. The activities/experiences herewith provided for becoming competent in knowing and imparting pre-school curriculum in the area of science, will be presented as "topics for teaching and learning."

WHAT ARE THE PROVISIONS FOR HAVING AN EFFECTIVE SCIENCE CURRICULUM IN THE PRE-SCHOOL?

An effective pre-school science curriculum must provide a holistic approach to teaching and learning for both the caregiver and the young child. Sequence and order are relevant factors to planning and implementing the science curriculum. Teaching science to pre-schoolers must be done spontaneously and deliberately by the caregiver. The spontaneous teaching during the daily routine at school or at home utilizes the resources at hand to provide learning experiences for young children. The leaf that the child finds and has questions about; or the curiosity built within the child when it thunders or lightning flashes; the rocks or sea shells collected by the child on a trip; or many other incidental objects or topics for discussion can be the basis for caregivers to provide information and exploration for gaining scientific knowledges, skills and attitudes. Yet this strategy for teaching science does not eliminate the teaching of science by planning deliberate activities for experimentation. The caregiver must be cognizant of the ways children learn science and provide directions and assistance for developing skills in scientific learnings concerning the world around them.

Young children learn through many scientific operations. The caregiver must make sure that these scientific operations (ways and means) are coupled with activities and experiences that are geared to the interest and maturity of the pre-schoolers. They (scientific operations) must be strategized to help the young children to find answers for themselves from direct, first-hand involvement. Correct names and terms should be used in order to build and increase the pre-schoolers' vocabulary. Many opportunities must be provided (by incident and planning) to encourage seeing, feeling, smelling, touching, listening, and tasting as key techniques for examining many different objects and materials. These sensori-motor experiences are dire to the facilitation of the scientific operations which are germane to "children's ways of learning science," cognitively.

Some scientific operations utilized by children for learning science are: (1) Observation--seeing animate and inanimate objects and actions in the environment stimulates interest and arouses curiosities in children for learning; (2) Exploration--handling and experimenting with objects and things to find out what will happen to motivate learning in children; (3) Invention--gathering new concepts beyond preconceptions based on exploring helps children to interpret observations which help them to learn; (4) Discovery--providing activities that require a child's application for a concept enhances the children's learning; (5) Discussion--talking among teacher and children clarifies concepts and increases understanding which is an important part of the learning process for children; and (6) Inquiry--asking questions of caregiver and of children by each other affects the children's work, skills, and attitudes. The kinds of questions asked, the way the questions are asked, and the reason behind asking questions can determine the usefulness of the answers given and/or found out for satisfying the children's curiosity for learning.

WHAT APPROACHES TO USE TO EXPAND/EXTEND CURRICULUM THEORY INTO TEACHING/LEARNING APPLICATIONS FOR EXPERIENCES IN SCIENCE?

Pre-school curriculum and teaching entails three major components:

- ° Learning Theories (possible ways child learn various subjects)

- ° Theories of Instruction (best ways to teach children)

- ° Teaching/Learning Process (rationale, purpose, strategies, methods, techniques, assessment, and resources)

A "curriculum model" in science is herewith provided to enhance the teaching/learning process in the pre-school. Approaches to expand/ extend curriculum theory into practical application are discussed in Chapter Four of the text. In the event that study and/or review is needed, the reader is directed to refer to Chapter Four for specific information, principally about process. The following charts are provided to show "curriculum experiences for teaching/learning science" in the pre-school.

CURRICULUM EXPERIENCES FOR TEACHING/LEARNING SCIENCE-CHART 10

(Subject) CONCEPTS	PERFORMANCE OUTCOMES	CHILDREN'S ACTIVITIES	TEACHING METHODS/RESOURCES
LIVING THINGS (Biology) - Plants, Animals, People, Insects, Bacteria	Gained awareness of the character- istics of living things to help interpret the environment, think critically, explore indepen- dently, increase vocabulary, and satisfy curiosity	-Classifying pictures of living and non-living things -Observing different liv- ing things -Discussing the behavior of living things	-Post a variety of meaning- ful science pictures. -Provide a science corner where many opportunities are available to touch, see, smell, feel, and use many different materials and objects. -Provide ample equipment, materials and supplies (bulletin board, pictures, table, books, films, film- strips).
Living things grow bigger			
Living things can move			
Living things can feel			
Living things can breathe			
Living things need air			
Living things need food			
Living things need water			
Living things reproduce			
Living things die			
Living things are organisms			
Plants are living things	Described care and elements of plants --leaves, stem, roots, flower, watering, light, etc.	-Planting seeds in class -Planting seeds in bed of soil in outdoors -Watching seeds grow -Taking a trip or walk to observe plant life -Bringing different plants to class to watch them	-Provide accessory materials: ½ pint empty milk containers, plastic & glass bowls, tin plates (pie pans), seeds, small plants, take trip to plant nursery, farm, etc.).
Plants grow from seeds			
Plants are used for food			
Plants give us food			

249

CURRICULUM EXPERIENCES FOR TEACHING/LEARNING SCIENCE-CHART 10

(Subject) CONCEPTS	PERFORMANCE OUTCOMES	CHILDREN'S ACTIVITIES	TEACHING METHODS/RESOURCES
Plants need food, water and air		grow and to care for them --water, fertilize, put in sunlight, re-pot, etc. and show those that give us food (carrots, peas, etc.)	-Provide resources and materials: classroom or home garden, small boxes to cover plant, living animal (fish, frog, gerbil, rabbit, etc.), aquarium, cages, large box, bowl, etc.).
Plants need care from people			
Some plants die in winter and when not properly cared for		-Watching plants, discuss and note changes in color of leaves, sizes of the plant, etc., in different seasons of the year	
Plants change in different seasons		-Observing and discussing pictures of poisonous plants and/or identifying them in the environment	
Plants give off oxygen			
Plants give us beauty		-Performing experiments with plants to show that they need sunlight--cover one or place in dark place and notice growth	
Some plants can grow in the dark			
Plants need sun light		-Sprouting vegetables in class	
There are different kinds of plants		-Feeding the classroom pet and seeing what food it prefers	
Some plants grow in water			
Some plants grow on land		-Observing falling leaves in autumn	
Flowers are plants		-Displaying leaves collected	
Some trees lose their leaves in winter		-Observing pictures of trees during different seasons	

CURRICULUM EXPERIENCES FOR TEACHING/LEARNING SCIENCE-CHART 10

(Subject) CONCEPTS	PERFORMANCE OUTCOMES	CHILDREN'S ACTIVITIES	TEACHING METHODS/RESOURCES
Animals are living things	Described care and elements of animals --kinds, characteristics, foods, use, etc.	-Taking field trips to zoo, jungle, country, etc.	-Provide live animals in good health for observation and care.
There are different kinds of animals		-Reading and listening to stories about animals.	
Animals need care		-Listening to records about different animals.	-Dramatize animal movement and have children imitate them.
Animals eat food		-Dramatizing proper care for animals	
Animals give us food		-Seeing films and filmstrips about different animals	-Show pictures of different animals.
Animals need air and water		-Collecting pictures of homes for different animals (pets, birds, lizzards, snakes, bees, butterflies, etc.).	-Show pictures of different meats for eating and the animals from which it comes.
Some animals work for us			
Some animals need little care		-Observing parent animals and their babies	
Animals live in different homes		-Digging in the earth (one foot) to see what animals are there (worms, insects, etc.).	-Provide resources--materials, trips, people, like films, pictures, filmstrips, records, neighborhood walks, Veterinarian, take a neighborhood walk and have children look for different animals.
Female animals have offsprings (babies)			
Some animals sleep during winter		-Identifying names of adult animals and baby animals	
Some animals have fur and some have hair			
Some animals get milk from their mothers			
Animals look like their kind			
Animals are used for games and sports			

251

CURRICULUM EXPERIENCES FOR TEACHING/LEARNING SCIENCE-CHART 10

(Subject) CONCEPTS	PERFORMANCE OUTCOMES	CHILDREN'S ACTIVITIES	TEACHING METHODS/RESOURCES
People are living things People are animals People use plants and animals for food People use plants and animals for clothing People use animals for pets People get oxygen from plants People help plants to grow People are boys-girls, men-women People need shelter (homes) People need medical care Some women have babies Babies are made by both men and women	Gained awareness of the characteristics and behaviors of human beings; and understood the concept of people belonging to the animal group (Kingdom)	-Observing people and discuss behaviors -Discussing how people and animals are alike and different -Seeing pictures, films, filmstrips about how people care for plants and animals -Observing pictures of basic food groups and identifying foods yielded by plants and by animals -Dramatizing home and family events -Discussing health, nutrition, safety, and hygiene	-Provide resources like: films, filmstrips, pictures, Nutritionist, Dietician, visit doctor's office, police station, hospitals.
Insects are living things Insects are helpful to people Insects compete with men for their food	Described elements of insects and their worth and harm	-Seeing pictures of insects -Searching the environment to find insects (ants, roaches, termites, bedbugs, crickets, hornets, beetles, mosquitoes, moths, grasshoppers, butterflies, flies, waterbugs, fleas, etc.)	-Provide resources like: pictures, nature walks, jars with lids, boxes, cotton, films and filmstrips, and a net.

(Subject) CONCEPTS	PERFORMANCE OUTCOMES	CHILDREN'S ACTIVITIES	TEACHING METHODS/RESOURCES
Some insects are pests to man There are many kinds of insects Insects live in many places Insects have six legs Insects are cold-blooded Insects can be friends and/or enemies to other insects, animals and plants		-Discussing functions of insects in reference to friends and enemies to man, plants and animals	
Bacteria are living things Bacteria are one-celled organisms Bacteria cannot be seen with the naked eye Some bacteria are mostly plants Bacteria are not always identified as plants or animals Most kinds of bacteria cannot make their food	Described elements of bacteria and how it plays a part in the environment.	-Discussing how animals waste is used for fertilization -Making buttermilk and butter -Observing milk on ice or in refrigerator and discuss how it keeps from spoiling -Observing milk that has not been refrigerated and discuss its spoilage (sour) -Observing mildew on bread, cheese, etc. -Making wine with yeast	-Show pictures of different kinds of bacteria. -Display plants (root crops: carrots, beets, fruits, etc.) and demonstrate the "decay" process. -Provide resources like: bread, a microscope, a bacteriologist, pictures, milk, plants, and so forth.

CURRICULUM EXPERIENCES FOR TEACHING/LEARNING SCIENCE-CHART 10

(Subject) CONCEPTS	PERFORMANCE OUTCOMES	CHILDREN'S ACTIVITIES	TEACHING METHODS/RESOURCES
There are four kinds of bacteria		-Discussing ways of pre-serving liquids, food, etc. (freezing, boiling, smoking, curing, etc.)	
Bacteria grow and multiply			
Bacteria move about in liquid			
Bacteria cause dis-ease in plants, animals, and people			
Some bacteria are called parasites			
Most bacteria live on the bodies of dead plants and animals			
Some bacteria are harmless and very useful to people			
Bacteria cause decay			
Bacteria cause fermentation			
Bacteria can be harmful			
Bacteria can be killed by methods used by people			
MATTER AND ENERGY (Physics and Chem-istry) Air (Wind),			-Use the environment and materials to explore and discuss.

CURRICULUM EXPERIENCES FOR TEACHING/LEARNING SCIENCE-CHART 10

(Subject) CONCEPTS	PERFORMANCE OUTCOMES	CHILDREN'S ACTIVITIES	TEACHING METHODS/RESOURCES
Water, Fire (light and heat), Sound, Chemicals, Temperature	Gained an awareness and understanding of matter and energy with specific competency level in the function of air and water.	-Using a straw and bowl of water to show that air is real--blow through straw into the bowl of water to show that air is mixed with water	-Perform experiments and demonstrations on concepts to show cause-effect relationships.
Air has pressure		-Using water to freeze in the refrigerator and make ice to show that a liquid can be made into a solid	-Prepare the environment to include many resources: natural surroundings, plants, small animals, containers of all shapes and sizes, soil samples, charts, calendars, telescope, thermometer, flashlight, sterno burner, hot plate, kettle, globe, maps, Meterologist, places for field trips, aquarium, balloon, straws, tissue paper, piece of water hose, etc.)
Air is all around us			
Air fills empty spaces			
Air can make things move			
Air can make sounds		-Setting up a weather station to observe and record information about weather--using pictures to show and discuss various types of weather	
Air can make us cold			
Air cannot be seen			
Air holds moisture		-Collecting samples of soil	
Air is a mixture of gases		-Visiting air and space museums	
Air is oxygen		-Visiting nature center	
Animals need oxygen		-Using shadows to show light not being able to go around or through an object	

255

CURRICULUM EXPERIENCES FOR TEACHING/LEARNING SCIENCE-CHART 10

(Subject) CONCEPTS	PERFORMANCE OUTCOMES	CHILDREN'S ACTIVITIES	TEACHING METHODS/RESOURCES
Water can move Water is wet Water can change forms (to ice, vapor) Rain is water Water is made of chemical elements (hydrogen and oxygen) Water can be seen Water is colorless, odorless, and tasteless Water can be mixed with chemicals that reduce smell, taste, and color other than hydrogen and oxygen) Plants need water Animals need water		-Using objects that will float and some that will not in a container of water to show force pressure	-Provide a picture file to use during discussions. -Use the rainbow to teach the concept of bent or broken light--drop duco cement into a pan of water and see it spread into a thin, rainbow-colored sheet, slide a piece of black cardboard under the sheet and lift it to see the rainbow colors.
Fire gives light Fire gives heat Fire needs air to burn Fire can be helpful Fire can be dangerous	Gained skills and abilities to use fire constructively in the environment	-Observing pictures, films and filmstrips about fire -Discussing health and safety principles, rules, and techniques -Doing experiments to see how fire functions	-Show ways fire can be used in a helpful manner, i.e., cooking, heating, welding; show ways it can be dangerous by being careless. -Demonstrate starting fires and stopping (putting out) fires (use candles, sterno burners, hot plates, etc.)

CURRICULUM EXPERIENCES FOR TEACHING/LEARNING SCIENCE - CHART 10

(Subject) CONCEPTS	PERFORMANCE OUTCOMES	CHILDREN'S ACTIVITIES	TEACHING METHODS/RESOURCES
Matter is material Matter cannot be destroyed Matter changes from one form to another	Gained an awareness of matter and its functions and changes	-Setting up a weather station -Observing and recording data weather and other earth facts -Doing anti-pollution project (clean up school yard, etc.) -Visiting nature center, air and space museum	
Sound makes music Sound makes noise Sounds help people and animals Sounds are different Sound travels Machines make sounds People make sounds Animals make sounds	Gained an awareness and understanding of sound and its properties	-Listening and describing sounds they hear -Turning back to class and identifying voices of peers -Using glasses (empty, half-full, etc.) to make sounds -Discussing unpleasant sounds (too many people talking at the same time, loud music, etc.)	-Tape record sounds of various objects-actions (siren, traffic, animals, electric fans, rain, footsteps, etc.) to be used in lesson. -Provide materials and resources like, records, tapes, tape recorders, record player, pictures, people to study voices, singers, actors, and so forth.
There are many machines Machines do work for us Some machines use chemicals Some machines use electricity	Gained sensory experiences in using and identifying machines and their functions and sources of energy	-Exploring parts of machines -Observing demonstrations on using machines -Using machines to accomplish tasks by the caregiver -Seeing pictures of different machines and matching functions of each	-Display simple machines like can openers, blenders, knives, etc. in the classroom. -Display pictures of machines and people at work on bulletin boards.

CURRICULUM EXPERIENCES FOR TEACHING/LEARNING SCIENCE-CHART 10

(Subject) CONCEPTS	PERFORMANCE OUTCOMES	CHILDREN'S ACTIVITIES	TEACHING METHODS/RESOURCES
Some machines use the wind Machines make work easier Energy is the capacity for doing work People use energy Energy should be used properly Food provides energy for people			-Display food groups and discuss nutrition and energy sources. -Provide resources--can openers, blenders, knives, empty cans, boxes, cartons, filmstrips, and slides
The sky is full of planets The moon is in the sky The sun is in the sky The stars are in the sky The moon gives light The sun gives light and heat Different colors are seen in the sky Clouds are in the sky Clouds make hail Spaceships and rockets travel in the sky	Gained skills, attitudes, and competencies in becoming aware and appreciating the solar system --planets, environment, weather, and so forth.	-Discussing each planet and solar object on a mobile solar system -Watching films about space -Visiting museums -Displaying pictures of the atmosphere -Telling stories about space -Painting pictures about space -Visiting the airport -Looking at pictures, films -Discussing rivers, lakes, streams, oceans, and continents -Observing samples of soil	-Provide an environment conducive to teaching and learning about space; include resources like, a solar system (model), places for field trips, compass, flashlight, clock, model rocket, airplanes, pictures of astronauts, magnets, binoculars, and mirrors. -Provide an environment conducive to teaching and learning about earth; include resources like, samples of soil, pictures of the earth and its waters, balloons, paper bags (small), garden tools, funnel, sifter, assorted sieves.

258

(Subject) CONCEPTS	PERFORMANCE OUTCOMES	CHILDREN'S ACTIVITIES	TEACHING METHODS/RESOURCES
Airplanes fly in the sky The atmosphere is everything in the sky The earth is made of water and soil Air is throughout the earth There are different kinds of soil The earth is made up of living and non-living things The earth is a planet The action of clouds make thunder and lightning There are four seasons: winter (cold weather), summer (hot weather), autumn (cool weather), spring (warm weather) Different plants grow during different seasons Different clothing is worn during different seasons		-Doing experiments to show how thunder and lightning happen. Fill two balloons with water to represent clouds; rub together-the-friction gives off electricity (lightning) and the bursting of the balloons make a loud sound (thunder) -Setting up a weather station -Displaying pictures to show "signs" of each season -Making displays of plants and leaves for different seasons -Reading and listening to stories about animals homes -Making snowflakes from cutting paper -Discussing the neighborhood -Discussing current events about pollution, waste, etc. -Collecting things (leaves, rocks, pebbles, shells, etc.) -Taking field trips to construction sites in the neighborhood	-Provide resources like, pictures of activities for various seasons, leaf samples, books, records, films, filmstrips, and slides, newspapers, pictures of snow scenes, waste projects, etc.

CURRICULUM EXPERIENCES FOR TEACHING/LEARNING SCIENCE - CHART 10

(Subject) CONCEPTS	PERFORMANCE OUTCOMES	CHILDREN'S ACTIVITIES	TEACHING METHODS/RESOURCES
Animals and birds find different homes during certain seasons			
The weather changes during different seasons			
It rains more during spring and summer			
It snows during fall and winter			
The environment is everything around us			
Litter is waste or trash			
Pollution is unclean air			
Litter pollutes the environment			
Man can help keep the earth clean			

HOW DOES SCIENCE CORRELATE WITH THE TOTAL
PRE-SCHOOL CURRICULUM?

Science experiences can and should be integrated with other subject areas. Some ways science can be taught through other subject areas are discussed in this section of the chapter.

In expressive arts science can be correlated through: experimentation with mixing paints and creating colors; mixing up paste and glue; constructing hand fans from construction paper; relating colors to the colors of objects, things, etc., in the environment; experimentation with sounds in the environment; using musical instruments to make sounds; drawing pictures and making sketches of concepts, experiments, and objects; making paper fans and windmills to demonstrate concepts of air and wind; relating the color chart (primary/secondary earth tones) to colors in the environment; and making charts, graphs, posters, scrapbooks, photo albums, and so forth.

In mathematics, science can be correlated by: counting animals, objects, people, plants; measuring objects; sorting objects into groups by various properties; recording data and making graphs and charts for information and study in counting, for designs, etc.; classifying pictures of plants and animals; making sets out of pictures by size, shape, colors, class, etc.; weighing objects and comparing and contrasting in view of size, weight, equality, balance, substance, etc.

Science is correlated with language arts in many ways. Children can label plants, animals; say names of plants, animals, and objects; record results of experiments on chalkboard, charts, posters by care-givers; other activities to correlate the two subjects include: story reading and story telling about weather, seasons, solar system, clothing, plants, animals, people, and things; building vocabulary from communi-cation modes, i.e. discussions, show and tell, listening exercises, and so forth.

Social studies are correlated with science by: examining climatic conditions (temperature, precipitation, etc.) in relationship to various living conditions for certain regions, states, etc.; identifying plants, animals, food crops, clothing, etc., from various regions; recognizing food nutrients, fibers, textile, etc., from plants and animals in various regions; exploring different living modes in reference to scientific facts and concepts (pollution, energy sources, health status of people in various regions according to employment, living conditions--housing, diets, working in factories, mills, mines, farms, and so forth.

ACTIVITIES FOR STUDY AND DISCUSSION

Teaching science is an ever-changing process which requires a person to keep abreast with an abundance of scientific concepts. In an effort to strengthen and expand the knowledge, skills, attitudes, and understandings of the pre-service teacher, these activities are provided for further study and discussion.

1. Collect a series of books and materials on the topic of science for review use.

2. Make a resource file on activities and experiments for science projects.

3. Develop a plan for a science fair where children can display their work and experiments with science tools.

4. Practice setting up science interest projects like aquariums, terrariums, animal shelters for rabbits, birds, etc.

5. Collect many objects to use in science activities. Use the sub-topics as a guide for organizing materials--biology, chemistry, physics, earth science, astronomy, and health.

6. Explain and discuss (by examples) the "scientific study" elements.

REFERENCES

Althouse, Rosemary and Cecil Main, **Science Experiences for Young Children.** New York: Teachers College Press, 1976.

Brandwein, Paul F., and Elizabeth K. Cooper, **Concepts in Science.** New York: Harcourt, Brace & World, 1967.

Brophy, Jere E., et al., **Teaching in the Preschool.** New York: Harper and Row Publishers, 1975.

Carin, Arthur and Robert Sund, **Teaching Science Through Discovery.** Columbia, Ohio: Charles E. Merrill Publishing Co., 1975.

Carmichael, Viola, **Science Experiences for Young Children.** Los Angeles: Southern California Association for the Education of Young Children, 1969.

Carson, R., **The Sense of Wonder.** New York: Harper & Row, 1965.

Cohen, Dorothy H. and Marguerita Rudolph, **Kindergarten and Early Schooling.** Englewood Cliffs, New Jersey: Prentice Hall Incorporation, 1977.

Croft, Doreen J. and Robert D. Hess, **An Activities Handbook for Teachers of Young Children.** Boston: Houghton Mifflin Co., Second Edition, 1975.

Devito, Alfred and Gerald Krockover, **Creative Sciencing.** Vols. I & II. Boston: Little Brown and Company, 1976.

Feldscher, Sharla, **148 Do-its for Early Learners.** Dansville, New York: The Instructor Publications, Inc., 1977.

Gale, Frank C. and Clarice W. Gale, **Experiences with Plants for Young Children.** Palo Alto, CA: Pacific Books, 1974.

Greenberg, Sylvia S. and Edith L. Raskin, **Home-made Zoo.** David McKay, 1952.

Harlan, J.D., "From Curiosity to Concepts," **Young Children**, May 1975, 30 249-255.

Haupt, Dorothy, **Science Experiences for Nursery School Children**. Washington, D.C.: The National Association for the Education of Young Children, 1980.

Hendrick, Joanne, **Total Learning: Curriculum for the Young Child** (Second Edition). Columbus: Merrill Publishing Company, 1986.

Hildebrand, Verna, **Introduction to Early Childhood Education** (Fourth Edition). New York: Macmillan Publishing Co., Inc., 1986.

Klausmeier, Herbert and Marcella H. Nerbovig, **Teaching in the Elementary School**. New York: Harper and Row Publishers, 1974.

Schickendanz, Judith A., Mary E. York, Ida Santos Stewart, and Doris White, **Strategies for Teaching Young Children** (Second Edition). Englewood Cliffs, New Jersey: Prentice-Hall, Inc., 1983.

Wortham, Sue C., **Organizing Instruction in Early Childhood: A Handbook of Assessment and Activities**. Boston: Allyn and Bacon, Inc., 1984.

EFFECTIVE TEACHING/LEARNING FOR ALL PRE-SCHOOLERS:
INTEGRATION, INTERVENTION, AND MANAGEMENT

(FOCUSING ON THE CULTURALLY DIVERSE, EXCEPTIONAL,
AND DISADVANTAGED)

CHAPTER 9

EFFECTIVE TEACHING/LEARNING FOR ALL PRE-SCHOOLERS: INTEGRATION, INTERVENTION, AND MANAGEMENT

- WHAT FACTORS MUST PRE-SCHOOL PROGRAMS CONSIDER IN MAKING CURRICULUM AND TEACHING/LEARNING FUNCTIONAL FOR ALL CHILDREN?: AN OVERVIEW

- HOW CAN WE INTEGRATE THE GOALS OF EARLY CHILDHOOD EDUCATION WITH INTERVENTION STRATEGIES AS AN INTEGRAL PART OF THE DEVELOPMENTAL CURRICULUM?

- WHY DOES FOCUSING ON TEACHING OBJECTIVES RATHER THAN ON DISCIPLINE AND CONTROL YIELD EFFECTIVE CHILD AND CLASSROOM MANAGEMENT?

- WHAT EFFECTS DO CURRICULUM AND INSTRUCTIONAL STRATEGIES FOR CULTURALLY DIVERSE CHILDREN HAVE ON THE TOTAL TEACHING/LEARNING PROCESS IN THE PRE-SCHOOL?

- ACTIVITIES FOR STUDY AND DISCUSSION

- REFERENCES

WHAT FACTORS MUST PRE-SCHOOL PROGRAMS CONSIDER IN MAKING CURRICULUM AND TEACHING/LEARNING FUNCTIONAL FOR ALL CHILDREN?: AN OVERVIEW

Preschool programs must continue to be developed and regularly revised to meet the educational needs of young children having various cultural and ethnic origins and special needs. These young children live under educational, social and economic conditions that are both common and diverse in the American society. The young Black child, other minority children, and in some cases children with handicaps are characteristic of this group. For the most part, the diversities of these young children present challenges to educational programs to provide effective curriculum and instruction that will encourage quality learning.

The challenges are underscored by the fact that the diverse child presents both the special characteristics of a diverse cultural group and his or her own individual differences within that group. These differences include sociopsychological aspects of the child's background and the educational needs to be addressed by the school systems. Therefore, the child's needs (abilities and disabilities) must be approached in terms of the "child as an individual" ("intra-individual"); not in terms that force comparison of the child with his peers. This will include effective planning, programming, and evaluating.

The key considerations to be undertaken in planning, programming, and evaluating curriculum and instruction for all children, regardless of their diversities are:

o Caregivers must be qualified and capable of understanding and accepting all children as unique persons first, each having the same basic needs, feelings, attitudes and interests as any other child.

o The cultural difference is just one aspect of the child's total spectrum to be considered in individualizing teaching/learning.

o Many ways exist for stimulating, teaching, and caring for children with special needs (handicapping conditions) so that they attain their maximum potential and live a productive life that fits their abilities and needs.

° Information, materials, resources, and strategies for pre-school special educators, parents and others, must be used in initiating, ameliorating, and implementing curriculum and instruction in programs for culturally diverse children.

The following factors are important ways of encouraging and cultivating an appreciation of ethnic heritage in the curriculum and instructional program:

° Have a rationale for your teaching and learning process for these children.

° Have a purpose for the particular programs.

° Coordinate goals and objectives for the growth and development of young children in the program with teaching methods and techniques.

° Use a system for measuring the outcomes of curriculum and instruction in behavioral terms, regarding their culture.

° Provide activities and materials (human resources) to give/provide opportunities to experience an appropriate cultural education which gives an intimate knowledge of, and which honors and respects, the history and culture of African Americans, Hispanics, Asians, and others.

° Make teachings and learnings a vital and integral part of the curriculum which deal with cultural excellence, as important as is reading, writing, etc.

Building curriculum and implementing teaching must be approached from a native (race, culture, sex, etc.) perspective, dealing with the diversities. To aid this process, implementing instruction presents a two-fold interrogative perspective on curriculum and intervention strategies:

° How can we integrate the goals of Early Childhood Education and Intervention Strategies as an integral part of the developmental curriculum?; and

° Why does focusing on teaching objectives rather than on discipline and control yield effective child and classroom management?

268

Each of these topics should be approached along with examples of principles and features that are germane to various curriculum areas, cultural differences, and handicapping conditions of the young culturally diverse child.

HOW CAN WE INTEGRATE THE GOALS OF EARLY CHILDHOOD EDUCATION WITH INTERVENTION STRATEGIES AS AN INTEGRAL PART OF THE DEVELOPMENTAL CURRICULUM?

Before curriculum is planned, goals must be established in order to determine what is to be accomplished. For the purpose of designing and modifying curricula and intervention strategies for all young children, let's use the basic assumption that "our goals mandate each child live a happy childhood, reach his/her potential, and become a happy, fully functioning adult." The primary theme of this chapter makes it necessary to include certain guidelines for attaining this goal. First, caregivers must understand and be aware of those aspects of the child's life--culture and heritage--that bring happiness to him or her. Second, caregivers must screen, assess, and diagnose the "whole" child's growth and development so that emphasis is not placed solely on the child's differences. Development occurs concurrently in physical, emotional, social, and intellectual areas and requires emphasis on all of these areas for the child to obtain, maintain, and strive toward his or her potential. Therefore, for this child who happens to be culturally different, educational planning must initially fit curriculum and instruction to each child's abilities and disabilities (intra-individual differences). Third, in order that this child may live a productive life from childhood to adulthood and thereafter, educational programs must be developed and improved and caregivers trained to implement curriculum and instructional strategies that are congruent with the child's needs, abilities, disadvantages and advantages. Information, therefore, will be presented here to assist the caregivers, parents, and others in teaching these goals.

The goals of early childhood education, as defined by Hildebrand (1975, 1986) and used randomly, will be the foundation for describing the developmental curriculum for the culturally diverse child. However, they have been modified with specific information to help planners specifically assist this child. The child for whom this curriculum and instruction are designed will have been screened, diagnosed and placed in the pre-school center and/or classroom as his or her least restrictive environment. So, reference to curriculum areas will include experiences in social skills, motor development, mathematics, science, language arts, creative areas (music, art, dramatic play, movement, block building, and field trips).

The major guidelines for using this material to improve the curriculum and instructional program include:

1. Adopt and use a rich curriculum having units in each subject area designed for pre-school children. There is a wealth of curricula (models, books, materials, etc.) available for programs to use in regard to the culturally diverse and special needs child.

2. Obtain and use knowledge, skills, and attitudes about young culturally diverse children in a diagnostic-prescriptive-intervention approach to teaching and learning. This can be facilitated through in-service training, utilization of support staff, and by involving parents and other related professional and community services.

3. Use caregivers who are capable, willing, able, and qualified to teach and help the culturally diverse and special needs child through curriculum and instructional strategies. There must be an acceptance of this child, as a child first, regardless of what he or she can and cannot do.

As this moves into the "goals of early childhood education and the developmental curriculum," remember that its intent is to facilitate (rather than supplant) the design and modification of curriculum and instructional strategies for all children (emphasizing culturally diverse and special needs children) through the foundation of goals for early childhood education.

Goal One: "To help the child grow in independence." The tasks for implementing this goal in preschool include providing the child the opportunities: to perform the task of dressing him or herself; to increase his or her ability to make wise choices and decisions in a consistent manner; to develop the ability to organize, plan, and follow through on simple assignments; to manage "self" as an individual and capable person; to establish routines and patterns of living that bring happiness; and to expect and cope with failures, as well as successes.

Curriculum and instructional strategies should permit children: to receive well-defined directions for performing tasks; to learn routines for functioning in the environment (hanging coats, washing hands, travel patterns for movement in classroom and home); to improve in learning on a developmental continuum based on ability to achieve;

270

to execute self-help skills independently (going to toilet, washing hands, etc.); to experiment with a wide array of curricula activities (art experiences, fixing puzzles, handling toys, playing in housekeeping area, riding the trike, etc.); and to use materials, supplies and equipment skillfully (design should be scaled to the child's developmental level, size, and interest).

The way the pre-school program develops this independence rests with the caregiver's attitudes and strategies for aiding the child with differences. If the caregiver and others act as if offering help is an imposition, the child is probably not being understood, appreciated, and cared for properly. This goal must be revisited continuously to make "independence" a reality for these young children.

Goal Two: "To help the child give and share as well as receive affection." This goal presents problems to all children at times, but it is even more pronounced for teaching a child who may look and/or act differently from his or her classmates or family members. The skilled, understanding caregiver can help children learn the necessity of sharing and cooperating with others and managing their feelings. The spiritual values (respecting others, sharing love and affection, etc.) imposed by the family and others also tend to aid children in obtaining this goal.

Since pre-school programs are charged with the responsibility of making this goal a reality, the first step is to plan a daily activity schedule which is followed in a classroom atmosphere of warmth and acceptance where children feel good, needed, and wanted. This includes having well-devised learning centers with materials and interests relevant to the cultural heritage, as well as other didactic materials to deal with special needs. All materials, supplies, and equipment should be plentiful and in good condition. The work of each child should bear his or her name, and conversation should occur with the child in which his or her work is described in a positive manner. Another way of fostering this goal is by putting each child in the driver's seat with giant ride 'em toys; by providing experiences in dramatic play and socio-dramatic play to act out real life scenes; by making provisions for children to console one another in unpleasant moments as well as in moments of joy and happiness; by stimulating conversation about how children felt in various situations, i.e., when the dog was stolen, or when someone laughed at his work, or when it was cold and there was inadequate clothing or fuel sources, or when parents did not take him or her shopping, or when he or she didn't get his or her way with the teacher.

271

Love and affection is present in the homes of all children, but for the diverse and special needs children, the methods of showing it sometimes vary from traditional society; therefore, careful listening and observation of (parent-child and child-child) interactions in both work and play situations will reveal this love and affection. The caregiver must understand the scarcity of commodities in some of the homes of the diverse children and the need for security in order to deal effectively with this aspect of goal implementation. Having an abundance of nonsexist, nonracist, and sensorial materials is central to combatting this dilemma for the diverse child.

Goal Three: "To help the child to get along with others." Developing interaction techniques that bring positive responses from within and outside the family unit is a developmental task for pre-school programs. The young child must be exposed to experiences that teach attitudes and abilities for functioning in a social group. Children from diverse groups with certain exceptionalities might need more than normal adult encouragement to fit into and/or to feel a part of a social setting. If the caregiver responds to the child's special needs, rather than expecting him or her to work and play with others cooperatively, the other children will treat the child differently and cause conflicts in the social interaction process. Therefore, caregivers must make sure that their attitudes are adjusted to show no prejudices toward the young culturally diverse or exceptional child which will mark him or her as being different.

Activities which involve group-living experiences--sharing materials, talking to each other, taking turns, obeying rules, accepting limits, responding to directions, etc.; and using dramatic play, water play, sand play, outdoor play, art, music, show-and-tell for language development, social studies, science, and mathematics--can be beneficial in operationalizing this goal. Refer to Chapters Four, Five, Six, Seven, and Eight for children's activities and instructional strategies.

Young children have tendencies to identify themselves, peers, and sometimes adults by "nicknames." Get children into the habit of identifying themselves and others by their real names--not "Buddy" and "Peaches," but Jim and Mary. The essence of "mainstreaming" different races of children into one educational setting may result in the nicknames being seen as "name calling" which oftentimes causes children not to get along well with each other. The caregivers must provide avenues for children to grow accustomed to using their proper names. This is possible in everyday greetings; performing singing games and poems or riddles where proper names are used; and having children record conversations and stories on tape from which children identify each other by putting a proper name with a voice. Getting along with others can also be fostered by using pictures of different racial groups, people with handicaps in various occupational roles and various pictures of ethnic groups in social settings to start conversations and build respect and appreciation for differences in people as they interact.

Consistent use of rules and procedures for interacting help children see the value of getting along. They must be taught to work together to get the job done--painting a mural, building a block structure, pulling a wagon, cleaning up the learning center, taking turns to perform activities and/or chores, and so forth. The caregiver is the key for making this concept a reality in the classroom or center. Also, by using parents and community resources in daily operations, the caregiver can help the culturally diverse and/or exceptional child see the team concept in operation, which should underscore the need to get involved and work together to be successful.

Goal Four: "To help the child gain self-control." Self-discipline, self-guidedness, and self-direction are essential elements in managing the behavior of all children. It is important to find the cause of behavior before enforcing consequences ("corporal punishment," "negative reinforcement by parents") or labeling ("hyperactive," "bad," "defiant") as is often done with the African American child (Hale-Benson, 1986). A child needs ways for understanding and responding appropriately to issues in order to protect himself or herself or "keep out of trouble." This means that the child must be given proper alternatives for expressing his or her emotions that are acceptable in terms of the group's socialization. Care must be taken to see that the child learns to respect authority through rational means rather than through fear.

The caregiver fosters this goal through curricular provisions and instructional strategies that include: many activities that require no right or wrong responses; many self-initiated activities; many instances of frequent praise; many chances for repetition of positive experiences; many ways of moving from one activity to another; and many anxiety-releasing types of activities (throwing bean bags, kicking balls, punching bags, painting pictures, pounding clay, hammering pegs or nails in boards, singing, running, tumbling, etc.). These aid the child in dealing with his or her inner feelings through what Piaget and others call displacement, positive acting out, and constructive behavioral responses. Self-expression of ideas and actions through dramatic and sociodramatic play are other means for building skills in self-control. The child can become very personally involved in his or her cultural and ethnic heritage through role playing, movement, improvisation, pantomime, puppets, dolls and object manipulation. These help the child remember, think, follow directions, make decisions, reach consensus, and solve/resolve problems. All of these are necessary for helping children, especially culturally diverse children, develop self-control.

This goal demands that the pre-school program work cooperatively with the home. Caregivers (including teachers, parents, and others) must make plans for activities and consequences regularly; these should be based on the various behaviors exhibited by children. This strategy will strengthen the child's mastery of self-control.

Goal Five: "To help the child develop a positive self-image and understand his/her relationship to the world." The way a child views himself or herself influences the way he or she behaves which does not always paint an accurate picture of the child. Self-image is learned from the way we are treated by principal caregivers and others in our environment. Personality types vary from one culture to another and from individual to individual. Research indicates the positive and negative effects of various child-rearing practices; tasks children are expected to perform or not perform and the praise, punishment, or regards for different competencies or lack thereof. Family members, as well as various outside sources, play a vital role in the development of the child's sense of self-worth. There must be a thorough understanding of cultural strengths in order to correct the effects of condescending attitudes and negative procedures in the teaching/learning processes culturally diverse children often go through. Sound educational practices have always stressed the importance of culture as a basic factor in curriculum and instruction (as suggested in the theoretical formulations of Erik Erikson). Yet culture has not always been considered in education for the minorities. Movements to motivate Black children, by stressing their cultural strengths and backgrounds, gave birth to the "Black is Beautiful" and "Black Power" concepts. While seen by many to be an adverse approach, the positive aspects of this "self-identity" theme were very beneficial.

As the child strives to preserve the integrity of the "self," coupled with desires for enhancing self-esteem, he or she also struggles to become a well-adjusted, motivated, adequate, competent, culturally-proud and social individual. This child must be given opportunities to adapt, adjust and control his or her environment and expanding world in terms of his or her own culture rather than in ways defined by the dominant culture. Caregivers must be constantly reminded of the minorities (especially Blacks) struggle for self-identity and recognition in the midst of racism and adversity throughout American history even into our present society (Hale-Benson, 1986). Different messages, ways of life, and love--a mechanism of strength for Black children can be extrapolated from the works and strifes of Countee Cullen, Paul Lawrence Dunbar, James Baldwin, Nat Turner, W.E.B. Dubois, H. Rap Brown, Gwendolyn Brooks, Dr. Martin Luther King, Jr., Malcolm X, Roy Wilkins and Marcus Garvey. Variations in Black culture and life are continuously being exposed through the works of thousands of Black contemporaries. Caregivers must consider the strengths of all minority children's culture and lifestyle in building positive self-images. Emphasis on pride and dignity in customs, traditions, cultures, values, and others, the influence of African, Latinos, and other heritages, and the strong focus of aesthetics in life (folklore; music in the form of spirituals, blues, jazz, poetry, dance; and art) can be positive parts of curriculum and instruction in the pre-school.

As curriculum and instructional strategies are considered and implemented for the culturally diverse child, caregivers must make provisions to screen, assess, and diagnose children. In this way, educators can provide activities in which children can perform well within their capabilities. Caregivers must make sure that critical comments are stated positively: the act and not the child is criticized. For example, say "If the doll were a real baby, how would it feel if someone hit it in the head?" rather than "You mistreated those dolls as a mean person would do" as this often happens. Then show the child the way to handle toys and objects. A caregiver should be a good model. There should be many activities available for fostering a positive self-image: (i.e., mirror play and printed materials for observations and conversations; ethnic identification through books, photos of children and others, pictures in magazines like <u>Ebony,</u> <u>Ebony Jr.</u>, charts and posters, etc.). Caregivers can also use manipulative materials to aid the child in mastering chores or tasks--easy-to-fix puzzles with knobs for easy handling, nesting cans, stacking cubes, building blocks, and many others. Caregivers can display photos of children in order to help motivate and develop feelings of self-worth. Activities in play that involve group interacting, sharing, talking and thinking also help develop a sense of self. "Show and tell" is a positive method for bringing the child's family into the teaching/learning process. Dramatic and socio-dramatic play are also curricula areas important to developing positive self-images. Positive reinforcement must be immediate and continuously used to show the young culturally diverse child that his or her contributions and performances are worthy and accepted; positive reinforcement is also used as a symbol of love and approval.

Goals Six and Seven and Eight: "To help the child to begin understanding his/her body and sex-role identification, as well as using large and small motor skills. Pre-school curriculum consists of materials and methods that aid children in identifying body parts and their functions. This step leads to understanding feeding, clothing, caring for, and appreciating the body. Activities are included in the curriculum that are appropriate to the developmental levels of the children. The child must be given opportunities to examine, manipulate, and enjoy materials in accordance with his/her sexual identity. Explorations and various activities germane to sex-role identification will begin as the child grows and develops in a world of social, emotional, physical and intellectual experiences. Caregivers must not allow their prejudices and values to affect the child's selection processes. More and more, society is becoming unisexual in roles and responsibilities and it can be considered a wholesome change. Various occupations are not just for any particular sex, family roles are more cooperative, and sports and aesthetics are more broadly interpreted for both males and females. This nonsexist approach is essential to teaching and learning.

The curriculum must provide opportunities for the child to get experiences for understanding his or her body. Use pictures of the human body for describing and labeling body parts and for discussing functions. Included in the pictures should be genital organs differentiating boys and girls. Motor development and music are areas where this goal can be accomplished easily: (i.e., movement, rhythmic exercises, small motor task, and running, climbing, jumping, swimming, and singing games). Through language arts, experiences in storytelling, show and tell, rhymes, and pantomime, the body can be thoroughly explored. An understanding of the care for the body can be obtained through health and science experience, like good grooming practices, eating proper foods, getting proper health tests, dressing properly and getting medical examinations and checkups.

Care must be taken to mold these activities to meet the needs (if necessary or different) of the minority child. There are biological differences in the body structure of Black children (Hale-Benson, 1986). Activities should be repeated such as saying the names of body parts and touching them. Break the tasks into small steps, allow for failure, but provide continuous practice through exercises. A lot of role playing where children can express themselves as others helps to foster sex and role identification. Conversations while washing hands, eating snacks and during lunch, can be related to the body.

The art activities (painting, modeling clay) provide avenues for large muscle development. Also, block building and dramatic play are areas that provide rich experiences for children with large motor involvement.

For small motor skills, use activities and materials like sewing, writing, drawing, cutting with scissors, snapping and fastening buttons, lacing and tying shoestrings, fastening zippers, playing with small toys, stringing beads and many other experiences requiring the use of the hands and eyes together.

Perceptual development is an integral part of motor functioning. Activities and materials that require using the senses for feeling, seeing, touching, smelling, and tasting are characteristic of perceptual skills. Curriculum activities include: using textile boards for feeling different materials such as sandpaper letters, numbers and figures; throwing balls for eye-hand coordination; coloring pictures within the lines; hearing and describing sounds; tasting various flavors of foods; and touching and naming body parts.

Culturally diverse children can benefit greatly from games, free play, outdoor play, dance, movement and many manipulative experiences. The methods and techniques used affect the effectiveness of the motor activity. The child will need guidance in adjusting to the exceptionality and finding ways to compensate for it (Bardwell, Kreig, and Olion, 1973). Much aesthetic appreciation for the arts-- dance, music, sculpture, crafts and painting--can be cultivated by focusing on and using cultural heritage.

Goal Nine: "To help the child to begin to understand and control his/her physical world. For the culturally diverse child, growth and development occur in the face of distorted life styles, underexposure of cultural contribution, racial conflict and adversity, inadequate portrayal of Blacks in the mainstream of society and historical accounts, and inequalities in the educational process. Obstacles thwart the child's understanding of and control over his or her physical world. It, therefore, becomes the developmental task of pre-school programs to provide a Black perspective in their curriculum and instructional design. This should be followed for other minority children (Hispanics, Asians, etc.).

Fostering this goal means that the curriculum and instructional design will help provide a background of experiences and attitudes that make living and learning meaningful. The child's world puzzle must be pieced together through careful planning, adequate provision and selection of materials, equipment and learning experiences. Instead of using many subjective, attitudinal, value-judgment or oriented approaches, caregivers must use scientific information to solve problems, encourage natural curiosity in children, and stimulate creative learning. This helps to develop intelligence--which includes thinking, reasoning, gathering, and using a variety of information. This is an excellent time for helping children develop good study habits and learn that successes are earned through repeated efforts. Understanding the physical world requires children to become interested, explore, examine, and appreciate their environments. The curriculum must foster this approach.

Fantasy play, dramatic, and socio-dramatic play help children to test their worlds. The use of housekeeping areas, unit blocks, large hollow blocks, and block accessories are useful materials for enhancing play. Through science, mathematics, and social studies experiences, the child is exposed to intellectual and scientific planning and discovery. Materials appropriate for this are: telescopes, telephones, microscopes, scales, thermometers, growhouses, mirrors, calendars, pictures of people, places and things, books for reading and conversation, musical instruments, games and puzzles, lotto games, work tools, field trips and neighborhood walks.

The utilization of families and community resources is important with this goal. Involvement of, and contributions from, parents, community helpers, and neighborhood establishments (churches, schools, businesses) are essential elements in operating sound, effective preschool programs for the young Black child (Dill, 1973; Hale-Benson, 1986). These involvements also make dealing with the cultural differences easier for caregivers.

Goal Ten: "To help the child to learn new language concepts and new vocabulary in his or her social and intellectual activity." Fostering the child's use of speech and language in his or her surroundings and developing meaningful vocabulary to use in communication are developmental tasks for achieving this goal. These activities are encouraged through vocalizations at very early ages by parents and family members; many opportunities for the child to express ideas through show and tell; and introduction to books and printed pages; storytelling, fingerplays, and dramatizations; musical activities; and media--television, radio, films, filmstrips and so forth.

Culturally diverse children in many cases are born into environments that make the acquisition of adequate communication skills difficult. These psychological and intellectual hindrances cause the children to become subnormal in developing skills in speaking and listening. Many children possess adequate communication and language skills, but, because of emotional problems, cannot use them properly in their social and intellectual activity. Then, there are children who are disabled by psychological, intellectual, and motoric malfunctions which cause them problems in speech and language development. Many professionals feel that language development and critical thinking are intimately related. Therefore, all children have the same communication needs. However, Smith (1969) noted that disadvantaged children, by definition and the nature of their lifestyles, have difficulty in becoming linguistically proficient in American society. Many Black exceptional children and others fit into Smith's description and are therefore in need of curriculum and instruction to help them attain language skills to cope in this highly verbal society. Success for these children in a pre-school program will prevail only when their educational experiences (models for language acquisition; curriculum and materials common to cultural heritage; respect for nonstandard English, but expectations that lead to learning standard English; use of words, terms, and reading materials that a child can comprehend, etc.) are designed to meet needs from a Black or Hispanic, rather than middle-class white, perspective. Immediate measures must be implemented to ameliorate or remediate language deficiencies.

Curricula provisions include using creative arts and crafts as a basis for communication and creative expressions--e.g., cooking, sewing, crafts, dancing and movements, singing; providing ample avenues for using oral language and listening (show and tell, audiovisuals, puppet shows, storytelling, science experiments, water and sand play, dramatic and socio-dramatic play). Stimulating conversation rather than accepting body language and gestures (i.e., pointing, touching) give the child a chance to finish his or her speech. Providing language and word games; puzzles; using dictionaries; and providing many books, magazines, and sensory materials--fabrics, scent jars, etc.--all help in developing language skills.

Instructional strategies include teaching auditory, visual, motoric, and verbal and listening skills through modeling and the use of concrete materials. The caregiver should use many examples and allow practice during instruction; he or she should show respect for nonstandard English insofar as it is a part of the child's cultural environment; he or she should then give opportunities for standard English tasks;

use the "language-through-experience-approach-charts" and real life stories; use all the media available and then be patient and understanding of the child having difficulty.

Summary

This goal-oriented approach for designing and modifying curriculum and instruction to facilitate positive appreciation of culture and ethnic heritage of minorities offers many pluses. The concepts provide information, curriculum materials, and resources that represent experiences and ideas gathered from the author's past and present endeavors in teaching, research, and personal involvement with parents and community resources. As an added feature to strengthening this goal-oriented curricular approach so that it is more responsive to the child with cultural differences, intervention strategies are vital to the developmental curriculum. The teacher and parents must consistently interact in the young child's play world, especially in dramatic/socio-dramatic play situations. The ten goals of early childhood education (Hildebrand, 1986) must be an integral part of the developmental curriculum for pre-school.

A Discussion of Intervention Strategies

Intervention strategies are approaches to teaching. They are structured around the needs of the child, which is essential for the culturally diverse child. They help the caregiver to focus attention upon the child's significant handicaps and strengths and they provide a consistent way of dealing with each learning situation. The intervention strategies are based on the child's developmental level and the tasks of which he or she should be able to attain; they assure, to a certain extent, that the child will successfully complete these tasks.

Intervention strategies encourage parent involvement and make provisions for parents to learn how to help the children through reinforcement procedures at home. The strategies work best when they are:

1. Developed as "prescriptions" which are based on the results from the diagnosis and the screening/assessment process.

2. Used in the design and implementation plan for teaching and remediation.

This process eliminates the guessing games and helps caregivers, parents and others develop specific tasks for each child based on his or her "individual education program" (IEP).

Intervention strategies for children with cultural differences, especially Blacks, should include planned opportunities for experiences and activities for the individual and group needs, likes, abilities, home life and experiential background of various children in the educational program. In planning and designing these strategies, the following TEN PROVISIONS may be used as a guide to help all children:

1. Teach new skills -- which is important to them as individuals as well as vital to the group's functioning.

2. Encourage personal-social opportunities -- which include sharing, laughing, consoling one another and being helpful to each other.

3. Share experiences with parents -- which involves parents observing and working in the learning process.

4. Encourage working alone -- which means being able to think, browse through materials and be quiet at varying intervals.

5. Help them make plans and decisions -- for special events, for daily activities, about behaviors and routine tasks.

6. Expand their interest -- by visiting places within the school and the neighborhood, and by being exposed to new adventures.

7. Get them "ready" -- in the areas of reading, speech, arithmetic, writing, and find a balance between active and quiet activities (indoor and outdoor play).

8. Develop social values -- which includes developing independence but guarding against aggressiveness, developing pride in ownership which is nonselfish and feeling secure about oneself and responsible in a group.

9. Help them inspect the natural environment -- by exploring, observing, investigating, experimenting and experiencing.

10. Let them grow -- through dramatic, socio-dramatic play, games, art activities, singing, rhythmic expressions, and personal creativity.

These provisions should be the basis of intervention strategies. Along with the goals for Early Childhood Education, they should be integral parts of the developmental curriculum. These provisions overlap as did the goals; but after all, social, emotional, physical, and intellectual development are interrelated. The provisions are a part of the ingredients needed to organize, manage and operate an effective classroom environment.

WHY DOES FOCUSING ON TEACHING OBJECTIVES RATHER THAN ON DISCIPLINE AND CONTROL YIELD EFFECTIVE CHILD AND CLASSROOM MANAGEMENT?

Planning is required for effective child and classroom management. Plans must answer some essential questions: "What are the rules?" "What are the consequences?" "How am I going to discipline, if needed?" Child and classroom management involve organizing and structuring the classroom, the day's activities, and the teacher's behavior. The physical environment and sequence of activities must support each other. Classroom organization and methods of instruction determine the degree of effective child and classroom management (Smith and Smith, 1978). The following strategies are offered to improve the learning environment of the minority child in pre-school programs. Teaching must be based on objectives or too much time will be spent on discipline and control.

Getting Started. Early in the process, write and display a set of rules. These may include: WALK IN ROOM AND IN HALL; RUN IN GYM AND OUTDOORS; BE POLITE; HELP EACH OTHER; PUT AWAY TOYS WHEN FINISHED; WEAR SMOCK WHEN PAINTING; SHARE WITH OTHERS; SAY PLEASE WHEN ASKING; and SAY "THANK YOU" WHEN SOMEONE GIVES YOU SOMETHING.

Remind the children of the rules by reading them to the children daily. Have children repeat the rules with you. Praise only when specific rules are followed. Make reference to the rules in comments, such as: "I like the way Johnny is walking in the hall." "Mary is really practicing using good manners. She said 'thank you' when Edward gave her the puzzle."

Helpful procedures for effective behavioral management in the classroom include:

1. Specifying, in a positive way, rules that are the basics for the reinforcement. Emphasize the desired behavior by praising

the children following the rules. (Rules are made important by providing reinforcement for following them.) Rules may be different kinds of work, study, or play periods. Limit the rules (taken from many) to three or less. As the children learn to follow the rules, repeat them less frequently, but continue to praise good behavior.

2. Relating the children's performance to the rules. Praise behavior, not the child. Be specific about behavior that exemplifies paying attention or working hard--"That's right, you are a hard worker," "You watched the pictures when I showed them. That's good paying attention." Relax the rules between work periods.

3. Catching the children at being good. Reinforce behavior that will be most beneficial to the child's development. In the process of eliminating disruptive behavior, focus on reinforcing tasks important for social and cognitive skills.

4. Ignoring disruptive behavior unless someone is getting hurt. Focus attention on the children who are working well in order to prompt the correct behavior from the children who are misbehaving or not attending to performing the tasks.

5. Looking for the reinforcer when a persistent problem continues. It just may be your own behavior.

In short, a caregiver's (or parent's) stock-in-trade method of handling day-to-day child classroom management in an effective manner is to: 1) specify rules, 2) ignore disruptive behavior, and 3) praise desired behavior (Becker, et. al., 1971). These are basic procedures. Variations must be made, however, for the individual child and the specifics of various situations.

General procedures for planning teaching and instructional operations are necessary for effective child and classroom management. Planning should take into consideration the fact that not all children finish a task in the same amount of time. For the culturally diverse child, providing a "cushion activity" between tasks will allow him/her, as well as all children, without regard to differences in performances, to complete the task. For example, the children may be told: "When you finish your table games, you may play with the wheel toys."

Plans should be made to provide "systematic prompts or reminders" about what each child should be doing or is to do next. Clear signals about what to do next can help eliminate confusion and wasted time. These items will assist in the prompting process: color-coded name tags, helper hands, lists on the bulletin board and chalk boards, verbal reminders, individual folders, and so forth.

Planning should provide for day-to-day "consistency in routine." The need for daily reminders of varying sorts is greatly reduced by establishing a routine. The completion of one task becomes the cue for the start of the next. For example, "Joe finished his art work. He went to the restroom and washed his hands. Then he went over to the block area and filled the truck with blocks and began to pull it." When the caregiver haphazardly moves from one activity to the next impulse, it becomes very difficult for the children to learn good work habits.

Planning can help in motivating children when one activity is automatically regarded by the start of another activity. For example, "Sue was browsing through the story books. Upon finishing, she walked over to the easel and began painting a picture of the animals that were in the story and asked the caregiver if she could tell the story to the class."

Planning should provide for a periodic "change of pace." Quiet work might be followed by talking or singing. Serious material might be followed by a game. Sitting might be followed by running or a more vigorous activity. This is all that is needed to ready a group for more serious work again.

Curriculum and instructional strategies for the culturally diverse child require that caregivers:

1. Use experiences that don't require RIGHT and WRONG performances and/or set answers. In order to alleviate "child failure," DO:

   ° let the child experience "success" in performing the task (even if you single out just one step done properly or almost properly).

   ° provide few choice (start with one).

   ° give directions in simple, clear words.

° give clues where needed.

° plan short-range tasks for immediate success, and long-range tasks for eventual success (developmental).

° use proper cues to get the child's attention on the task.

° avoid cues that lead to learning that is irrelevant to the task being presented.

2. Provide experiences that require brief tasks. In early learning stages, DO:

° present tasks that require only one response.

° make sure that the response is overlearned through sufficient repetition of experiences.

° avoid leading the response into a sequence of interrelated concepts.

° limit the number of concepts presented in any one learning set.

° show as well as tell.

3. Know the child on a personal basis. Make sure that the materials start from an early level and graduate to a more challenging one, DO:

° plan from the tasks the child can already do.

° follow his or her lead for discovering interests.

° extend the activities in degrees of difficulty.

° observe child's responses to detect early frustration (when detected go back one step or level).

° utilize a systematic, step-by-step technique in providing a simple to a more complex sequence of tasks.

4. Avoid quick, drastic change from one task to another. Learning is best facilitated when you, DO:

º   gradually move into activities that change tempos (quietly to active).

º   present a task in a sequence of small steps, each one built upon a previously learned one.

º   help the child generalize from one situation to another.

º   present the same concept in various settings and in various relationships (transference of common element in each).

5. Use immediate and continuous reinforcement. It is important that the child knows whether or not his or her response is correct. For him or her to have this knowledge, DO:

º   reinforce the child when he responds correctly (social activity and/or token reinforcement).

º   provide immediate feedback so that the child knows that he or she has responded correctly.

º   let him or her know if responses are incorrect along the way; this is part of the process of finding the correct response.

Child and classroom management which focuses on teaching objectives rather than on discipline and control makes the pre-school learning environment come alive and promotes happiness, health, and successful growth and development of the children who attend. Proper and consistent care and attention must be given to planning, using rules, ignoring disruptive behavior and praising desired behavior, and focusing on teaching objectives.

WHAT EFFECTS DO CURRICULUM AND INSTRUCTIONAL STRATEGIES FOR CULTURALLY DIVERSE CHILDREN HAVE ON THE TOTAL TEACHING/LEARNING PROCESS IN PRE-SCHOOL?

The approaches used for helping caregivers deal effectively with curriculum and instructional strategies as presented in this chapter are holistic; it involves planning, programming and evaluating. It is the key to helping children, especially Blacks with cultural differences, compete and function in society to their fullest potential.

Furthermore, these approaches tend to keep the education realistic; programs for pre-schoolers must take into consideratiion that young Black minds may not be totally prepared for a pre-school educational program based solely on their historical continuity.

As we look at the Black experience, as well as other minority experiences, and convert it into curriculum, warning has been given that the pre-school program cannot be a panacea in and of itself, for all of the ills which confront our children. Care and consideration must be given to planning programs that provide curricula that will have an effect far beyond the pre-school years. Therefore, the goal-oriented curricular mechanism, offered in this chapter, should be used to foster effective instruction and lead to sound, long-range, positive effects for learning. At the same time, curriculum and instructional strategies must be designed from a native (African-American, Hispanic, Asiatic or other) perspective which ensures cultivation and appreciation of the ethnic heritage.

The following poem by Marilyn Wilke appropriately describes the importance of the caregivers in the total teaching/learning process for the culturally diverse, as well as for all of the children in pre-school. It reads as follows:

> Look at the children
> They're counting on you.
>
> The toddler, the runner
> The jammer, the funner
> They're counting on you.
>
> The cute ones, the sly ones
> The bold ones, the shy ones
> They're counting on you.
>
> The dark one, the small ones
> The light ones, the tall ones
> They're counting on you.
>
> You're important to them,
>   give all you've got
> Don't measure the time,
>   just love them a lot.
> They're counting on you.

Guide them, forgive them
   again and again.
Be their helper, their teacher,
   their mentor, their friend.
They're counting on you.

You are the hope for their plans
   for their schemes.
You are the link to their future--
   their dreams.
Look at the children,
They're counting on you.

ACTIVITIES FOR STUDY AND DISCUSSION

1. Select an appropriate pre-school curriculum (model) and modify it to fit the culturally diverse child, using this chapter as the guide. This should be a long-range developmental task for group work.

2. Have discussions on this statement: "Intervention strategies are structured around the needs of the child rather than the child being expected to fit the needs of the program."

3. Study and learn the goals of early childhood education. Make this learning functional by assigning the tasks of identifying each of the goals in operation in real pre-school settings.

4. Compile a list of guidelines to be used when designing, modifying, and implementing curriculum and instructional strategies for culturally diverse children, or the dominant race of children in the program.

5. Define "intervention strategies" in reference to curriculum and instructional strategies for culturally diverse children. Link the definition to "provisions" for facilitating teaching/learning for this diverse culturally different pre-schooler. List these provisions from study and discussion of this chapter.

6. Discuss the rationale for "focusing on teaching objectives rather than on discipline and control in order to assure an effective child and classroom management system."

7. Have students design a "child management" project from observation/participation experiences in the pre-school. Use information and materials from class discussions, research, and experiences. Use books and materials from the bibliography. The format for the project should be specified before it begins (i.e. stating problem, summarizing behaviors, identifying treatments, implementing the treatments, recording results, drawing conclusions, summarizing, and so forth).

8. Discuss the cognitive styles of Black children as presented by various researchers/educators (i.e. Asa Hilliard, Rosalie Cohen, Janice Hale-Benson, etc.) and match them with the children in pre-school classes and practicums.

REFERENCES

Bardwell, A., Fred Kreig and LaDelle Olion, **Knowing the Child With Special Needs: A Primer.** Chicago: Head Start (The Office of Child Development, Region V, 300 South Wacker Drive), 1973.

Becker, W.C., S. Engelmann and Donald R. Thomas. **Teaching: A Course in Applied Psychology.** Chicago: Science Research Associates, Inc., 1971.

Berger, Eugenia H., **Parents as Partners in Education: The School and Home Working Together.** St. Louis: The C.V. Mosby Company, 1981.

Cook, Ruth E. and Virginia B. Armbruster, **Adapting Early Childhood Curricula: Suggestions for Meeting Special Needs.** St. Louis: The C.V. Mosby Company, 1982.

Dill, J.R., "Basic Principles of Good Child Development," (A Workshop sponsored by The Black Child Development Institute, Inc.--Curriculum Approaches from a Black Perspective), Washington, D.C.: The Black Child Development Institute, Inc., 1973.

Ellis, M.D., "Black Children and Literature," An unpublished speech presented at the Annual Meeting of Black Child Development Institute, Inc., October-November, 1974.

Fraiberg, S., **The Magic Years: Understanding the Problem of Early Childhood.** New York: Charles Scribner and Sons, 1959.

Fromberg, D.P., **Early Childhood Education: A Perceptual Models Curriculum.** New York: John Wiley and Sons, 1977.

Frost, J.L., and G.R. Hawkes, (Eds.) **The Disadvantaged Child: Issues and Innovations.** Boston: Houghton Mifflin Company, 1972.

Hale-Benson, Janice E., **Black Children: Their Roots, Culture, and Learning Styles.** Baltimore: The John Hopkins University Press, 1986.

Hankerson, Henry E., "Curriculum and Instructional Strategies" (Chapter 2) **In The Young Black Exceptional Child**, Eloise Jackson (ed.), TADS, The Frank Porter Graham Child Development Center, 500 NCNB Plaza, Chapel Hill, North Carolina, 27514, (1980).

Hendrick, Joanne, **Total Learning for the Whole Child.** Columbus: Merrill Publishing Company, 1986.

Hildebrand, V., **Introduction to Early Childhood Education.** (Third and Fourth Editions) New York: Macmillan Publishing Co., Inc., 1975 and 1986.

Huel, B.P., **A Model for Developing Programs for Black Children.** Washington, D.C.: Black Child Development Institute, Inc., 1976.

Jones, Vernon and Louise Jones, **Comprehensive Classroom Management.** Boston: Allyn and Bacon, 1986.

Karnes, M. Et. Al., **Not All Little Wagons Are Red.** Arlington, Virginia: The Council for Exceptional Children, 1968.

Kendall, Frances E., **Diversity in the Classroom.** New York: Teachers College Press, 1983.

Kirk, S.A., **Educating Exceptional Children** (Second Edition). Boston: Houghton Mifflin Company, 1972.

Miller, L.P., "The Importance of Cultural Awareness in the Development of Positive Attitudes Among Black Children," an unpublished speech presented at the Annual Meeting of the Black Child Development Institute, Inc., October-November, 1974.

Passow, A.H., (Ed.), **Education in Depressed Areas.** New York: Teachers College Press, 1966.

Smith, D.H., "Language Training for Disadvantaged Youth," an unpublished speech presented at a meeting of Flint Community School personnel on the "Disadvantaged" in Flint, Michigan, 1969.

Smith, J., and D. Smith, **Child Management: A Program for Parents and Teachers.** Champaign, Illinois: Research Press Company, 1978.

Thomas, R.M., **Comparing Theories of Child Development.** Belmont: Wadsworth Publishing Company, 1979.

_____, "Saving the African American Child," A Report of the National Alliance of Black School Educators, Inc., Task Force on Black Academic and Cultural Excellence, November, 1984.

ABOUT THE AUTHOR

Dr. Henry E. Hankerson is the Chairman of the Department of Curriculum and Teaching and Graduate Associate Professor in the School of Education, Howard University. He was the Director of Undergraduate Teacher Education for six years prior to becoming Chairman. He has accumulated over twenty years of teaching, administrative, and supervisory experiences. His educational background includes the Ph.D. from the University of Michigan, the M.Ed. from the University of Illinois, the B.S. from Florida A and M University, and graduate and post-doctoral studies at Florida State University and Harvard University (extension program).

Dr. Hankerson is actively involved in professional organizations (i.e., National Association for the Education of Young Children, Phi Delta Kappa, American Association of Colleges for Teacher Education, National Alliance of Black School Educators, etc.) and serves as a presenter at many professional conferences on an annual basis.

He has to his credit over fifty (50) research and scholarly publications and teaching aids. Some recent publications are: 1) Author of research reports in the 1987 Black History Month Kit, "Education and the U.S. Constitution: Historical Effects and Perspective Implications for Blacks;" 2) Author of book chapter, "Black Parents and Children, and Teachers: Partners in Teaching and Learning" (in **On Being Black: An In-Group Analysis**--Being Essays in Honor of W.E.B. DuBois, (ed.) David Pilgrim, Wyndham Hall Press, 1986); 3)Author of an article, "Parenting the Minority Handicapped Child: Developing Awareness, Knowledge, Attitudes, and Skills," (in **Early Child Development and Care Journal**, Volume 15, Number 4, pp. 349-360, 1984); and 4)Co-author of 1984, 1985, 1986 Black History Kits on "Afro-Americans and Education," (1988 topic - "Schooling and the U.S. Constitution: Segregation, Bussing and Magnets"), and a Book Review, "Black Children: Their Roots, Culture, and Learning Styles" by J. Hale-Benson (in Journal of Negro Education, Spring 1987).

Dr. Hankerson has traveled extensively, completed a study tour of England (British Infant Schools), and has always been an advocate of excellence and equity in education for all, but particularly for Blacks and minorities.